PARAGES

Cultural Memory
in
the
Present

Mieke Bal and Hent de Vries, Editors

PARAGES

Jacques Derrida

Edited by John P. Leavey
Translated by Tom Conley, James Hulbert,
John P. Leavey, and Avital Ronell

STANFORD UNIVERSITY PRESS

STANFORD, CALIFORNIA

Stanford University Press
Stanford, California

English translation © 2011 by the Board of Trustees of the
Leland Stanford Junior University. All rights reserved.

Parages was originally published in French under the title
Parages © 1986, Éditions Galilée.

Derrida, Jacques. "Living On / Border Lines" (translated by James Hulbert).
In *Deconstruction and Criticism*, edited by Harold Bloom. © 1979 Continuum
Publishing. Reprinted with permission. Derrida, Jacques. "Title (to be specified)"
(translated by Tom Conley). Originally published in *SubStance* 31 (1981): 5–22.
© 1981 by the Board of Regents of the University of Wisconsin System. Reproduced courtesy of the University of Wisconsin Press. Derrida, Jacques. "The Law
of Genre" (translated by Avital Ronell). In *Glyph* 7, edited by Samuel Weber, pp.
202–9. © 1980 The Johns Hopkins University Press. Reprinted with permission of
The Johns Hopkins University Press.

No part of this book may be reproduced or transmitted in any form or by any
means, electronic or mechanical, including photocopying and recording, or in any
information storage or retrieval system without the prior written permission of
Stanford University Press.

Printed in the United States of America on acid-free, archival-quality paper

Library of Congress Cataloging-in-Publication Data

Derrida, Jacques.
 [Parages. English]
 Parages / Jacques Derrida ; edited by John P. Leavey ; translated by Tom
Conley . . . [et al.].
   p. cm. — (Cultural memory in the present)
 "Originally published in French under the title *Parages*, 1986, Éditions Galilée."
 Includes bibliographical references.
 ISBN 978-0-8047-3581-0 (cloth : alk. paper)
 ISBN 978-0-8047-3582-7 (pbk : alk. paper)
  1. Blanchot, Maurice—Criticism and interpretation. 2. Literature—
Philosophy. 3. Philosophy. I. Leavey, John P., 1951– II. Conley, Tom.
III. Title IV. Series: Cultural memory in the present.
B2430.D483P3713 2011
194—dc22

2010013218

Contents

Editor's Note	*viii*
List of Abbreviations	*ix*
Introduction	
translated by John P. Leavey	1
*Pa*ce Not(*s*)	
translated by John P. Leavey	11
Living On	
translated by James Hulbert	103
Title to Be Specified	
translated by Tom Conley	193
The Law of Genre	
translated by Avital Ronell	217
Notes	*251*

Editor's Note

As Derrida explains in the introduction and notes to the various texts included in this volume, three of the following four texts appeared in English or in publications outside France first. Only "Pas" ["*Pa*ce Not(*s*)"] appeared originally in France. The original English translations of those three texts have been revised to reflect the French versions that were published in *Parages* in 1986 and 2003 (new, revised, and augmented edition). In general, works cited by Derrida are given in the available English translations, which have been modified where necessary to follow the emphasis of his text. In addition, where necessary, the English translations of Blanchot's texts that have been published since the appearance of the original English translations have been incorporated within the revised translations; those translations too have been modified where necessary to follow the emphasis of Derrida's text.

Abbreviations

Works by Maurice Blanchot.

A	*L'amitié.* Paris: Gallimard. 1971.
AM	*L'arrêt de mort: récit.* Paris: Gallimard. 1948.
AMV	*Au moment voulu: [récit].* Paris: Gallimard. 1982.
AO	*Awaiting Oblivion.* Trans. John Gregg. Lincoln: University of Nebraska Press. 1997.
AtOu	*L'attente, l'oubli.* Paris: Gallimard. 2000.
CQN	*Celui qui ne m'accompagnait pas: [récit].* Paris: Gallimard. 1953.
DS	*Death Sentence.* Trans. Lydia Davis. Barrytown, NY: Station Hill Press. 1978.
ED	*L'écriture du désastre.* Paris: Gallimard. 1980.
EI	*L'entretien infini.* Paris: Gallimard. 1969.
EL	*L'espace littéraire.* Paris: Gallimard. 1955.
F	*Friendship.* Trans. Elizabeth Rottenberg. Stanford, CA: Stanford University Press. 1997.
FJ	*La folie du jour.* Montpellier: Fata Morgana. 1973 [1980].
FP	*Faux pas.* Paris: Gallimard. 1975.
IC	*The Infinite Conversation.* Trans. Susan Hanson. Minneapolis: University of Minnesota Press. 1993.
MD	*The Madness of the Day.* Trans. Lydia Davis. Barrytown, NY: Station Hill Press. 1981.
MH	*The Most High.* Trans. Allan Stoekl. Lincoln: University of Nebraska Press. 1996.
OW	*The One Who Was Standing Apart from Me.* Trans. Lydia Davis. Barrytown, NY: Station Hill Press. 1993.

PAD	*Le pas au-delà.* Paris: Gallimard. 1973.
PF	*La part du feu.* Paris: Gallimard. 1949.
SL	*The Space of Literature.* Lincoln: University of Nebraska Press. 1982.
SNB	*The Step Not Beyond.* Albany: State University of New York Press. 1992.
TH	*Le très-haut [roman].* Paris: Gallimard. 1948.
ThIo	*Thomas l'obscur.* Nouvelle version. Paris: Gallimard. 1983.
TO	*Thomas the Obscure.* New version, trans. Robert Lamberton. Barrytown, NY: Station Hill Press. 1988.
WD	*The Writing of the Disaster.* Lincoln: University of Nebraska Press. 1986.
WF	*The Work of Fire.* Trans. Charlotte Mandell. Stanford, CA: Stanford University Press. 1995.
WTC	*When the Time Comes.* Trans. Lydia Davis. Barrytown, NY: Station Hill Press. 1985.

Would I not [*pas*] be bound, going against usage, to say in the first place disparity?

Dissimilar and discontinuous, these writings nevertheless appear together [*paraissent ensemble*], bound as allies or in a book.

Doubtless they try to describe one and the same motion. Proceeding *in view* of a unique *oeuvre*—Maurice Blanchot's—they would attempt thus to draw near it, even if they have to give up getting there [*l'aborder*].

Doubtless too they are part of one and the same time: they were written and published, in their first versions, between 1975 and 1979.

They appear to have this in common as well: they all take their departure from a certain *situation*—in language and between languages, *in translation*. They also speak [*parlent*] about this, they incessantly recall it, perhaps they say nothing else. This results doubtless from reasons internal and specific to each text, but also from this other necessity: for a long time unavailable in France, with the exception of just one, "*Pace* Not(*s*)," they had to be published abroad, sometimes in French, sometimes in a bilingual edition, sometimes in translation.

Apparently, then, one and the same time. In that case the continuity of an experience and some principle of gathering together [*rassemblement*] are supposed. And in fact, over the course of these years, I had thought I would reread Maurice Blanchot's works of fiction. In truth I was discovering them. For [*par*] convenience let's still call them *fictions*. At times [*parfois*] they bear the mention of *récit*, elsewhere that of *novel*. Occasionally, this sign of belonging [*appartenance*] does not appear or is effaced from one version to another, from one edition to another.

How are we to legitimate these names?

The question will incessantly come up again, under one form or another; I let it go here. It remains [*demeure*] inseparable from other motives [*motifs*] of this book. Motives rather than themes, *motives* in order to point in particular to what sets in motion, and first of all [*d'abord*] toward *citation*, which I sometimes hear in the sense that comes from the Latin. Incitation or solicitation, it calls for or gives rise to motion.

These motives lead back to places where, the criteria of decidability no longer being assured, a decision can finally begin to engage.

And the event can take place. More than one time. No more of just once. [*Plus d'une fois.*]

For a start, what is to be said here about these places?

On first approach [*d'abord*], they leave no chance to, and no right can be recognized therein of, some parti(cipa)tion [*partage*] between literature and philosophy. A proposition that does not ban, on the contrary, requires some new and rigorous distinctions, a complete redistribution of spaces (let this be said for those who would want to derive an advantage from the aforesaid proposition, all sorts of advantages and they are always the advantages of confusion).

If one was trying by anticipation to follow here a trajectory from the questions that have just cropped up, those of genre, gender, of the title or the law, of *récit* or novel, of simulacrum, of fiction or truth, of motion and citation, one could multiply the handoffs passing the baton. One example among others: the law *and* the law of genre, genre *and récit*, *récit and* citation (with or without coded mark, with or without quotation marks), citation *and* the "first time" of an event, event and the/her coming [*la venue*], the/her coming, the making-come (again citation) or the letting-come, the coming [*le venir*] and address (come, *viens, venez*), address and destination, destination, distance or approach, approach and appropriation—or pace [*pas*], or not [*pas*], and so on. Another such metonymic chain will associate the law of genre and of sexual difference, for example, and it is the trailblazing [*frayage*] of another *récit*. Another such chain will pass from the word "*pas*" to negativity, from negativity to dialectic, to denegation, still another such, and so on.

These fictions—let's keep this name—I thought I had already read them. Today, when, having studied then cited them at length, I dare to publish these essays, I am less sure about that than ever. Other works of Blanchot have been accompanying me for a long time, those that are situated, also improperly, in the domains of literary criticism or of philosophy. Not that I have become familiar with those works. At least I had been able to think, in the course of the years I am speaking about, that I had already recognized an essential motion of the thought there. But the fictions remained inaccessible to me, as though plunged in a fog out of which only some fascinating glimmers, and sometimes, but at irregular intervals, the light of an invisible lighthouse on the coast reached [*parvenaient*] me. I will not say that from now on these fictions have left this reserve, indeed on the contrary. But in their very dissimulation, in the distance of the inaccessible *as such*, because they open onto it in giving it names [*elles donnent sur lui en lui donnant des noms*], they presented themselves to me again. With a now inescapable force, the most discreet and then most provocative force, force of obsessive haunting and conviction, injunction of a truth without truth, always beyond the fascination that one speaks about regarding them. They do not exercise this fascination. They traverse it, describe it, give it to be thought rather than using or wielding it. But before speaking about a law of fascination, we should be attentive to a fascination *of* the law. The law always appears fascinating; one will have to ask oneself why the law can also be fascinated, which seems unimaginable or inconceivable, if not unthinkable.

Why disparity?

One always expects—this is the author's presumption at times— that preliminary pages have the value of forewarning, of foreword. In order to respect the genre, I shall content myself then with a warning. It will forestall without prohibiting [*previendra sans interdire*]: it would be better to hold these texts to be dissociable bodies, apart and disparate.

No one should expect in effect some organized, *theoretical* discourse on Blanchot's fictional *oeuvre* as a *whole* or *set* [ensemble]. Rather, some *situations* of speaking [*parole*] that are not theory or totality or set, a topology at times impracticable that would not be without relation, at least indirect and analogical, with some paradox or other in what is called *set theory*.

4   *Introduction*

First, then, the voices that become entangled in this book do not carry a discourse, one sole discourse that in the final analysis may be of a theoretical nature. There are several discourses herein; none of them proposes conclusions in the form of theorems, whether those theorems fall under literary criticism, poetics, narratology, rhetoric, linguistics, semantics. And in the end, for the most part, the concern of this book would be neither hermeneutical nor philosophical. Will it be called foreign to every discipline?

No, for two reasons: (1) One of the questions that lets itself be heard most insistently, across this multiplicity of voices, concerns the law, in particular, the law that norms the theoretical, the thematic, or the thetic in order to constitute them, precisely, as disciplines, in order to find in them, rather, the condition of all teaching. How to recognize their frontiers, functioning and institutional effects? How to evaluate the competencies, the regime of statements, the specific rule, the proper authority? Is it possible to decide, indeed to submit to them in all rigor? Where does the line of parti(cipa)tion pass between the event of an inaugural statement, a citation, a paraphrase, a commentary, a translation, a reading, an interpretation? (2) All these texts were associated, for me, with an experience, an experiment, a testing, rather, of teaching. A counter-rule has, certainly, dictated them: how to write what does not let itself be reduced, from one part to the other [*de part en part*], to the injunctions of a didactic speaking, however liberal or free? But these texts explain themselves unceasingly, and perhaps by [*par*] that very thing have it out with the academic institution. In their turn they make of teaching a theme. A *theme* to be elaborated in the vicinity of what Blanchot says about this, for example, in "Thought and the Exigency of Discontinuity" (*Infinite Conversation*), but also a *position* to be interrogated or disturbed, for example, in the masculine figure of mastery [*dans la figure masculine de la maîtrise*]. For, what's more, while I was striving to withdraw this writing from the didactic norms, a limit essentially inaccessible, it turns out that simultaneously, in a parallel manner, I was teaching. In the course of different seminars in which certain wakes in reading could be followed, I was attempting an introduction to the *oeuvre* or the thought of Blanchot. It was always a matter of translation, in the most conventional sense and in other senses of this word; and these seminars took place sometimes in Paris, sometimes at Yale University. Between these two shorelines [*rivages*], as between two tongues, the invisible parti(cipa)tion but also the abyss of an ocean. One of the seminars bore on the gift and time. "Given Time" was its title, and readings of Mauss, Benveniste, Heidegger, Baudelaire led up to a concluding analysis of *La folie du jour* [*The Madness of the Day*]. Another, distributed over three years, had for its title "The Thing": two series of readings apparently independent or parallel, one dedicated to Heidegger, the other, in succession, to Ponge (1975), Blanchot (1976), Freud (1977). Another still, "Of the Right to Literature / From Right to Literature" (1978), passed in particular through an interpretation of "Literature and the Right to Death." Another finally (1979) took pains to compare the two versions of *Thomas the Obscure*. The project that I still have to postpone was at first to recast and order one day in a single work all the notes of these seminars. What I am venturing today to publish resembles more the discontinuous score [*partition*] of heterogeneous writings. They would have in common at least that they are not able to let themselves be accredited [*habiliter*] or rehabilitated by the teaching word.

Second. If they do not devote themselves, for the most part, to theory, these texts no more claim to delimit a *set*, the corpus of Blanchot's fictions. That not only stems from some paradoxical structures that would discredit in advance [*par avance*] the values of set and corpus. Such paradoxes doubtless harass this work. But they do not explain everything. There were also, of course, more contingent limits that I do not want to dissimulate. Perhaps all Blanchot's fictions are cited or evoked in one moment or another; I am not even sure about that. Certain of them, however, will have left a much more visible imprint than others, whether it be a matter in particular of the two versions of *L'arrêt de mort* [*Death Sentence*] or of the two publications of the same *récit* finally entitled *La folie du jour*. Even if my analyses are not yet up to, and far from, the measure of these two works [*oeuvres*], they leave the greater part of the others in the shadows [*dans la pénombre*]. Such disproportion betrays an immense injustice. Despite the rule of recurrences, however legitimate at times the *analogical* temptation may be, each fiction remains incommensurable, as does the event of each version for one "same" work.

Disproportion, then, and disparateness. Carried beyond what is asked about in a theoretical, continuous, and monological treatise, each of the texts gathered together here places itself on scene, if one can say that, following the law of its dissemblance and always in a fictional mode. Each of them parti(cipates)tions itself otherwise. Whence its isolation, let's say rather its insularity. It does not communicate with the others except by the sea [*par la mer*]. Here ("*P*ace Not(*s*)"), two voices of which one, manifestly masculine, at times catches itself in the traps of the teaching or magisterial authority whereas the other, feminine on the whole, cites to appear the citation that calls her—and says *come, viens*. Elsewhere ("Living On"), triumph of life as triumph of death, a double procession advances itself—such a double file [*théorie*]—in the concurrence of two superimposed discourses: at the bottom of the page a long, underlying band of writing accompanies the other. In the form of a Note to the translator, a "Journal de bord" (translated as "Border Lines") murmurs the dates and the deadlines below the principal discourse, naturally more audible and articulate. Here again ("Title to Be Specified"), an academic lecture finds itself entirely occupied with interrogating, playing, foiling, flaunting the titles or contracts that authorize an allocution of this genre. Elsewhere, in "The Law of Genre" precisely, another communication broaches [*aborde*] the question of genre in the course of a colloquium. It tries to treat it according to a mode that, in a fashion at once constrained and deliberate, catches itself in the nets of its very own performativity. Like the other texts, it ventured beyond the too well-received parti(cipa)tions between performative speech and constative speech, in those parts, in those waters off [*dans ces parages*] where a borderline sets itself trembling. It regularly undecides itself between the event of the citation, in advance divisible and iterable, and the desire of the/her coming itself, before all citation. But the event—encounter, decision, call, appeal, nomination, initial incision of a mark—can come to pass [*advenir*] only from the experience of the undecidable. Not the undecidable that is still part of the order of calculation, but the other, the one that no calculation would know how to anticipate. Without this experience, would there ever be the chance of a pace crossed [*d'un pas franchi*]? A call for the event (*come*)? A gift, a responsibility? Would there be a thing or cause other than causality? Wouldn't all this be booked in the program?

Parages/Waters/Parts: to this single word [*mot*] let us entrust what *situates*, very near or far, the double motion of approach and distance, often the same pace/not (*pas*), singularly divided, older and younger than itself, always other, on the brink of the event, when it arrives *and* does not arrive, when it happens *and* does not happen, infinitely distant as the other shore [*rive*] approaches.

For the shore—let us hear the other—appears in disappearing from view. One part only of this book, its lowest note, is called "Journal de bord," as if to keep the register of a sailing, but all the borders, edges, brinks, from one text to the other, are also shores [*rivages*], inaccessible shores or inhabitable shores. Not that it—landless landscape, opened onto the absence of the fatherland, seascape, space without territory, without reserved path, without locality[1]—lacks these, but if it takes place, and *it must*, it will first have to open itself to thought of the earth [*terre*] as to blazing a path. Page after page, as you will verify, but I clearly realized this only after the fact [*après coup*], everything seemed [*paraît*] to wait here on the brink [*au bord*] and by the edge [*au bord*] of the sea, at times very near to losing itself there or letting itself be battered by it. If I had had to choose in this place an exergue, perhaps I would have cited this passage, the first lines of *Thomas the Obscure*:

Thomas sat down and looked at the sea. He remained motionless for a time, as if he had come there to follow the movements of the other swimmers and, although the fog prevented him from seeing very far, he stayed there, obstinately, his eyes fixed on the bodies floating with difficulty. Then, when a more powerful wave reached him, he went down onto the sloping sand and slipped among the currents, which quickly immersed him. [7/ *ThlO* 9]

Or that other, the incipit of *The One Who Was Standing Apart from Me*:

I sought, this time, to approach him. I mean I tried to make him understand that, if I was there, still I couldn't go any farther, and that I, in turn, had exhausted my resources. [1/ *CQN* 7]

And farther on:

I could recall, as an intoxicating navigation, the motion that had more than once driven me toward a goal, toward a land [*terre*] that I did not know and was not trying to reach, and I did not complain that in the end there was neither land nor goal, because, in the meantime, by this very motion, I had lost my memory of the land; I had lost it, but I had also gained the possibility of going forward at random, even though, in fact, consigned to this randomness, I had to renounce the hope of ever stopping [*arrêter*]. The consolation could have been to say to myself: You have renounced foreseeing, not the unforeseeable. But the consolation turned around like a barb: the unforeseeable was none other than the renouncement itself, as though each event, in order to reach me, in that region where we were navigating together, had demanded of me the promise that I would slip out of my story. [7/ *CQN* 18]

Parages/Waters/Parts again: this name seems to emerge alone, that is at least the appearance, in order to consign the economy of themes and sense, for example, the indecision between near and far, the casting off in the fog, in view of what arrives or not, what happens or not in the vicinity of the coast, the impossible and necessary cartography of a littoral, an incalculable topology, the phoronomy of the ungovernable.

In truth the name is never alone. Each one of its syllables receives in an underwater wave the coming [*la venue*] of another vocable—which, imprinting on it a motion at times imperceptible, exchanges there as well its memory [*mémoire*]. And it is the souvenir of *words in* [mots en], as one says strangely in order to accentuate the beginning or end of a nomination: here the names in *pa, par, para, ra, rage, age*. With their value as signifiers, as one used to say not long ago. In the collusions of a glossary that never remains aleatory, syllables or entire words disturb the unconscious perhaps and the body proper of a title. The list and genealogy of these *other words* ought not to become established here—neither table nor chart [*tableau*]. The deduction would be long and would not know how to be closed. Apparently fortuitous, the occurrence of each vocable would come to cross [*croiser*], in these parts, in these waters, both chance and necessity: brief glimmer, abbreviation of a signature hardly sketched, immediately effaced, a name of which one no longer knows to whom it comes back, to what author or to what tongue, to one or the other.

Note: The first version of this text appeared in the journal *Gramma* (Cahiers 3/4, *Reading Blanchot*, 1) in 1976. At that time it was preceded by two letters addressed to me by Frédéric Nef and published by the journal, then by a preamble that I reproduce here.

" . . . as if there is always a little less in the response than in the question." (*Awaiting Oblivion* [18/*AtOu* 39])

"The call always takes place, it doesn't need anyone to answer, it never really takes place, that is why it isn't possible to answer it. But he who does not answer, more than any other, is enclosed in his answer.

"When did I give myself up to this risk? Perhaps while sleeping . . . " (*The One Who Was Standing Apart from Me* [64–65/*CQN* 122])

In its first and incomplete version, here is the fragment of a text that I write "right this moment." Indirect and, as much as possible, fictive, it would describe the *preamble* of a response to the two letters of Frédéric Nef.

*Pa*ce Not(*s*)[1]

Translated by John P. Leavey

—*Viens* 'Come.'

Viens: what do you call what I've just, in French *je viens de*—what I just what? what I just said? Is *viens* a word? A word in French? a verb? On the face of it, it's an imperative, necessarily present, a mood here conjugated in the second-person singular. This definition seems to be as reliable as it is inadequate. What do you call what I just—what? said?[2] What did I do? I called. What do you call *that*?

You've [*As-tu*] remarked how that, how "*Viens*"—let's say that strange word [*mot*]—in *Death Sentence*, right near the end, before those last two paragraphs that disappeared from one edition to the other and that provoke more, by their disappearance . . .

—I have to interrupt you [*vous*]; you are losing me. Did you say to me "come," or have you already stopped talking to me in order for you to converse with whomever, about this—let's say this word [*mot*]—and about knowing what it—it what in fact? I'm lost [*perdue*].

—I no longer know. No verb here can measure up to this word to describe what it does. *Operate, function, play* irk me. Bad enough to wear them out by use, tiresome "modernity" hasn't even succeeded in withdrawing them from the ancient history it no longer recognizes in them. This "word" "*come*" as it is said . . .

—I no longer hear or understand it. Did I hear it? Has it been said? By whom? It is written already, and that's why I'm lost. The word that would have been said, isn't it the one you would have addressed to me, to me alone [*seule*], exclusively, the word in the present, just once leaving no written trace, in any case not becoming confused with any, but explaining that now I'm there to respond to you? Otherwise I wouldn't respond to it. Besides, whatever you do in order to cite it, to write it, to take it up again within quotation marks, and quotation marks within quotation marks, haven't you *said* it, already, anyway, even before pronouncing it, so that I'm there, as if at sea, drowned [*noyée*], but still responding to you?

—Yes, yes. But if I had been able just to *say* it, you wouldn't be disturbed by this citation, already at work, through [*par*] which I began to speak of another "come," addressed by the other to the other, then kept within its quotation marks. It was—already—in quotation marks in *Death Sentence*, right near the end, not at the end, neither in the first nor the last version, but near the end, already divided. Whence, nevertheless, come my force and my desire to repeat, to cite, to recite for you: "and in the end she has always been equal to me. I have loved her and I have loved only her, and everything that happened I wanted to happen, and having had regard only for her, wherever she was or wherever I might have been, in absence, in unhappiness, in the inevitability of dead things, in the necessity of living things, in the fatigue of work, in the faces born of my curiosity, in my false words, in my deceitful vows, in silence and in the night, I gave her all my strength and she gave me all her strength, so that this strength is too great, it is incapable of being ruined by anything, and condemns us, perhaps, to immeasurable unhappiness, but if that is so, I take this unhappiness on myself and I am immeasurably glad of it and to her I say eternally, 'Come,' and eternally she is there" [*DS* 80/*AM* 146–47].

He does not say "Come," he says that he says it, "I say eternally, 'Come,'" and I ask myself if the immeasurability [*démesure*] of unhappiness is not already involved, if its eternity is not there, in the division of that, of this "Come"—there, which means "she is there" eternally. He says *now* that he says it, but that he says it, thus has said and will say it, eternally.

—Yet I've come [*je suis venue*], already. The citation hasn't banned me; it escaped you [*vous*] as soon as it called me, me alone, uniquely, called me by the familiar *tu* in its very drift. I arrive; I happen [*arrive*] . . .

—Yes, yes. I called you, uniquely, in order to speak to you of (her) coming [*la venue*], of what does or does not come about [*arrive*]. This citation or re-citation [*re-citation*] of the *come*, for example, in *Death Sentence*, does not intend it only as a defeat, as if the living force of a name [*appellation*] were exhausted, decomposed, doubled over as well, on the bias, oblique, indirect. Reciting [*récitation*] *come*—what makes it possible in its first event, what enfranchises it in its frankness [*franchise*] and opens it to the energy of these *récits*—that's the repeated affirmation, isn't it? If *come* is *on first approach* cited, that does not so much depend on some loss [*déperdition*] of the authentic speaking act into citational writing as on the force of affirmative repetition, on the self-affirming affirmation, that produces itself as the unique call [*appel*] of the to-come only as the will to repeat itself, to ally itself with itself in what it affirms, eternally. Another thought of the eternal return starting from which to reread this citational or *réci*tative [*récitative*] writing. Why would I, in my turn, have loved to cite *Death Sentence*, if not to reaffirm it? " . . . I have loved her and I have loved only her, and everything that happened I wanted to happen. . . . " The *yes* that makes a hole in the language as strange as *come*, this *yes* approves, affirms, countersigns everything "that happened," hurls itself ahead of what has not yet happened; this *yes*, the one it gladdens, who "[is/am] immeasurably glad of it" (one must not say *it*, here, but *I*), approves nonetheless an "immeasurable unhappiness." So one must think here, as the same, the joyous eternal repetition of the *come*, the reciting and the *récit* that bre/oach themselves in it, the immeasurable unhappiness, the commensurable and the immense ("and in the end she has always been equal to me [*à ma mesure*]. I have loved her and I have loved only her, and everything that happened I wanted to happen . . . condemns us, perhaps, to immeasurable unhappiness, but if that is so, I take this unhappiness on myself and I am immeasurably glad of it . . . "). The measureless excess of unhappiness and of the re-enjoyment depends on the redoubling of the strength [*force*], of the strength as given strength, strength as gift [*force de don*]. "Strength is too great," he said, and indestructible from then on ("incapable of being ruined"): this indestructibility is an "incapacity," the strange passivity of nonpower [*impouvoir*] proceeding from this, that the strength is given, from the other received, received from the other to whom the strength is also given, whence the eternal annulus, the endless annulment restarting an alliance without debt, a gift without credit. He collapses into bottomless unhappiness, the sole disproportion that was "always equal to me." A disproportion works (over) the singular present in which nothing singular ever presents itself, the present of "to her I say eternally, 'Come,' and eternally she is there." The present of this "there"—*là*—the last word that *presents* "her," can be defined only as the response to the *come*. Who is there? What is there? What is the "there"? the "*là*"? Who is the "there," if not what can respond to the *come*? What announces itself: nothing will have been able, *as such*, to measure itself against what can be said of the disproportion of this "present" in grammatical terms (verb in the imperative mood, present in its tense, bound to this person, this adverb, etc.), in semantic, linguistic, psychological, psychoanalytic, philosophical terms. Not that the disproportion remains inaccessible to them, rejected like a beyond. Rather it dislocates the unity of the *as such* that defines, as a last resort, the identity of the region or of the object. The disproportion derives from the necessity to *repeat* the affirmation, an affirmation that does not say *yes* to a being, a subject or an object, the state or the determination of some thing, but to what/whom is to come *again, again* that the eternal repetition will always have called from a "she is there" already. Between what/her who "is there" *to respond*, not only *in order to* respond but also *on account of* responding to *come*, and what/her who *already* will have given all its/her strength and called *come*, there is no incompatibility, no contradiction, but no synthesis or reconciliation either, no dialectic. Whence the immeasurable unhappiness. Whence also the impossibility of cutting through to a decision between, *on the one hand*, an eternal repetition of the affirmation that saves the recited (henceforth I shall be able to say *récit* to recall only Blanchot's-*récit*, and I read it also as a new thought of the citation according to the eternal return, the repetition of the *yes* that begins only by doubling itself—yes, yes—by citing itself one more time, the *récit*, then, is unharmed, being of value just one single time, unique force of a *come* that never reproduces itself: *come*—save/safe [*sauf*]) and, *on the other hand*, but at the same time, a repetition of what is already republished in the quotation marks, writing and citation in the current sense. The contamination by the current sense is not an accident, is part of the structure of the affirmation, is always risked inasmuch as it requires the *récit*. Writing is also this irreducible contamination, and the *récit* this immeasurable unhappiness about/from which he/it can say "I am immeasurably glad of it." He/it says this of/from the *récit* itself, as of/from that to which *come* is said, and of/from the *come* itself, then.

It is to speak to you of (her) coming, of what comes about or does not come about that I called you, uniquely. I could not converse with myself about (her) coming before saying *come*, to you. But will I have been able to say, to you, *come*, without knowing, without having, without seeing [*sans savoir, sans avoir, sans voir*] in advance what "come" ["*venir*"] means to say?

My hypothesis: the sense, the status, the function, as they say, of *come*, of the event *come*, cannot be derived or construed starting from what is thought to be known of the verb *come* and its modifications. *Viens* is not a modification of *venir*. On the contrary. To be sure, this contrary is no longer simply a contrary; rather it is a completely other relation. And consequently my "hypothesis" no longer designates a logical or scientific operation, in the usual sense of these words that would have to be verified or invalidated. Rather my hypothesis describes the unusual advance of *viens* over *venir*. It is one pace/not more or less under *venir*.³ This no/pace comes down to subtracting something in every position, such that my hypothesis is propagated and recited through the moods and modes of *venir* or *la venue*, of come or (her) coming, for example, the to-come (*avenir*), event, advent, etc., but also through all the verbal tenses and moods of coming-and-going.

Come doesn't give an order; it proceeds here from no authority, no law, no hierarchy. I do indeed say *here*. And in order to recall that only on the condition of a context, of a very determined operation of writing— here Blanchot's-*récit*—a "word," ceasing to be entirely a word, disobeys the grammatical or linguistic, or semantic, prescription, which would assign it to be—here—imperative, present, in this person, etc. That is the riskiest possible writing, subtracting something from the order of language it in return yields to with a very gentle and inflexible rigor. But what is to be subtracted in this way? "Thought"? A thought "outside language [*langue*]"? There would be enough here to scandalize a certain modernity.

That's a risk to run, the price to pay for thinking otherwise the "outside language" of thought. *Come* is not [*pas*] an imperative, is not a present. Not to be such does not confer on it a kind of nonlinguistic savagery leaving the event *come* free. On the contrary, that, singularly insistent in the language, disquiets all the linguistic, grammatical, and semantic securities. If *come* does not give an order in the present to someone, what is a present imperative in the second-person singular?

Giving no order, receiving no order from the law of laws, from the order of language, giving none because it receives none, *come* exchanges nothing, does not communicate, says nothing, shows, describes, defines, states [*constate*] nothing, the instant it pronounces itself, nothing that may be something or someone, object or subject. *Come* does not even call someone who would be there before the call. To say that it calls the call, that it calls itself, that would be more exact, provided no specular reflection is understood thereby, and would have to be specified shortly. For the same reasons—I would like to put it clearly, simply, in limpidity—*come*, which is not an order, is not a prayer, a demand, or a desire either. Although *come* makes possible all these modes, it is nonetheless not anterior to them, upstream like a transcendental origin, pure and for itself as a primitive word or an *a-priori*. Each time it is a singular event on the condition of a *come*, each time unique but eternally repeated, saying *tu* . . .

—Would you dare address Blanchot as *tu*?

—Let's leave that question for later. Why is that the easiest and most impossible thing? Why is the easiest thing impossible here? And why can one read his writings (and not only the *récits*) as a patient and interminable meditation on *tutoieing* [*le tutoiement*], in him? Saying that, I am not reducing everything to a question, a sense, or a theme. The question of using *tu* where it acts on the question of the *come*, leaves nothing outside itself, nothing of reality, of the symbolic, of history, of political economy, of the unconscious, of sexuality; I accumulate in order to forestall the prejudice [*prévenir la prévention*]. This question leaves nothing outside itself without ever totalizing anything. I would like you [*tu*] to approach slowly what is at stake in this *viens*.

He not only says *viens*, but also, much later, in *Awaiting Oblivion*, *venez*.[4] Contrary to the code and appearances, the *vous* does not hold the other at a greater distance than does the *tu* implied in *viens*. Each time, in one and the other, the opposition of near and far, with the immense, semantic network it orders, finds itself annulled, not in the confusion or the circle of the annulus, but according to what I call, provisionally, *la démarche d'un pas*, the (dis)approach of a no/pace.⁵ What happens when the near be-comes far, when the near comes-from far? An event with unlimited consequences. (With another step [*pas*], all "Heideggerian" thought proceeds, in its decisive "turnings," by the "same" de-distancing bringing-near of the near and the far. *Entfernung* de-distances the far it constitutes, brings the far near therefore in holding the far far. The eventual propriation [a forced or risky etymology for *Ereignis*] of the far is de-distant from itself.) The nearness of the near is not near, therefore is not proper, and you [*tu*] see all the dams bursting announced step by step [*de proche en proche*]. When I say *distance* from now on or read it in one of his texts, always hear the invisible trait that holds this word open on itself, de-distant from itself: with a *pas* that distances the far from itself. *Pas* is the Thing, *la Chose*. "Here the distance is in the heart of the thing" ("The Two Versions of the Imaginary," in *The Space of Literature* [255/*EL* 347]).

If *venez* does not place at a distance, according to the code of civility, if *viens* supposes distance, one must not hasten to distinguish them. And the repetition of the unique, if it is inherent to *viens*, pluralizes the *viens* in advance, a kind of singular plural that calls itself: as it does not precede her who, "eternally," "is there," its call to her already comes from the other, is a response. Such coming-and-going is not a specular circulation. The room or hotel, the place of all his *récits*, constitutes their topic according to the no/pace [*pas*] of this coming-and-going. We do not know what a room is (so anonymous, so paradigmatic, beginning to become what it is, a room, for example, in the neutrality of a hotel and its guests) "before" the logic—or rather, the atopic phoronomy—of this *pas*.

In *Awaiting Oblivion*, to cite some more, I cut out above the articulation, according to an artifice that is not prohibited: " . . . Naturally, he is free to believe that by responding to his invitation in a seemingly mechanical and obligatory way, she is merely complying with the customary usage of the place, if it is true, as he has reason to believe, that a part of the hotel is reserved for such comings-and-goings. This idea does not displease him.

"❖ When he had said to her: 'Come' [*Venez*]—and immediately she approaches [*s'approche*] slowly, not in spite of herself, but with a simplicity that does not make her presence closer—shouldn't he have gone to meet her instead of formulating this imperious invitation? But perhaps he was afraid of frightening her with his gesture; he wants to let her be free, and if she is not free in her initiative, at least free in her movement. (She chooses a very slow movement, the one most foreign to hesitation for the very reason of its slowness, movement in which the immobility that is particular to it and that contrasts with the brevity of the authoritarian invitation is held back.) So it is an authoritarian word?—But also an intimate one.—A violent word.—But one carrying only the violence of a word.—Carrying it far.—Reaching the far-off without harming it.—With this word, doesn't he wrest the violence from the far-off?—He left it there.—The violence is, therefore, still at the farthest possible distance [*loin*]?—But it is the farthest distance [*le lointain*] that is close.

"The word is only the extension of the sign he made to her. The sign, in enduring, is changed into a word of appeal necessarily pronounced in a low and impersonal tone of voice in which the attraction of the expanse is affirmed. But did the sign say anything? It made a sign by designating. But is the appeal more demanding? It goes toward that to which it appeals. But does it make something come? Only that which asks to come in the appeal. But is it an appeal that questions [*interpelle*]? It responds by appealing" [*AO* 63–64/*AtOu* 120–22]. Coming-and-going in this very passage. Passage of a coming-and-going where the origin of the movement, action, sign, or word never lets itself be arrested, assigned. One voice says "He/*Il*" (When he had said to her: "Come" . . .) in order to cite him who will have seemed to take the initiative: *come/venez* on first approach passes for a word of initiative without past. But he is, from the apparent present of the *récit*, cited in the past: "When he had said to her: 'Come' [*Venez*]. . . . " Now immediately, another (sur)passing [*dépassement*] that dismembers the origin in the synchrony that should adjust the origin to itself, the movement of the approach ("he had said to her: 'Come'—and immediately she approaches slowly . . . ") is described in the present, in a present contemporaneous, apparently, with the *récit* and not with the event it reports. Which no doubt makes a cinematographic image (visible present whereas the sayable is past), but remark above all that the approach, which should respond to the appeal and then follow it, is, very nearly, immediately simultaneous with it. The word *venez* is not at the end of itself than the response, she, has begun to approach, as if she/it had arrived before what provokes her/it: as it [*il*] is said at the end ("But is it an appeal that questions? It responds by appealing.").

Venez is already a response: to another *venez*, that is, to the same [*même*], which calls itself from an infinite distance. That which responds to *viens*.

—She who responds to *viens*, I who am (following) there, even [*même*] before . . .

—She who responds to *come* seems sometimes to accompany the call in its present (before the end of the "word" she is there), sometimes to precede it, indeed to provoke it, she coming from farther off and for a longer time than it, sometimes to follow it, as a movement obeys a past that placed it in motion, here a past most indefinite ("he had said to her: 'Come'—and immediately she approaches slowly . . ."). The slowness is no longer very simply a certain relation of time to movement, a slower speed. It achieves, accelerates, and delays at once infinitely a strange displacement of time, of times, of continuous (non)paces [*pas*], and of movements rolled around an invisible axis without presence, which pass into one another without rupture, of one time in the other, while they keep the infinite distance of moments. This displacement displaces itself, in all the complexity of its network, across *Awaiting Oblivion*. The *récit* always recites, on first approach, the displacement of these displacements. It de-distances them from themselves. You heard and understood one time "he had said to her: 'Come'—and immediately she approaches slowly. . . ." The approach is described elsewhere according to other times and other relations to the apparent time of the utterance *venez*: here a simple past ("She approached slowly . . ." [*AO* 30/*AtOu* 60]), there a pluperfect ("and she had immediately drawn near" [*AO* 35/*AtOu* 71]).

Here they are:

"❖ 'Come' [*Venez*]. She approached slowly, not in spite of herself, but with a kind of profound distraction that made him wondrously attentive.

"She had spoken, but he did not listen to her. He listened to her only so that he could attract her to him by his attention" [*AO* 30/*AtOu* 60].

Farther on: " . . . and when I said to her, 'Come' [*Venez*], she immediately drew nearer with a profound distraction that made me extremely attentive. He then disappeared for good. At least, it was more practical for me to think that he did. Does a god disappear?" ("The dream of a dreamless night": three, he that says *I* and "Two beings from here, two ancient gods. They were in my room, I lived with them.") [*AO* 31–32/*AtOu* 63–64]

Farther on still:

"❖ He knew what his first word had been; he was certain that by saying to her: 'Come' [*Venez*]—and she had immediately drawn near—he had made her enter this circle of attraction where one could begin to speak only because everything had already been said. Was he too close to her? Was there no longer enough distance between them? And wasn't she too familiar in her strangeness?

"He had attracted her, that was his magic, his fault. 'You did not attract me; you haven't attracted me yet'" [*AO* 35–36/*AtOu* 70–71]. That's also why it [*il*] ("Come" [*Viens*]) upsurges from a groundless ground of an indefinite past ("When he had said: 'Come' [*Venez*] . . . "). The approach that responds to him/it—in advance—is immediate and infinitely delayed nonetheless. Infinitely, since the approach that responds to *venez* is an approach that "does not make her presence closer." The pace (*pas*) that brings close de-distances, reduces and opens at the same time, with the same not (*pas*) that denies and removes itself, its own proper distance. This *pas*, this no/pace, is not [*pas*] even divided by a self-negation or self-denegation. Nothing dialectical in this "*pas*"—that can immediately be placed, like "Come," like "*Viens*" or "*Venez*," within quotation marks—since it will never be present to itself, close by self, near self in some self-return: *pas de réappropriation*, (non)pace of (no) reappropriation. The impossibility for "presence" to be "nearer," to be the nearest, even though she/it "approaches," this impossibility is reimprinted in the disjointed time of the *récit*: not only does one not know who is at present speaking (to say "When he had said to her: '*Venez*'—and she approaches immediately . . . "), but also who is speaking within parentheses, poses the objections (But, But . . .) and the responses in a dialogue that at times resorts to the conventional signs of the change of person—the dashes—and sometimes dispenses with them, in the last paragraph. The presence of the present (*récit*) is that presence, impossible, of this strange "*pas*" of distancing, this strange no/pace of distancing.

From the place of him who says *venez* (but he responds by calling out—and this place is also hers—to her, who responds by approaching without getting nearer), the apparent continuity, the patience of the discourse is also from a response to the accusation, that is, to the logic of category identity. Not the discourse of ethical self-justification (no/pace of authority, no/pace of violence, leaving her free, etc.—and, besides, the response does not oppose itself, does not oppose the argument contrary to the objection; it suspends and only disquiets the objection), but an infringement of the categorical, of the self-identity of the category—accusation or judgment—itself under the law of the identity of the "is" in predication. Now it is not indifferent that this "first" infringement affects the "*pas*," the one that is found provoked by *venez*, but as well the one that provokes *venez*. By reason—a new reason—of this *pas* that approaches without bringing nearer, each time the "is," or the "it is," takes form in the text, it is in order to subtract itself from the logic of identity, indeed from the dialectics of contradiction ("a movement in which is retained the immobility that is proper to it," "But it is the farthest distance [*le lointain*] that is close," etc.). *Venez* on first approach says the provocation of a *pas* affecting without return the being of the "is." Forgetting would be another name for *pas*.

In every *récit*, in every *récit* of Blanchot, this *pas* is at stake. *Awaiting Oblivion*, since we are there: "❖ For a long time he had believed that the secret counted less than his approach. But here the approach was without approach. He was never closer to or farther from it. Thus, he did not have to approach it, but only to direct his attention toward it" [*AO* 56/*AtOu* 107].⁶

"Thus, he did not have to approach it, but . . . ": one could show—this perhaps will happen of itself—that in this statement [*énoncé*], the syntax of stress [*insistance*] privileges no word, absolutely none, in the least, ever, each one playing there an irreplaceable role. Farther on still in *Awaiting Oblivion*:

"❖ 'There is still a long road ahead.'—'But not one that will take us far away.'—'One that will lead us to what is nearest.'—'When everything that is near is farther away than any far-off place.'

"It is as if she [*elle*] carried the force of proximity in herself. Far away—when she is standing against the door—necessarily close and drawing ever closer, but near to him, still being only close and, nearer, placed completely at a remove [*éloignée*] by the proximity that she makes manifest. When he holds her, he touches this force of approach that gathers together proximity and, in this proximity, the far-off and the outside in their entirety.

"'You are near; she is only present.'—'But I am only close, whereas she is presence.'—'That is true: only close; I will not deny this 'only,' thanks to which I am holding you here.'—'Because you are holding me?'—'Well, you are holding me too.'[7]—'I am holding you. But close to whom?'—'Close: close to everything that is close.'—'Close, but not [*pas*] necessarily to you or to me?'—'To neither the one nor the other. But that is how it must be. That is the beauty of the attraction [*attrait*]: you will never be close enough and never too close; and yet always held [*tenus*] and contiguous [*attenant*] to each other.'

"Held and attracted in this contiguity [*attenance*]. What attracts is the force of proximity that holds under attraction, without ever being exhausted in presence and dissipated in absence. In proximity, touching not [*non pas*] presence, but rather difference.

"'Close even if I do not speak?'—'Then letting proximity speak.'

"What spoke in her was the approach, the approach of speech [*parole*], speech of the approach, and always approaching speech in speech.

"'But if I am close, then you are too.'[8] —'Of course. And yet, one cannot really say it.'—'What can one say?'—'That I am here.'—'Whereas I am not really here?'—'You are here, in proximity. That is your privilege; that is the truth of the attraction.' The attraction, the manner in which the approach responds to everything by approaching.

"'So, we shall never cross proximity?'—'But always meeting ourselves in proximity'" [*AO* 60–61/*AtOu* 115–17].

Twice *force* is named. In the necessary rarefaction of the lexical where everything is reduced to the twists and sly, syntactic turns [*à l'entors et au retors syntaxique*] of de-distancing, what puts in movement, approaches, gathers together proximity and in proximity, outside it, the far, is *force*, or rather *the difference of force*, the force always different and thus always excessive in relation to itself, disproportionate [*démesurante*]. ("I gave her all my strength [*force*] and she gave me all her strength, so that this strength is too great, it is incapable of being ruined by anything, and condemns us, perhaps, to immeasurable unhappiness, but if that is so, I take this unhappiness on myself and I am immeasurably glad of it and to her I say eternally, 'Come,' and eternally she is there" [*DS* 80/*AM* 147].) Being *there* is not simply being near. The force is excessive because it is different, different from itself, and double, force of a movement as it were of a given force, force of a movement that can be *described*, in the sense in which a trajectory is described, only from the de-distancing of the *come* and not the reverse. The disproportionate force of *Death Sentence* is as well the "'force of approach that gathers together proximity'" or "'the force of proximity that holds under the attraction'" in *Awaiting Oblivion*. Resorting to the noun "force" is not an appeal to some occult virtue. The *récit*'s context never lets the force be defined other than "starting from" the de-distancing of the near, of what approaches, gathers together proximity and, in proximity, according to an inclusion without interiority, the far. "Starting from," to think starting-from divides itself and de-distances itself at the same split time, in a redoubled stroke [*du même coup dédoublé*]. It is a thought that no longer thinks starting-from, having departed from this line of thought so reassuring to philosophy; it is a thought that thinks, a completely-other thinking, "starting from"—this de-distancing; this thought leads back without return to the coming/starting and to the having-just-started (*venir-de-partir*). In the same way, if one *does not know* what force there is *before* the proper de-distancing of the near, so that these statements, "'the force of proximity that holds under the attraction'" or "'this force of approach that gathers together proximity and, in this proximity, the far-off and the outside in their entirety,'" would be statements that cannot be decomposed—one would have said they were "analytic" statements, if they were not aiming at the inappropriate inclusion of the completely other in the same—then one can no more say that one *knows* what force there is *after* having thought the distancing of this *pas*, if at least *knowledge* has always been looked after [*gardé*], as knowledge of the object or self-knowledge, by this formal or dialectical logic that chances [*vient*] here to de-distance itself. If this custody [*garde*] were in its turn distanced, the word *knowledge*, like every other moreover, would be affected enough by this to be folded to that re-employment. All of Blanchot's language [*langue*], lexicon and syntax, keeps [*garde*] its classic appearance only to implement, silently and with the most necessary discretion, this formidable refolding [*reploiement*].

In this refolding the present is also disjoined from the near, but the mode of disjunction parts [*s'écarte*] from simple opposition, as well as from hierarchy, the value of value also finding itself distanced in this: the two "only"'s—"'only present,'" "'only near'"—make the too much and the not enough [*le pas assez*] oscillate without promising any stopping: "'I will not deny this "only."'"

The disjunct of the near and the present produces, engenders, and reveals at once a fissure without limit: in knowledge or in philosophic discourse. But it is a fissure that still holds together, near and present to each other, the two that it separates. That it separates without separating, keeps up without keeping together. The altogether singular syntax of *without* (*sans*) in the writing of his *récit*, along with the syntax of *pas*, is what will henceforth hold us under the fascinating power of its attraction. But I won't speak to you [*te*] about that directly yet.

—When will you [*vous*] speak directly? When will you speak to me? In rectitude, a word I would like to understand without morality, duty, right, law . . .

—The syntax of *sans*, in his *récit*, is apparently, as syntax, altogether normal and regular. The word "syntax" then is not suitable to describe an operation, without operation, that is no more lexical. But let's leave that for later. I take up only an example of it, still in *Awaiting Oblivion*, because it marks the *sans* in the movement of de-distancing and when, as *venez* a moment ago, what happens is neither an "action" ["*geste*"], nor a "word," not even simply a "sign." And the bare "room" always names (neither nature nor architecture) this other topic, this other phoronomy. "❖ In the room: when he turns back toward the time he made a sign to her, he feels that he makes a sign to her in turning back. And if she comes and he takes hold of her, in an instant of freedom about which there is nothing to say and that he has long since marvelously forgotten, he owes the initiative to which her presence responds to the power of forgetting (and to the necessity of speech) that this instant grants him.

"'I do not remember.'—'But you come [*venez*].'—'In distancing myself.'—'You come closer in this distancing.'—'Remaining motionless.'—'You are at rest through the strong attraction of the movement.'—'Restless rest'" [*AO* 78/*AtOu* 148–49].

This lawless law of de-distancing is not the essence, but the impossible topic of essentiality. Let's take the most economical way to come to understand this. It is the route that cuts across a discursive schema of Heidegger and prepares us to think at once proximity and—this will appear only later—the chiasm powerfully distancing these two thoughts from each other: *Entfernung*—which I proposed to translate in French by *é-loignement* [and following Stambaugh by de-distancing in English]—and *Ereignis* (event, a word in which the *proper* [*eigen*], indeed the proceedings of the near [*prope*] or of appropriation have doubtless abusively come to be read, a word around which I would like—here—to get you to hear the coming-back [*sous-venir*] without memory of a *come*), in this collusion without identity of the near and the far we tackle with this *pas*, this no/pace. Thus: some thing (what? some other-thing) draws near (itself). We think we understand what that means (to say), as plain as day: the thing tends to get near. Near what, what other thing? Let's leave this question aside for a moment. Near some other thing or itself as an other thing, the thing can appear near only to what anticipates what the near and proximity are there. Not [*Non pas*] according to the general concept proximity, but to the essence of the near "starting from" which such a concept can be formed. What then is the "near" or the relation near-far? What is the proximity of the near? The thing certainly can be near, but the near or proximity is not near. The proximity of the near is not any *other thing* but the near thing, but it is not near. The essence of the near is not any more near than the essence of red is of the color red. Let's at least submit to the law of this truth, to this manifestation of the essence *as such* that dominates the most powerful philosophical tradition, up to Heidegger who finds next to it thought's most decisive aid. Consequently, the more one tries to approach the proximity of what approaches, the more the completely other—and therefore the infinitely distant—of proximity opens up. Since as much can be said of the far, no *opposition* is more pertinent between the near and the far, no identity either. Now this contraband or double-band (*double-bind*)[9] bivalence affects *all*, all that *is*, that is, all that presents itself, *is present*, comes, comes to pass, arrives, happens, exists, the essence of event and the event of the essence, so many indissociable semantic values of a nonregional topic of the near and the far. Thus you sense what is at stake in this *pas d'é-loignement*, this no/pace of de-distancing. And what expends itself (unthinking itself) in such (dis)-

approach [*Et ce qui se dépense en telle démarche*]. And the strange rhythm this (dis)approach imparts to our discourse, to the choice of words, to the construction of our phrases and sentences, to the idiom of the word "*pas*." Rarefaction, a strict and rigorous law: the other is at stake. It can approach *as other*, in its phenomenon as other [*phénomène d'autre*], only in distancing itself and can *appear* in its far of infinite alterity only in drawing nearer [*se rapprocher*]. In its double *pas* (pace, not), the other dislocates the opposition of the near and the far, without however confusing them. It subjugates the phenomenal presence to its (dis)approach.

This *pas*, multiple of itself, does not displace itself *in* a labyrinthian *topos*: this *pas* carries itself along as labyrinth; it has the structure of the labyrinth. Not only because it brings nearer in distancing and gives the misleading appearance of a dialectics in which the *pas* denies itself, is not the proceeding it is, without this double *pas* . . .

—You are going to do what he/it never does: play with an indiscreet insistence on the language, exhibit an economical mastery, render yourself untranslatable in the very proposal [*propos*].

—To do right to an other text, a text of an other, one must assume in a certain way, a very determined way, the fault, the weakness; one must not avoid what the other will have known how to avoid: in order to make it appear from this withdrawal (*retrait*). The text he will have signed, without signing, is one of the very few before which I will gladly take upon myself and delight in my withdrawal, my weakness, about which you talked to me and which can take the form of an indiscretion of mastery. Why not? Why *pas*? Why (not) *pas*?

It's also because I want to speak, later on again, about the inconspicuous but so much more effective way in which on another scene he lets be or play the powers of language, of the French language: at that point where untranslatability closes off nothing, on the contrary, where the whole economy of *Witz*, essentially slavish and commonplace, complacent when consciousness deliberates on it, finds itself sovereignly thwarted, defeated [*déjouée, défaite*], broken open at the moment of its greatest force. Without this double *pas* ever arresting itself in the dialectical negativity of its proceeding, nor likewise in the trope that accords de-distancing to the march, to the way of marching [*démarche*], to method, to a movement supposing being-upright, the advance of one foot on the other. At least the *pas-à-pas*, the *step-by-step* is only a "metaphor" for de-distancing and never appears in its movement of going or having come except "starting from" a thought of de-distancing. *Le pas n'est donc pas même un pas, pas même.* The no/pace therefore is not even a no/pace, (not even) *pas* itself. In all these senses *pas* is labyrinthian and immediately, singularly multiple, *digressive* of itself. She, to whom he responded *come*, she knows it/him in advance. I will already cite *Thomas the Obscure*, farther on than the first access [*abord*] at which we'll try to arrive, again later on. For example, he: "... on all sides his way was barred, an insurmountable [*infranchissable*] wall all around, and this wall was not the greatest obstacle for he had also to reckon on his will that was fiercely determined to let him sleep there in a passivity exactly like death. Madness therefore..." [*TO* 13/*Thlo* 15]. The barrier, what is opposed to proceeding, does not hold itself before the *pas* or outside it, but within it, in the mortal "passivity" that does not [*pas*] authorize *pas* to be what it is. But this "passivity" on its own surmounts [*franchit*] itself, enfranchises itself in the immediately transgressive nature of *pas*, of the no/pace. An affirmative transgression that—*pas*'s negation of negation—does not come down to a double negation. "What dominated him was the sense of being pushed forward by his refusal to advance. So he was not very surprised, so clearly did his anxiety allow him to see into the future, when, a little later, he saw himself carried a few paces [*pas*] further along. A few paces: it was unbelievable. His progress was undoubtedly more apparent than real, for this new spot was indistinguishable from the last, he encountered the same difficulties here, and it was in a certain way the same place that he was distancing himself from out of terror of being distanced from it" [*TO* 13–14/*Thlo* 15–16].

For example, farther on, she: "... there came a moment when, brought forward by this endless wandering [*vagabondage*] before a reality without reason, she stopped suddenly, emerging from the depths of her frivolity with a hideous expression. The issue was still the same. It was vain for her to search out her route at the ends of the earth and lose herself in infinite digressions—and the voyage might last her entire life; she knew that she was coming closer every minute [*à chaque pas*: also, with each pace] to the instant when it would be necessary not only to stop but to abolish her path, either having found what she should not have found, or eternally unable to find it. And it was impossible for her to give up her project. For how could she be silent, she whose language was several degrees below silence? By ceasing to be there, ceasing to live? There were just more ridiculous strategies, for through her death, closing off all the exits, she would only have precipitated the eternal race in the labyrinth from which she retained the hope of escape as long as she had the perspective of time. And she no longer saw that she was coming imperceptibly closer to Thomas. She followed him, step by step [*pas à pas*], without realizing it, or if she realized it, then wanting to leave him, to flee him, she had to make a greater effort. Her exhaustion became so overwhelming that she contented herself with mimicking her flight and stayed glued to him, her eyes flowing with tears, begging, imploring him to put an end to this situation, still trying, leaning over this mouth, to formulate words to continue her *récit* at all costs, the same *récit* she would have wished to devote her last forces to interrupting and stifling" [*TO* 59–60/ *Thlo* 63–64].

The forces then seem to have force only in opposing themselves to the *récit*. And she, only in "mak[ing] a greater effort" to distance herself from him/it. But the *récit* is interminable because the force opposed to him/it, all as the effort of distancing, produces just what the force contradicts without hope of any exit [*issue*] in gathering together, in the negation of negation or denegation. *Pas de récit, pas de mort*, (non)pace of (no) *récit*, (non)pace of (no) death ("There were just more ridiculous strategies, for through her death . . . she would only have precipitated . . . "), *pas* without dialectics, only differences of *pas*, only differences of (non)paces ("wanderings," "labyrinths," "infinite digressions," "language . . . several degrees below silence"). What is described in this way is the *récit*, the "same *récit*." *Pas de mort, no/pace of death*. As always, for it/him, the immeasurable unhappiness is the impossible death.

And time (the possibility of the lure, of the "hope of exiting there") names here the digressive difference, this disjunct of the *pas*, between *pas* and *pas*, between *pace* and *no*, the *pas à pas*, the step by step, that promises *pas*'s final transgression, its overstepping, its beyond [*au-delà*]. There is no (*pas*) time outside the distancing movement from/of the near.

Immediately after "the same *récit*" I just [*viens de*] cited, after the *pas* of the impossible *récit*, the moment she is, literally, abandoned by her paces [*ses pas*], she glides into the water [*eau*].

Eau: I pronounce thus to name at once the letter [O], the syllable or the word (name or element of the name) and the thing [water] in this passage where they flow into one another. And in(to) his text so regularly, immensely, beyond measure. Where we will unceasingly meet again, find our bearings, lose them, ourselves, get bogged down, drown.[10]

The water [*eau*] sets free the movement of the *pas*'s: she/it authorizes a movement foreign to the inner turmoil that comes to divide the *pas*—it is finally a *paceless movement*, a *mouvement sans pas*. But as the *paceless* [*le sans pas*] certainly says that *pas* is only a trope warning of a distancing that no longer walks or works, well, to be abandoned by one's paces [*de ses pas*] in order to glide into the water [*eau*] is also to set the pace [*pas*] free, to free it precisely from *pas*, to complete it, to occasion it, I'll even say to pass the Rubicon [*franchir le pas*], she/it, naked, unveiled, while doing this: while doing this beyond [*au-delà de*] all crispation of activity, and even up to melting into the element "*eau*" "water" (or *o*, since *eau* is also there for the other thing—in a certain manner, it/she is nothing, no [*pas*] more a thing than a letter, a syllable, or the element of a name: the degree zero of an infinite metaphor), that is to say, while drowning herself naked, unveiled, in being "drowned" rather, which can take place—that is why it's necessary to say *o*—"among the stars and the spheres," the moment "her paces left her": " . . . the same *récit* she would have [*aurait*] wished to devote her last measure of strength to interrupting and stifling.

"It was in this state of abandonment that she allowed herself to be carried along by the feeling of duration. Gently, her fingers drew together [*crispèrent*], her paces [*pas*] left her, and she slipped into a pure water where, from one instant to the next, crossing eternal currents, she seemed to pass from life to death and worse, from death to life, in a tormented dream that was already absorbed in a peaceful dream. Then suddenly with the noise of a tempest she entered into a solitude made of the suppression of all space, and, torn violently by the call of the hours, she unveiled herself. . . . First she climbed down into the [*au*] depths of a day totally foreign to [*aux*] human days, and, full of seriousness, entering into the intimacy of pure things, then rising up toward sovereign time, drowned among the stars and the spheres, far from knowing the peace of the skies she started to tremble and experience pain. It was during this night and this eternity that she prepared herself to become the time of men. Endlessly, she wandered along the empty corridors . . . incapable of seizing again the reason for these metamorphoses and the goal of this silent walk [*marche*]. But, when she passed . . . " [*TO* 60–61/ *Thlo* 64–65].

—Why *she* [elle]? Why is this movement entrusted to this figure, to *her*? And these "shores," this "shipwreck" [*naufrage*]? these "dams" [*barrages*]?

—I must tell you unceasingly, "it's too soon" and "it's necessary": it's necessary to learn to read him/it with an infinite patience, to be immobilized endlessly in each passage and to come back to it indefinitely, to recite it in this way. "But, when she passed before a door that looked like Thomas's, recognizing that the tragic debate was still going on, she knew then that she was no longer arguing with him with words [*mots*] and thoughts, but with the very time she was espousing. . . . It was in this situation that she penetrated as a vague shape into the existence of Thomas. Everything there appeared desolate and mournful. Deserted shores where deeper and deeper absences, abandoned by the eternally departed sea [*mer*] after a magnificent shipwreck gradually decomposed. She passed through strange dead cities. . . . She thought she understood—oh cruel illusion—that the indifference that flowed the length of Thomas like a lonely stream [*eau*] came from the infiltration, in regions she should never have penetrated, of the fatal absence that had succeeded in breaking all the dams, so that, wanting now to discover this naked absence, this pure negative. . . . she prepared to go out so far in front of herself that on [*au*] contact with the absolute nakedness, miraculously passing beyond [*au travers*], she could recognize therein her pure, her very own transparency. Gently, armed only with the name Anne that must serve her to return to the surface after the dive, she let the tide of the first and crudest absences rise . . . " [*TO* 61–62/ *Thlo* 65–68].

The element in which it will be said that she "could no longer find any foothold" [*TO* 63/ *Thlo* 68], element liquid or marine, galactic or seminal ("Anne . . . ascended the course of waters where obscure origins floundered" [*TO* 83/ *Thlo* 93]), "after the dive" or when the "tide" rises, is the element of "absences" [*TO* 63/ *Thlo* 68]. But also the element of "sovereign time" [*TO* 60/ *Thlo* 65] in which she swims or drowns as she penetrates. When her paces [*ses pas*] have left her, her movement is always entry or penetration, in water [*eau*], in time, in absence, in Thomas: "she entered. . . . entering. . . . she penetrated. . . . in regions she should never have penetrated" [*TO* 60–62/ *Thlo* 64–67]. Now the element of ocean [*eau*] ("oh cruel illusion" [*TO* 62/ *Thlo* 67]), that of sovereign time as the illusion of the pace-less [*du sans-pas*], of the absence of space, lets resound pure sonority, the phoneme *o* ("she hurled herself against the extraordinary sonority of nothingness that is made of the reverse of sound [*son*]" [*TO* 61/ *Thlo* 66–67]) in which she recognizes herself in her [*son*] name, Anne, that is, in her [*son*] nothingness. Immediately after: "In this exploration that she had undertaken so naively, believing that she might find the last word on herself, she recognized herself passionately in search of the absence of Anne, of the most absolute nothingness of Anne." The moment she recognizes herself in search of the absence of Anne, absence of her name to her existence, or of her existence to her name, is also the moment a stream [*une eau*], the tide of absences, succeeded in passing, breaking all the dams: "of the most absolute nothingness of Anne. She thought she understood—oh cruel illusion—that the indifference that flowed the length of Thomas like a lonely stream came from the infiltration, in regions she should never have penetrated, of the fatal absence that had succeeded in breaking all the dams . . . " [*TO* 62/ *Thlo* 67].

Among the "eternity" of *come*, the distance of "*pas*," "name," and "*eau*" is announced a lure [*attrait*], the set of an attraction that we will slowly have to learn to read. Let us leave for now what determines *eau* (name, thing, element of name or thing, syllable or letter) as ocean, sea, tide, with rhythms and edges [*bordures*], shores or wrecks [*rivages ou naufrages*]. We shall try to approach them later. Here, when she could recognize "herself" "in search of the absence of Anne" or "recognize . . . her pure, her very own transparency," it is the force of her name, a name without inner dam, that draws her or that draws her/itself from the water (*eau*), its medium of resonance: "she could recognize therein her pure, her very own transparency. Gently, armed only with the name Anne that must serve her to return to the surface after the dive . . . " [*TO* 62/ *Thlo* 68]. She ends, as you [*tu*] well know, and it is necessary to give up citing, it is necessary to allow for reading, in the conflagration of her name; she bursts into flame, "a complete torch," howling Anne. But her corpse then becomes, "at the heart of nothingness," "an inassimilable nothingness." Perhaps nothing could be resolved, dissolved, reconciled, relieved into the simple of a "passion." The *no/pace* of [*le* pas *de*] this ultimate "intrud[ing]" would be neither the univocity nor the dialectics of desire in this passion: "... she began to howl 'Anne, Anne' in a furious voice. At the heart of indifference, she burst into flame, a complete torch with all her passion, her hate for Thomas, her love for Thomas. At the heart of nothingness, she intruded as a triumphal presence and hurled herself there, a corpse, an inassimilable nothingness, Anne, who still existed and existed no longer, a supreme mockery to the thought of Thomas" [*TO* 64/*ThIo* 70].

There it's a matter of a moment of the *récit*. And even though this moment is justly not that of a (hi)story, in whatever sense one understands this word in literature or in philosophy, the cutting out I have submitted this moment to is absolutely unjustifiable and in fact impossible. I only wanted to begin to make the *go* and *come* [*le* va *et* viens] of Blanchot's no/pace [*pas*] resonate, not in order to extract it as the law that would come to dominate his text or his name, but in order to approach slowly the event of his unheard-of signature and to plunge it back into its water [*eau*]. Anne, on the following page, "came around" "into another body" ("her body had mingled with the pure void, thighs and belly united to a nothingness with neither sex nor sexual parts, hands convulsively squeezing an absence of hands, face drinking in what was neither breath nor mouth ... " [*TO* 67/*ThIo* 71]), and one could follow, so arbitrarily, so necessarily, all the no/paces, all the *pas*'s that carry the text, carry it off rather. Anne is not one of those (women) to whom he has said "Come," but "Go." The voice that says to her "Go" nevertheless gives her no order and above all commands her not to go somewhere, not even somewhere else, only toward Anne, the other Anne, she or her name through which she must again "flow" after the penetration ("she entered") into a place where she "appeared bathed in the intoxication of recovery.... She ... saw approaching ... the moment when, regaining contact with the earth, she would again grasp ordinary existence, would see nothing, feel nothing, when she could live, live finally, and perhaps even die, marvelous episode! She saw her very far away, this well Anne whom she did not know, through whom she was going to flow with a gay heart. Ah! Too dazzling instant! From the heart of the shadows a voice tells her: Go.

"Her real illness began" [*TO* 76–77/*ThIo* 82–83].

"Go" that goes from one Anne to the other is therefore also the call come from her name as from another (woman) [*d'une autre*], from a single breath [*souffle*], without barrier [*barrage*], without inner occlusion (it is also true of "Anne" or of "Come," indivisible monosyllables or vocalisms). "Go" says nothing other than "Come," and it moves away [*éloigne*] from/ with the same no/pace [*pas*]. Toward a place without passage [*sans passage*], without beyond, toward a *living* finally intransitive that is equivalent to "perhaps even d[ying]" [*TO* 77/ *Thlo* 83]. *Pas d'au-delà*, no beyond: it is in *Thomas the Obscure* too (1940) that one will have been able to read this, much farther on: "It [night] does not allow anything other than itself to be attributed to it; it is impenetrable. I am truly in the beyond, if the beyond is that which admits of no beyond [*pas d'au-delà*]" [*TO* 104–5/ *Thlo* 123]. This no-beyond that would be the beyond itself, *Thomas the Obscure* names it, in this place, the "supreme relationship"; this relationship "imparts to me the desire of a wonderful progress": "In this absolute repetition of the same is born true movement that cannot lead to rest" [*TO* 105/ *Thlo* 124]. This statement ("if the beyond is that which does not admit of any beyond, *pas d'au-delà*") inscribes the *pas* (not, adverb of negation) in the very place and in the movement gathering momentum in which the substantive *pas*, come to uphold the negation from deep down in the language, crosses the line without crossing it, in its name and under the title *Le pas au-delà*: in which, this time, according to a chiasm traversing the whole "corpus," *beyond* (noun on first approach: "if the beyond . . . ") will have become adverb (the pace/not beyond), whereas the adverb *pas* will have become noun.

In order that "I am truly in the beyond, if the beyond is that which admits of no beyond [*pas d'au-delà*]," the pace [*le pas*] that carries me there must clear itself [*se franchisse*], annul in preserving the beyond; and yet the structure of *pas* excludes that the double effect of the *pas* (annulment/ preservation of the beyond) be a negation of the negation coming back to include, interiorize, idealize for (it)self the *pas*. This is the strange proceeding in which the negation of the negation remains in its powerful system a determined effect of *pas*, a *pas*, a pace.

More than thirty years after *Thomas the Obscure*, in which we would have been able to reread again all the *pas d'éloignement*, all the no/paces of distance (for example, but return these fragments without totality to their *récit* and recall that it itself never underlines: "since I was real only under the name of death, I let the baneful spirit of the shadows show through, *blood [sang] mixed with my blood*, and the mirror of each of my days reflected the confused images of death and life. . . . This Thomas forced me to appear . . . a body *without* life, an insensitive sensitivity, *thought without thought*. At the highest point of contradiction, I was this *illegitimate* dead person. Represented in my feelings by a double for whom each feeling was as absurd as for a dead person, at the pinnacle of *passion* I attained the pinnacle of estrangement, and I seemed to have been removed from the human condition because I had truly accomplished it. Since, in each human act, I was the dead person that at once renders it possible and impossible and, if I walked [*marchais*], if I thought, I was the one whose complete absence alone makes the *pace* and the *thought* [*le* pas *et la* pensée] possible, before the beasts, beings who do not bear within them their dead double, I lost my last reason for existing. There was a tragic[11] *interval* between us" [*TO* 92–93/ *Thlo* 105–6]. This interval has the form of the absence that makes possible "the pace and the thought," but it *intervenes* first of all as the relation of *pas* to *pas*, of pace to not, or of thought to thought, as the heterological inclusion of *pas* within *pas* (pace or not within pace or not), of thought within thought, pace without pace (not without not), or "thought *without* thought" [*de pas à pas, de pensée à pensée, pas sans pas ou "pensée* sans *pensée"*]. This play (without play) of the *without*, of the *-less* in his texts, you just saw that it disarticulates every logic of identity or of contradiction and that it does this ever since "the name of death" or the nonidentity of the double in the name. That reading must again be patiently reserved. Another "example": "Death was a crude metamorphosis beside the indiscernible nullity that I nevertheless coupled with the word[12] Thomas. Was it then a fantasy [*chimère*], this enigma, the creation of a word [*mot*] maliciously formed to destroy all words? But if I advanced within myself, hurrying laboriously toward my precise noon, I yet experienced as a tragic certainty, at the center of the living Thomas, the inaccessible proximity of that Thomas that was nothingness, and the more the shadow of my thought shrunk, the more I conceived of myself in this faultless clarity as the possible, the willing host of this obscure Thomas. . . . I felt this nothingness bound to your extreme existence as an unexceptionable condition. I felt that between it and you [*toi*] undeniable ratios were being established. All the logical couplings were incapable of expressing this union in which, without *then* or *because*, you came together, both cause and effect [*fils*] at once, unreconcilable and indissoluble. Was it your opposite? No, I said not. But it seemed that if, slightly falsifying the relationships of words, I had sought the opposite of your opposite, having lost my true path I would have arrived, without turning back on my paces, proceeding wondrously from you-consciousness (at once existence and life) to you-unconsciousness (at once reality and death), I would have arrived [*abouti*] . . . " [*TO* 97–98/ *Thlo* 112–14].

I cut out this passage in the middle of the one that displaces the *pas* (the not [*le ne-pas*] rather, for the *pas* of *ne-pas* is not in itself negative) between the *I am* and the *I think* ("and, rather than murmur, 'I am, I am not,' mix the terms together in a single happy combination and say, 'I am, while I am not,' and likewise, 'I am not, while I am,' *without* there being the slightest attempt to force contradictory words together, rubbing [*usant*] them one against the other like stones. As voices were called down upon my existence, affirming in succession, with equal *passion*: He exists for always, he does not exist for always, that existence took on a fatal character in their eyes. It seemed that I was walking [*marchais*] comfortably over the abysses and that, complete in myself, not half-phantom half-man, I penetrated my perfect nothingness. A sort of integral ventriloquist. . . . I wrote on the wall these sweet words: 'I think, therefore I am not'" [*TO* 96–99/ *Thlo* 110–14]) until the alternation of the not affecting the *I am* or *I think* lets itself be described as paceless non-walking [*dé-marche sans pas*], counting certainly his paces [*ses pas*], but paces carried beyond themselves: neither movement nor legs. The pace [*pas*] is nevertheless not simply denied, not simply affected by a not [*ne-pas*]; it describes another topic and escorts the statements *I am* or *I think* there: "I think, said Thomas, and this invisible, inexpressible, nonexistent Thomas I became meant that henceforth I was never there where I was, and there was not even anything mysterious about it. My existence became entirely that of an absent person who, in every act I performed, produced the same act and did not perform it. I walked, counting my paces, and my life was that of a man cast in concrete, with no [*pas de*] legs, with not even [*même pas*] the idea of movement" [*TO* 100/ *Thlo* 114]. *Farther*: "I was absurd, not because of the goat's foot that permitted me to walk with a human pace [*un pas d'homme*], but because of my regular anatomy, my complete musculature that permitted me a normal pace, nevertheless an absurd pace, and, normal as it was, more and more absurd" [*TO* 101/ *Thlo* 118]. Every transgression operates from then on against or beyond transgression to the extent that it would be the fact of a (non)pace; transgression transgresses the (non)pace itself, steps across a pace beyond the pace, across a not beyond the not; and what we might call the digression of distance diverts, from *Thomas the Obscure* on, every logic of the limit, of opposition, of identity, of contradiction, but as well sets free, under the apparent normality of his language (vocabulary and syntax), the contamination of noun (*pas*, pace) and adverb (*pas*, not, no)—which alters at the same time, subterraneanly, in the simulacrum of the "same" "word," the respective identity of signifiers and signifieds, of semantic proprieties and improprieties. Of course, for reasons you [*tu*] understand right here, the proceedings of language, on the scene of consciousness, need to seem to leave everything intact, must dislocate everything without appearing to displace anything in its discursivity—and on a completely other scene will increase the violence of the effect. Because the scene is then completely other, mastery and the amortization of effects will have to be renounced. It is through the law—this going-through will be our question—through the unscathed and assured normality of language that the general catastrophe of de-distance is irresistibly provoked. The logic, the syntax, the vocabulary, the rhetoric appear impassive when they are forced to enunciate what in advance will have ruined them from top to bottom, or, rather than ruined, expropriated and subjugated them. Never do the logical conjunctions, adverbs, nouns cease to play their proper role. Never, for example—because everything must not [*ne faut pas*] be escorted back there as to the truth of the *récit*—does one *pas* (the noun "pace") touch the other (the adverb "not"), nor even suggest the least semantic or homonymic familiarity. Not [*Pas*] even in the imperturbable irony or rigor of "The '*pas*' of the completely passive—the 'pace beyond'?—" of *Le pas au-delà* [167/*SNB* 122], twice. Thus, still in that "first" *récit* (*Thomas the Obscure* [55/*Thlo* 57]): "What she said to him took the form of direct speech. . . . 'Yes,' she said, 'I would like to see you [*vous*] when you are alone. If ever I could be before you and completely absent from you, I would have a chance to rejoin you. Or rather I know that I would not rejoin you. The only possibility I would have to diminish the distance between us would be to remove myself to an infinite distance. But I am infinitely far away now, and can go no further.

As soon as I touch you, Thomas. . . .'" Much farther on [*TO* 106–8/*Thlo* 125–28]: "Any distance between us is suppressed, but suppressed in order that we may not come closer one to the other. . . . The being of a nonbeing of which I am the infinitely small negation that it instigates as its profound harmony. . . . All of us are condemned by the same logical proscription, all three of us (a number that is monstrous when one of the three is everything). . . . Now, in this night, I come forward bearing everything, toward that which infinitely exceeds everything. I progress beyond the totality that I nevertheless tightly embrace. I go on the margins of the universe, boldly walking [*marchant*] elsewhere than where I can be, and a little outside of my paces [*mes pas*]. This slight extravagance, this deviation toward that which cannot be, is not only my own impulse leading me to a personal madness, but the impulse of the reason that I bear with me. With me the laws gravitate outside the laws, the possible outside the possible. O night. . . . You [*Tu*] become a delicious passivity . . . "

—Does he *tutoie* with the night alone? Did you say *come*, *viens* to the night just a short while ago? Why sometimes *viens*, sometimes *venez*? A short while ago, in *Awaiting Oblivion*, you remember, he said "*Venez.*"

—But "*Viens*" too: "Forgetting a word, forgetting in this word all words.

"❖ 'Come [*Viens*], and give back to us the becomingness of [*la convenance de*] what disappears, the movement of a heart'" [*AO* 46/*AtOu* 88].

—If *come* is always preceded by another to which it singularly responds, how are we to hear and understand the *becomingness* in this phrase that uses the familiar? Doesn't it make *come* [venir] into the alliance, pace in accord with pace, not with not, one to the other, one in the other, one and the other together? Is the word *coitus*, the moment or the movement of a *coire* . . . ?

—Leave in reserve too the enigma of *tutoieing*, of its bondless bond to a language, of the supplement of discretion that distances from itself all modesty. In using the familiar with him (the question from a short while ago), I would not inevitably be violent or indiscreet, and if I want to be—which I do—I must be more violent or indiscreet than he, in a different way from him. His text—this perhaps has not yet sufficiently been recognized about him—unchains the law of absolute discretion, pushes it forward with the most intractable rigor, and on its own proper scene violates it with a measureless obscenity. But to surprise his indiscretion with the sole discretion that would have remained impossible for him would be still to remain [*demeurer*], in friendship, under the law of the other: the sole sign of friendship, but as if effaced in advance. This machineless machination is what interests me, fascinates me, as does fascination. I again put that off until later—a debt that annuls itself in being infinite. It is a matter of what, of whom? Ever since I've read him—for as long as I can remember—I keep putting off until later the moment of speaking directly about him, about anything at all that comes back to him, and of speaking to him.

I come back to before. I was on the point of remarking the immobile progress that—ever since the paces not beyond [*les pas d'au-delà*] in *Thomas the Obscure* (1941–1950)—is insistent up to *Le pas au-delà* (1973), lays stress on its pace or not, the same, the other. As a sort of response on first approach to your question of the present moment, here is, on the same double page of *Le pas au-delà* [184–85; overleaf in *SNB* 135–36], announced by those lozenge hallmarks (quadrilaterals here, four points there) and sometimes in one type sometimes in the other: "◆ *Taking three paces [*pas*], stopping, falling, and, all of a sudden, becoming sure of himself in this fragile fall.* . . .

"◆ Praise (of the far near) from the near to the far.

"◆ *Come, come, come [*viens, viens, venez*], you for whom the injunction, the prayer, the wait could not be becoming.*

"◆ 'Be at peace with yourself.—There is no one in me to whom I can speak familiarly.— . . . '"

Also count the *pas*'s in his titles. They are displaced and carried away from themselves, but are reprinted also endlessly.

"*Faux-pas*": working (over) the surface of normed intelligibility, other semantic and syntactic forces require other methods. *Faux-pas* of error, errancy, or mistake [*faute*] are not to be committed (*faut-pas*, must-not). *Il faut, ne faut pas* [must, must not, need not], *il faux* [he/it false], etc., get derived straight away from "*pas*" as noun with "*pas*" as adverb of a suspended negation still on hold; and from then on it is the noun that is "false" or simulated. Invisible quotation marks ("*Faux 'pas'*"). *Pas* (the other) is put in *pas* but in order to mislead it and bring it down [*le faire tomber*], to mix the signifier with the signified, to cross the noun and nounless, the categorem and syncategorem, to scramble the syntactic and the semantic, and to announce thereby a *pas*, a pace beyond the language that comes down to some prediscursive phoneme or grapheme. Thus, in *Celui qui ne m'accompagnait pas* [*The One Who Was Standing Apart from Me*], a suspended relation (a relative proposition) simulates in the negative *not* [ne pas] the pace [*le pas*] of *Celui qui ne m'accompagnait pas*; of the one who moreover receives in his title, in his definition (apart from his sex, don't forget), only the definition of walking [*démarche*], of a pacing-with [*un pas-avec*] that does not take place. Or whose pace, not there, denied pace [*le pas n'y est pas, niait* pas]. But once the forces beyond discourse are unleashed, the *pa* in the middle of *Celui qui ne m'accom*pa*gnait pas* is remarked. And if everything is implemented, discreetly, so that this effect is set free in the pace beyond sense and language, one can welcome (to stick to the titles) *La part du feu* [*Work of Fire*], *L'espa*ce *littéraire* [*The Space of Literature*], or *Faux* pas, as legitimately as one welcomes, according to the semantic affinity that leads from *venir* to *viens*, *Le livre* à venir [*The Book* to Come]. And if we gave way to the necessary drift, the recurrence of the *a*'s would propose a whole fiction of theory, for example, apropos this genesis, genesis of color itself—the most extraordinary that I know—recited by Anne and Thomas the Obscure, from the blanched [*le blanc*], the pale, the rare. Later on there will be the *rat* of *Thomas the Obscure* to be recognized, "what seemed to him to be a word, but resembled rather a gigantic rat" [28/*Thlo* 32], etc.

With regard to the possibilities of this writing, to the powers or rights of such a fiction of theory, a science must be determined, measured, transformed. "*Le pas au-delà*" (I am speaking of the title and place it within quotation marks, although what is said through the interminable indirection of language may also be the other of language, its beyond that never lets itself be regulated by the language and reinstitutes the maddest referential opening) accumulates all the economic reserves we have just designated too quickly, but while marking the surplus. No economic circulation, no dialectic can snap shut on a determinable quantity of forces.

Suspended in a context still undetermined (the title's function), the definite article (le *pas*) requires being *pronounced*—the writing of speech too in which the quotation marks are not heard or are heard everywhere, but in which no pronouncement can ever be made on them: the *word* or the *thing*, the word *and* the thing. *Pas* then is the word *pas* AND *pas*, OR *pas*.[13] And the same can be said for the whole title *Le pas au-delà*. What finds itself thus named, entitled, as referent, can be a statement, as much as a referent beyond the statement. The possible transformations of the statement (and so of the title) bre/oach a process of endless dissemination that is just what and therefore some other thing than what comes to the title as title. The word *pas* is noun or adverb, an indecisive adverb as to negation (half-pair of the negation that announces, in the immediate and inevitable doubling of *pas*, of the other *pas*, in *pas* itself, a double *pas* without negation of negation and without denegation), negationless *pas* (not without negation), this proceeding determining the "beyond" but also letting itself be totally carried away by it, in each case, all the better as it is a matter there (*beyond*) of an adverb that lets itself, more easily than another, be nominalized (*Le* pas *au-delà*).

An analysis of *pas* that would stick here to the morsel *ne-pas*, that is, to the functioning of negation or negativity, even if unusual, nonnegative, nondialectical even, would risk interrupting the force of the *récit* in several ways. But the risk of interruption is run, programmed in the night, *by* the *récit*. The reader would miss the text, first, by sticking to the logical and signified side, to the content of a discourse held in its strict limit; second and consequently, by no longer taking into account what is called in the classic code the signifier. One defends oneself then against the homonymic but also prelinguistic contamination that the text calls for or lets come about; that is why the signified/signifier [*Sé/Sa*] opposition is left stranded. Third and consequently, one gives up [*s'interdit*] giving an account of this: the double *pas* is neither a dialectical reappropriation nor a denegation, or at least draws them beyond. Fourth, remaining with the logic of the language ("normally spoken") and consciousness, one excludes all the "unconscious" processes (drives or representatives) that take turns in *pa* and *o-de-la/o-2-la*, etc. Fifth and above all (I say above all because it's a matter here of the sole strategic lever capable, it seems to me, of forcing all the previous limitations), by isolating, in order to give pace [*pas*] over to, the logical or semantic functioning of the not [*ne-pas*], by separating it normally from both the semantics of a walking pace [*du pas de marche*] and the nonsemantics (contaminations, anomalies, delirium, etc.), one gives up all that takes the problematic of logic, of dialectics, of sense, of the being of beings (philosophy and its pace [not] beyond, thought) toward a coming of the event (as de-distance of the near) (*Ereignis, Entfernung, Enteignis*) "before" which philosophy and its pace (not) beyond, thought, are striving without success to close themselves. Now this coming or this arrival [*ce venir ou cette venue*] of the event—going-to-come rather than coming-and-going—does not appear "starting" [*ne paraît pas "à partir"*] from the onto-logic, even if nondialectical, of the not [*ne-pas*]. Onto-logic proceeds from the event (to come and more than past) of a *come* of which we here, you and I, recite the *pas*.[14] Beyond because the instant I say *come*, if I say it, the whole system of limits (*faut pas*, must not) that would prohibit placing one *pas* in the other (for example, the *pas* of walking in the *pas* of negation and reciprocally), is found to be crossed in a single *pas*, without even the *pas*, the activity of walking, what one does with the legs (see above) taking place. *Le pas au-delà*: "Transgression transgresses by passion, patience and passivity" [*SNB* 119/*PAD* 162].

—How would you [*vous*] translate this displacement, this play of words and things, I mean in another language? And there where this play slips without being remarked, leaving it discreetly to its chance to appear or be lost, you come back with a heavy and insistent pace [*pas*] . . .

—I told you my parti pris of effacement by indiscretion, of withdrawal [*re-trait*] slipping away in passing again over the line [*trait*] of the other. And then I want to explain, yes, explain by insisting why he does not insist, for that is not clear. On the one hand, a certain exhibition of the play of words or of homonymy could, stressed in a certain way, give one to think that the primitive identity (for example, by etymological filiation) or even the semantic affinity of the two *pas*'s procures in the end a reassuring foundation, a general and saturating economic law to all this strangeness of de-distancing. Now this strangeness goes beyond the semantic, the etymological—and in general beyond simple language—therefore as well beyond the logical, the rhetorical, etc. And he has himself remarked it enough to have written (to my knowledge only in his latest publication,

I discovered it too late to have taken it into account up to here): "This is what is strange: passivity is never passive enough. It is in this respect that one can speak of an infinite passivity: perhaps only because passivity evades all formulations—yet it seems that there is in passivity something like a demand that would require it to fall always short of itself. There is in passivity not passivity, but its demand, a movement of the past toward the unsurpassable.

"Passivity, passion, past, *pas* (both negation and pace—the trace or movement of an advance [*marche*]): this semantic play provides us with a slippage of meaning, but not with anything to which we could entrust ourselves, not with anything like an answer that would satisfy us." And the following paragraph, which describes a "knot [*noeud*] of refusal" short of all negation, all decision, all denegation, and finally of all saying, appeals to the "I would prefer not to . . . " of Bartleby the scrivener: "'I would prefer not to . . . ' belongs to the infiniteness of patience; no dialectical intervention can take hold of such passivity. We have fallen out of being, outside where, immobile, proceeding [*marchant*] with a slow and even pace [*pas*], destroyed men come and go." ("Discours sur la patience," in *Le Nouveau Commerce* Nos. 30–31 [Spring 1975]: 27–28.[15] The paragraphs in "Discours sur la patience" are preceded by two solid lozenges.)

What he rejects, and from this "knot of refusal," is the complaisant semantic triumph that could take place in the play of words in *pas*, in the play of *pas*'s, if we asked him for a foundation, a certitude, or a mastery, that is, the wherewithal, simply and finally, to limit, with a reappropriating denegation, its madness. He warns us about play as "semantic play," about slippage as "slippage of meaning." But this warning, instead of imposing a limit on the contamination, hands it over to all the excesses of force, beyond every genealogy, every *etymon*, the semantic, ontological or, as well, signifying economy. Finally, there is always in *Witz*, when it is used, authorized, cultivated, this economic vulgarity, very precisely the vulgarity of *our* epoch, which claims to condense in *advance*—in order to master ideally at the least cost, appropriating and paraphing in the blank spaces [*en blanc*] just what will not yet have been thought in the language—some "effects of meaning." Psychoanalysis should have led us away from rather than rush us toward this: *Witz*, conscious and deliberate, perceptible or mastered, always comes in a situation of denegation or apotrope, in resistant relation to the other, to the unconscious. Psychoanalytic discourse, which presents itself as such, in practice or in theory, should be the first to suspect this.

As much as possible, he has never yielded to the mastery or the economic slavishness of *Witz*—and without any retreat, as we shall confirm, in relation to the advances of the epoch, provoking, preceding, accompanying them on all the breaking lines, on all the frontlines. For convenience let's call them literature, philosophy, psychoanalysis, political thought and practice, etc. He has maintained this impassive, neutral, transparent surface of the language of writing [*la langue de l'écriture*]. But in such a way that this exigency prohibits nothing, on the contrary, and unleashes what the scared exhibition of *Witz* often comes to contain or deny. If there were, which I don't believe, some pertinence to praise him for this, if there weren't in that a coarse attribution of mastery and if *Le pas au-delà* did not make such a metaphor out of date in advance, I would say that never have I imagined him so far in front of us as I have today. Awaiting us, still to come, to be read, to be reread by those very same ones that do it ever since they knew how to read and *thanks* [grâce] to him. Do not hasten to refuse this word. Read what he says himself, on grace and chance, at the beginning of *Le pas au-delà* [37–43/*SNB* 24–28].

Therefore the two *pas*'s do not touch in the same. Must not, need not [*Il ne faut pas*]. That's how it works and blows up, just like that [*C'est comme ça que ça marche et que ça saute*], and how the other *pas* inhabits, marks, and effaces that very *pas* it does not appear to touch or tamper with. This absence of contact or contiguity between the *pas*'s, within *pas* itself, is where Blanchot's *pas* leaves a mark. *Le pas*. Marking time, *pas* marks *pas*. To reestablish the continuum, it would simply efface it. Which would come down to nearly the same. Since they no longer appear to touch, never to have done so, one *pas* effaces better the other with its erasure without negation, without denegation, without remains [*reste*], without contrast [*relief*], without relief [*relève*]. Which would come down to nearly the same, then. Save [*Sauf*] the *récit*. (No) more *pas*. " . . . the slight derision of his words: 'Are you writing, are you writing *at this moment*?'

"What is going to come about [*arriver*], then? Did I really have this desire to steal away, to unload myself on someone else? or rather to conceal in me the unknown, not to disturb it, to efface its paces [*ses pas*] so that what it has accomplished may be accomplished without leaving any remains, in such a way that it not be accomplished for me who dwells on the edge, outside the event, which no doubt passes by with the brilliance, noise, and dignity of lightning, without my being able to do more than perpetuate its approach, take its indecision by surprise, maintain it, maintain myself in it without yielding" (*The One Who Was Standing Apart from Me* [67/*CQN* 126]).

When I say to you [*te*] *come* once more, for example, what is going to come about then? And at the moment the other, who does not accompany him, asks him, "'Are you writing, are you writing, *at this moment*'"? Going to come about: the strange future of the coming about (the coming [*arrivée*] of what?), the future [*avenir*] of imminence, is marked in French and English [*dans la langue*] by recourse to the present of a verb (*aller*, going, *va*, is going), which should say what distances-itself-from in order to get-closer-to—here to what would de-distance, from itself—the to-come in order to make it come about, etc. The whole is suspended in the indecision (remarked farther on in the word "indecision") of the question, the question itself potentialized by the impersonal neuter (what? what is going to come about? or rather, for it is not something that is going to come about, but that *there* [*il*] is going to come about: what is *there* going to come about, then?)[16] and in a sort of a-semy of the *come(s) about* [*arrive*: arrive, happen] whose analysis I defer. Going to come about: restrained imminence of the future [*l'avenir*], no/pace of coming about [*pas d'arrivée*]. It has just come about [*Il vient d'arriver*]: past hardly restrained in the present pace [*pas*]. Untranslatable text, to be sure, and riveted, each time, to the unique event of one single language, one single syntactical and lexical normality. And yet this untranslatability is as accessory as essential. At stake is a pace (not) beyond the language that walks/works [*marche*] only with a language, doubtless, but in order to open to a transgression of the linguistic *without* metalanguage. What I would like to give you: *Come* without any language overhang, without anything that can in its turn designate it from a third place, that can name it. And in effect each time one says, within quotation marks, "Come," the "Come"—what we will not be able to avoid, unfortunately for us—is missed, not spoken of. But one runs the chance of repeating the alliance.

The impact of the walking *pas* [*pas de marche*] on the negation *pas*

[*pas de négation*] tilts yet otherwise: so that the interdictory negation (not, must not, need not, you must not, etc.) comes loose from itself, in a "sweet, gentle" ["*doux*"] movement. See what he says under that word as to "not—you will die" and as to "Not—I know" in *Le pas au-delà* [148, 154/*SNB* 108, 112]. The limit of both negativity and interdiction is crossed there, remaining nonetheless "saved" in a sense that we shall still have to reread.

The *pas* extra—the other *pas*—works (over) silently its homonym, haunts or parasitizes it, steps over the two limits all at once in both senses and directions. *Its* transgression is not yet labor or activity; it is passive and transgresses nothing, "empty transgression" [*PAD* 143, 146/*SNB* 104, 106], "Transgressive passivity" [*PAD* 167/*SNB* 122]. "The '*pas*' of the completely passive" (*Le pas au-delà* [167/*SNB* 122]) that carries along to the limit, to the internal border where every transgression comes about itself [*s'arrive*], leaves that border nevertheless unharmed: border without border, *without* ever any dialectic reappropriation.

It is not only his *récit*, or how it works and walks according to Blanchot's no/pace, that takes here its strange departure, its so singular possibility; it is the system (without system) of all his redoubled affirmations. For example, the affirmation of the discretion *without* discretion. Here I underline without discretion:

"*Walk, go forward*—I could certainly do that, and I had to, *but* rather like an ox that has been hit over the head: *my paces* were *the paces of immobility.* . . . The hallway led to the *room that was at the other end.* Everything seems to indicate that I looked terribly distraught, I *went in* more or less *without* knowing it, *without* any feeling of *going from one place to another*, filled with a motionless falling, I couldn't see, I was miles from realizing I couldn't see. I probably stopped on the *doorsill*. After all, there was a *passage* there, a thickness that had its own laws or requirements. Finally—finally?—the *passage* became free, and *I forced the entrance*, and I took *two or three paces* into the room. Fortunately (but maybe this impression was accurate only for me), I *walked with a certain discretion*. . . . This is the reason for my desire to abbreviate, at least its nobler aspect. *To pass over the essential*—that is what the essential asks of me, asks of me through this desire. . . . (so I had taken several *paces* into the room in order to reach the *foot* of the bed). . . . It was also true that I had taken *a few paces*; passing near the armchair. . . . What is strange about *not* [ne pas] seeing something distant when nearby things are still invisible?" (*When the Time Comes* [4–7/*AMV* 15–21]).

The *room*—bare topography of this (non)walking, without nature and without culture—at *the other* end. It is necessary to get [*arriver*] there through the "paces of immobility." No paralysis however, nor interdiction. Nothing remains finally on the doorsill. The paceless pace (not without not) does not stop at a simple thought of *limen* [*Le pas sans pas ne s'arrête pas à une simple pensée de* limen]. Two or three paces are taken: into the room. But one must get to the other end, this time into the room and to "the foot of the bed." The *almost*, the proximity of the *almost* does not simply keep at a distance; it crosses over, and "the wild statement [*l'affirmation sauvage*] that has no rights" [*WTC* 8/*AMV* 23] takes place there, a place that cannot be situated in a topography that would only receive it or would have preceded it. Before this affirmation leaps out, after he had passed "near the armchair": "Things appeared to resolve themselves (appeared? that was already a great deal). At the moment I was *closest* to her, two paces from the armchair, she could not only see me better, my face livid rather than pale, my forehead cruelly swollen, but *almost* touch me" [*WTC* 7/*AMV* 22].

The wild affirmation that leaps out from these "two or three paces" is not, simply, nondialectic. The insistence on the two or three (non) paces [*pas*], here and in *Le pas au-delà*, does not stop at a relation that is negative, indeed critical, suspensive or denegative to all dialectics. There is no dialectics *there*. What if, on the other scene, the scene that did not represent itself as philosophy (idealist or materialist), it were (not) *pas*, it, dialectics [*c'était* pas, *ça, la dialectique*]?[17] But also the dissimulation *of* dialectics? What if it were necessary, as the philosopher would say, to re-think its possibility from ("starting from") such a de-parture, finally, or from its *faux-pas*? Or from its double *faux-pas*? There are *always two pas's*. One in the other but without possible inclusion, one affecting the other immediately but in crossing while distancing itself from it. Always two *pas's*, crossing up to their negation, according to the eternal return of the passive transgression and of the repeated affirmation. The two *pas's*, the double *pas* disunited and allied with itself nonetheless, one passing the other immediately, passing into it and provoking from then on a double instantaneous but interminable preterition, that is what forms a singular limit between keeping and loss, between remembering too and forgetting. They are no more opposed, in their infinite difference, than *pas* to the other *pas*. According to the simulacrum of the circle—eternal return of the double *pas*—he/it that says *come* inaugurates only in already responding. He/it follows her/it that he/it seems to call and whose call he/it remembers. "Faux-pas" of desire, as is said in *Le pas au-delà*, and crossing of the circle: no/pace of circle.

Pas is forgetting, no/pace of forgetting doubly affirmed (yes, yes). "A hurried, eternal *pas*" (*Awaiting Oblivion* [39/*AtOu* 77]). Elsewhere: "❖ She forgot more slowly than any slowness, more suddenly than any surprise.

"'I sometimes have the impression that you [*vous*] recall only so that you can forget: so that you can keep the power of forgetting perceptible. It is rather forgetting that you would like to remember [*vous souvenir*].'—'Perhaps. I remember when I am two paces away from forgetting. It is a strange impression.'—'A dangerous one as well; the distance of two paces is quickly crossed.'—'Yes, but there will always be two more paces, and each time I sense that you are following me, you who are nevertheless in front of me.'—'I am following you; I would like to follow you'" [*AO* 54/ *AtOu* 103–4].

—I have long ceased to understand you [*vous*] and no longer know what I am listening to and who is speaking to me. As *pas* is not a word, nor a thing, a cry maybe, short of language (even though the manner in which the cry is opposed to language makes this word cry inappropriate here), a movement beyond everything and itself, without origin and without goal [*but*] that precedes it, it occasionally comes about that the word "*pas*," already pluralized in itself (its writing without an article does not allow distinguishing between the singular and the plural, a rather rare phenomenon), starts to signify, beyond all the content of the noun and the adverb, just what is not signifiable in a language: even less a metalinguistic gesture conferring all power over language. Would it signify, once more overlapped in itself, one of those syllables or phonic elements that, before the civilized [*policé*] order of language, on the side of phantasm or drive . . .

—Not/*Pas* before (proceed here with that infinite patience that in one stroke, however, crosses its limit), not/*pas* before having drawn the conclusion from what he hears and understands by "forgetting" and that overflows all the philosophical and psychoanalytic determinations of forgetting. Without omitting anything, however, of their pertinence. What is said of the "psychoanalytic" determination will have to be said—later, therefore, as well—of the "political."

—I've ceased understanding you [*vous*] right from the start. Why do you detain me after I've left you?

—I am trying, once more, to say *come*.
Remember.

This so that you [*tu*] remember at last. For you, this should be but an interminable digression to *approach* [aborder], one more but always unique time, *come*. Remember. It's a matter of your name. For what the name *name* will not have sufficed.

The affirmation that leaps out just now from these "two or three paces," analogous in this to the *come* that remains an affirmation beyond its grammar, he calls it a "cry," and it bears relation without contract, *wild*, without filiation to the name—his name for her who cries out the affirmation. There is excess of strength [*force*] again: "and suddenly she had the strength, the *immense strength* to cry out at me, and while I leaned over the objects on the dresser, she actually did utter a *cry* that seemed to her to be born, to leap out, from the living *memory* of her *name*, but—why?—valiant though this cry was, it did *not surpass* [*ne* dépassa *pas*] its limits, it did not reach me, and because of that, she herself *did not hear it*. . . .

"Pride also! The wild statement has no rights, the pact signed with what defies the origin, oh strange and terrible tranquility" [*WTC* 8/*AMV* 22–23].

How does this affirmation of the double *pas*, the alliance without contract of one to the completely other (yes, yes), how does it expend a force without measure to cry out a name, and above all a name that the cry does not invent, that comes from a memory already, comes back in the memory [*souvient dans le souvenir*] of who nevertheless has right from the start forgotten it, separated from her own proper name up to not hearing it? What does this double *pas*, this double band of a pact without pact (without subject and without origin, without object either since nothing is enunciated in it, nothing is treated in it but the name) have to do, to see or hear, to lose or to win with the fascination of water [*eau*]? I wanted to ask you that in the course of this endless digression. And not so that you may respond to it as to a question—the affirmation that comes back to us [*nous souvient*] will have exceeded [*débordé*] in advance such an exchange—but so that you may hear only an other *come*...

—Why would it be, each time, the image, at least, of a woman?

—Perhaps not [*pas*]. Not yet. They [*elles*] are...

—Women?

—In any case, three times at least (as you [*tu*] read in *Death Sentence* and in *Awaiting Oblivion*), someone *tutoies* them only to say *come*.
The other *come*: in *Celui qui ne m'accompagnait pas* [145/*OW* 77]—gentle rule, that is, without law, of our reading: to comment on, to read, to write it *with* it (in the camera) without accompanying it, from the place and the walk of the one that does not accompany, from/with another (non) pace—"Come" occurs [*se passe*] not far from the "water" [*eaux*] [*CQN* 144/ *OW* 76], from a drowning, in other words, from what misses the shore, fails to arrive [*ce qui manque la rive, n'arrive pas à arriver*]. Come: how would that provoke the coming of what comes, the coming of the event, for example, if *come* itself does not arrive, does not come itself about [*n'arrive pas, ne s'arrive pas*]?

—Is that so assured? *Come* calls nonetheless, and I am there; you came up to me [*par vous abordée*]. *Come* also proceeds from my place, no matter what you were able or meant to say. And she who is called, to whom it would be enough that the event were *come*, she too can re-cite:
"*We should not, by means of sacrifices, pretend to carry on a dialogue.*"[8] And on the same page: "... *the final discretion, and it is on the basis of this discretion that the precaution of friendly words* [paroles] *calmly affirmed itself. Words from one shore to the other shore, speech* [parole] *responding to someone who speaks from the other edge and where, even in our life, the measurelessness* [démesure] *of the movement of dying would like to complete itself. And yet when the event itself comes, it brings this change*..." (*Friendship* [291–92/*A* 329]).

—Whence the right to interrupt? Do you [*tu*] imagine a dialogue, a plural speech [*parole*] without the always unjustifiable violence of an interruption? *Come*, is that an interruption? I interrupt you to say: one should not be able to cite *Friendship*. Everything should be dated in it: sealed by the absolute singularity of a single friendship, Maurice Blanchot's and Georges Bataille's. There is nothing more vulgar and more servile, indiscreet, unspeakable than the arraignment [*arraisonnement*] by which in citing, extracting, teaching, one generalizes the hijacking [*détournement*], one thinks one appropriates the unique.

—He exposes himself to that, and far from refusing this nonsecret, he specifies again, starting from another anonymity, renouncing the right of property/propriety as well as the lesson, teaching, generality.

—Yes, yes, as soon as death—which has arrived, happened (you [*tu*] remarked that he always regards it as just what fails to come [*n'arrive pas à venir*] ["Dying (the non-arrival of what comes about [*advient*]), the prohibited . . . " and on the same page, in *Le pas au-delà* [132/*SNB* 95–96]: "The work of mourning: the inverse of dying"])—as soon as death fails *to* come, does not arrive as soon as it comes, or does not reach the coming [*n'arrive pas au venir*] or what comes in the coming or *come* ("and eternally, she/it is there"), death, arrived at the other, frees speech from speech that, as he also says, is proffered uniquely in *tutoieing*: "this *tutoieing* that seems to designate only the lack of anyone, restores the intimacy and the singularity of the relation. Chance joins these two traits. Chance comes [*arrive*] only through playing. And the game does not address itself to anyone in particular. He who is lucky [*a la chance*] is not lucky and is not so for himself or because of himself. The 'without you' of chance frees, through *tutoieing*, for the anonymous" (*Le pas au-delà* [39–40/*SNB* 26]). For the event that you have cited, and that arrives, has arrived in the other alone (*"when the event itself comes, it brings this change . . . "*), isn't that what is also called (as) death? Isn't what is always called, to whom *come* is said, isn't that death, the other's death, come from the other that calls and names itself?

—The shore too, impossible. What arrives would always arrive *at the edge* [*au bord*]. Would affect the edge. But by remaining at the edge: by not arriving. Come, you told me: that does not arrive or happen, if I have understood right. Because of the repetition—even if affirmative (yes, yes, come [*venez*]) and allied to itself from one yes to the other—to itself, which divides the unique, gives a sense, from then on, to this singularity that should have none, refolds the other to which that—*come*—is addressed.

In order to announce the impossible arrival of *come*, you said that *eau*, either it [*elle*, water] or the word [*mot*] "*eau*," had to affect, in some part, immediately, the departed-from, the shore that emits *come*, that is, always the other shore, the one as well that you [*vous*] have just let be called death.

—*Eau* (water): neither it nor the word "*eau*" nor simply the syllable or the letter (oh, *au*, o) would be enough to signify here the element of this affection by which what departs from a *come* relates to itself (*m'* . . .) from the other, the *eau*, the oh, the *au*, the o, the word, the *m'ot*,[19] the bit [*le mors*], death [*la mort*], etc. "The conviction that there was, in fact, no water. . . . Was it actually water?", that is what is said in the first three pages of *Thomas the Obscure* [7/ *ThIo* 10] toward the waters off [*parages*] of what I would like to get at with you [*toi*], so that we can approach [*aborder*] according to his name's double o: water and o [*l'eau double*].

—The other *come*: since you [*vous*] are making it resound from *The One Who Was Standing Apart from Me*, recall the first words of the *récit*: "I sought, this time, to approach him" [1/*CQN* 7].

Waters [*Parages*], you say. Farther, this floating movement, time as if suspended from apprehension, every machine stopped, the coast in fog, a vicinity without proximity, without distance, between the silence and the murmuring of language, very gently (I know now the rigor of this word), very violently, defines the coming [*la venue*] of the event or rather, since the event does not simply arrive, its (non)pace, its gait, that from which it goes in the coming [*le venir*] of an event, the unique as relation to the other, the (non)pace that does not accompany, each *time* uniquely unique and inalterably other, the "time" ("*fois*") being always this time here, here and now, as when you said to me, without context or possible anticipation, without the least shoreline or riveting [*rivage*], *come*, and always other, but *always* (all the same) other. This first sentence, however inaugural it seems, recites itself in advance. Some eight[20] pages farther on, the question is raised of knowing whether the inaugural would not be the goal, the end, the other end, being-at-the-end-of-one's-strength, the *end result*: "was all this destined to result in that one sentence: 'I sought, this time, to approach him'? 'This time,' I saw clearly how unjustified such a remark [*mot*] seemed. It appeared there because I wanted to be at the end of my strength. But for my part, I was not, and for such a part 'this time' was not 'this time,' but another time, a time that was always another. I can't hide the fact that the desire to approach him could only with great difficulty be reconciled with the idea that this could ever take place 'this time.' He did nothing to ward off such an event. It may even be that he awaited it with a sort of hope. But I felt that the whole enterprise was entrusted to me alone, and I must say I wasn't managing it, I wasn't managing it [*je n'y arrivais pas, je n'y arrivais pas*].

"'You get by rather well,' he remarked. 'You're astonishing, you know.'

"Yes, I got by quite well, but this in itself cast a not very engaging light on everything I could imagine doing; I got by all too well, whereas the best that could have happened [*arriver*] to me would have been not to get by at all" [*OW* 5/*CQN* 14–15].

I got by all too well, he says. The "too well" comes to him from the fact that he does not manage, to be sure, to approach finally, one time that would no longer be another, and that, nonetheless, he manages to not manage and insists on it and repeats it. It is rather in this repetition ("I wasn't managing it, I wasn't managing it") that, as he attracts the familiar and ironic remark, he gets by not bad, "'rather well,'" and that the worst passes into the best or reciprocally. The event does not manage *to* happen [*n'arrive pas* à *arriver*], but that is because he himself gets by rather well: because he is not himself disabled enough. He does not manage to let the event come. The best that could happen to him himself is to be disabled enough, on the brink of wrecking, no longer getting by at all, for the chance (the failure and the due date) of the event: something (other) that would happen (to him) finally, the best and the worst. His mastery is put in check for what is called to come: *come*. Perhaps then he could cease citing, repeating, dividing, as you have done, even before beginning, your (word) *come*, in order to affirm it finally without possible return or as the eternal return of the other; cease placing it, as one says so easily today, adrift. The drift [*dérive*], to be sure, puts one on guard against all the securities of anchorage, shoreline, riveting, property, propriety, but puts one on guard, precisely, and keeps guard still, perhaps, against what arrives, the best or the worst, coming from in front or from the abyss, in the center's baseless center. "*Drifting without shoreline* [Dérivant sans rivage]" (*The Step Not Beyond* [64/*PAD* 91]). Vague, essentially, in these waters [*parages*], indeterminate proximity, the other shore . . .

—Surprising locution. As in *the other thing*, I sense in it a certain order always veering, and the noun exchanging its place with the indefinite adjective, then the noun with the verb. All the better since these two nouns are the most singularly indefinite. The other becomes thing or shore. Both shore and cause as well under fascination. The figure of the other, without figure, the split-in-two face of the shore ("I found myself with two faces, glued one to the other. I was in constant contact with two shores. With one hand showing that I was indeed there, with the other—what am I saying?—*without the other*, with this body that, imposed on my real body, depended entirely on a negation of the body, I entered into absolute dispute with myself. . . . And so on, for all my organs. I had a part of myself submerged, and it was to this part, lost in a constant shipwreck, that I owed my direction, my face [*ma figure*], my necessity. . . . Between this corpse, the same as a living person *but without life*, and this unnameable, the same as a *dead person but without death*, I could not see a single line of kinship. No poison might unite me . . . " *Thomas the Obscure* [96–97/ *ThIo* 111–12; Derrida's emphasis]), the figure of the shore is insistent when he speaks of the other, the other that one does not reach, whose distance one does not manage to cross, beyond that element of which the two waters (two O's) (synonyms and homonyms for what remains without name) would be then the best "representation." Face, shoreline, wreckage—that is the same seascape, a landless landscape, without familiarity, rootless.[21] Thus: "But we are led through the teaching of Lévinas before a radical experience. *Autrui* is entirely Other; the other is what exceeds me absolutely. The relation with the other that is *autrui* is a transcendent relation, which means that there is an infinite, and, in a sense, an impassable distance [*distance*] between myself and the other, who belongs to the other shore [*rive*], who has no country [*patrie*] in common with me, and who cannot in any way assume equal rank in a same concept or a same whole . . . " (*The Infinite Conversation* [52/*EI* 74]). We find ourselves here, without landing, in waters off [*parages de*] thought where conceptual vicinity is indeed impossible, and "family resemblance"[22] . . .

   —But can one, ought one to, *must one* land on [faut-il *aborder*] this other shore? Wouldn't it immediately cease to be the other? Would the event still come about? Wouldn't it be hit with an interdiction (*not! ne pas!*) on its very arrival, according to the double no/pace of the law, its double bond [*lien*], its circlelessly circular double knot that is on first approach crossed? "The circle of the law is this: there must be a crossing in order for there to be a limit, but only the limit, inasmuch as uncrossable, summons to cross, affirms the desire (the false step, the *faux pas*) that has always already, through an unforeseeable movement, crossed the line" (*The Step Not Beyond* [24/*PAD* 38]). Just like death ("always the horizon of the law" [*SNB* 25/*PAD* 38]) "that prevents us from dying" and from which is withdrawn "in advance the benefit of an *event*" (*The Step Not Beyond* [93–94/*PAD* 129]). Mustn't one leave the shore, instead of landing, for the event to come about? Then the "waters" (the O's), the wreckage in "them" without possible parry, and those that let themselves *tutoie* . . .

   —Mustn't one leave the shore, you say, for it to come about [*pour que ça arrive*]? And for it no longer to go on [*ça ne marche plus*], from one *pas* to the other? The play of words can always dissimulate what terrifies us the most; we needn't push it. The *must* [il faut] you just this instant pronounced to enjoin the greatest risk, mustn't one try to lose that for it to come about? It is nearly impossible, but yet has already come about.
   Yes, the drowning in these waters [*parages*], and then, this time in the course of *The One Who Was Standing Apart from Me*, *come* is not launched, but again cited, evoked as an eventuality, as what "it would be enough for me to say to one of them—but only to one" [77/*CQN* 145]. The preceding page enunciated this absence of law that *would have to*, yes, again, be prescribed when one accompanies such a *récit*, such a signature, from which I get the absence of law as the sole possible gift, in the *tutoieing* that *The Step Not Beyond* opposes to the law's use of it, in the *tutoieing* that, saying "'without you'" instead of "'in spite of you,'" "grants itself," like "sovereignty," "in forgetting itself" [25/*PAD* 38–39].

—I am wondering if this is not yet a bit more complicated, twisted, ensnared, if there is not (I am following your discourse there) something like a gift-knot [*un pas de don*]²³ that has to recall itself in order to come about [*advenir*], however little is a bit more, and from then on start to be ensnared in the trap of the law, in its very own trap. The trap then would not be nearing the knot but would be confused with the very structure of the knot [*du pas*], with the truth of the knot as the knot of truth. But the knot of truth becomes irreversible in the truth of the knot, just as there is no longer any essence for the distancing as the topic of the essence. The *I* that he lets speak in the exergue of *The Most High* would come about then there where there was (k)not: "'I'm a trap for you. Even if I tell you everything—the more loyal I am, the more I'll deceive you: it's my frankness that'll catch you.'

"'Please understand: everything that you get from me is, for you, only a lie—because I'm the truth.'"

—But I affirm, without this truth of the truth, in saying *come*, the gift that from him, from "you" . . .

—From whom?

—I get as the sole gift possible. Forget the question. Here is the page preceding the other *come* and that I was going to cite (*The One Who Was Standing Apart from Me*): "I mustn't alarm them, nor tame them. I must remain [*demeurer*] still so that they will remain still. Deal with their presence in a loyal way, and 'loyally' means without attributing any law to them, without attributing myself to this presence as to a law—and perhaps not taking them into account. . . . In return, and because, in a way I don't understand, I fascinate them, I have to remain within their fascination. This isn't noticed, doesn't disturb appearances, is nothing but an uncertain expectation [*attente*]. Next to them, I am like a man who has already held himself up in the water [*eaux*] too long and who sees, coming to meet him, what appears to be the body of a drowned man: only one? perhaps two, perhaps ten. . . . The circle they form around me encloses me on the outside and yet always within me still. It is infinite, and because of this I suffocate inside it. . . . but I am really touching them, they hold me against myself, as I hold them desperately beyond me.

"The feeling I am left with: I will not yield, I can't do otherwise.

"Strange impression of daylight in this feeling, not that of any sort of hope, but of an accurate direction, of confidence that doesn't alter, of affirmation that persists: I will go in that direction, never in another.

"A feeling that is immediately disturbed, for the thought goes through me that if I wanted to, I would get an increase in strength [*forces*] from them [*elles*]."

—From them? From whom? The increase in strength as in *Death Sentence* before the *come* of the end: "I gave her all my strength and she gave me all her strength, so that this strength is too great . . . ," and in *Awaiting Oblivion*: "as if she bore in herself the force of proximity. . . . this force of approach that gathers together proximity and, in this proximity, the far-off and the outside in their entirety." She is defined only by this bonus of force; this difference to be given, what is it?

—". . . an increase in strength from them. But this is the strength to which I can't consent; why? I don't know more precisely; nevertheless, I still know that this depends on me, on me at each instant; I know it even in forgetfulness and even when, looking at them, I have the presentiment that it would be enough for me to say to one of them—but only to one—'Come,' for it to cry out its name, and right away I would emerge from that reserve in which, even if the instant doesn't stand there, I stand in its place, in that spot where, in the confidence that is suitable to the abyss, I await the instant that will say to me: 'Now everything is all right, you don't have to talk [*parler*] anymore'" [*OW* 76–77/*CQN* 143–46].

—The upsurge (I will not say the baptism although it is a matter of calling someone to his own proper name in the water, of calling someone starting from the water: it would be rather a matter of analyzing baptism from this gift of the name) . . .

—And of recalling that elsewhere the gift is defined as that alone that hands over to anonymity, to the forgetfulness of the name, to the without-name, to the no name, to the (non)pace *of* the name [*au pas de nom, au pas du nom*], in him.

—The name still has the form of a cry uttered by who is named for the first time. And this cry is the wild affirmation, without pact, of *When the Time Comes*. Then "you don't have to talk anymore." How are we to understand that? Have to? Have to not talk anymore? Don't have to? Have to not? Prohibition? Or else "it is not necessary anymore"? You don't have anymore the need, the desire, the lack "you don't have . . . anymore"?[24]

—Why do you always want to decide the sense? arrest it, gather it, bring it near to itself? And then one would have to leave the text alone. Not accompany it. These citations, already, from a moment ago, deported outside a unique *récit* in which they have a unique place, should not be possible, above all should not be suitable for these new linkings, these simulacra of demonstration, these other configurations. They are possible, however, and suitable, that is what makes them readable, in the very uniqueness of their place. This *récit* here being a *récit* of double affirmation, one can always catch in midair, between two affirmations, in the legendary suspense in which the undecided lets itself be lured . . .

—But why pretend from then on to leave it undecided? What economy—and what ruse, what new mastery—is hidden in these parts [*parages*], behind the undecidable? What new technics? What parry?

—None in any case that doesn't expose itself and remove itself. The undecidable is only a phase, a (non)pace of the *récit*, the one here that thwarts a certain relation to dialectics and neutralizes it. But this movement of the neutral is evidently neither negative nor dialectical. It must pass, at a certain moment, in a natural manner, that is to say without possible convention, through the very form of what it neutralizes or passes: here, for example, dialectics, binary or triadic thought, the logic or grammar that would confine the *ne-uter* in negativity, or would make of the "*pas*" a noun *or* an adverb, and so on. One must not [*Il ne faut pas*], and besides one cannot come to a stop at this value of the undecidable once one has let it come into play. But one does not let it [*elle*] come into play; it comes. Itself just now not having come about, in order not to come about [*De ne pas s'arriver*][25] . . .

—Will he, at the end of the account, say *come* to those that drowned [*ces noyé(e)s*]? Will he have let them cry out their name? Or only, once more and in advance, will he have commented on, accompanied the eventuality of what would come in the event ("it *would* be enough for me to say to one of them [*l'une d'elles*]—but only to one—'Come,' for . . . ")?

—That is not for him to decide. *Come* is in the response, which is also just what says *come* and gives the gift as she hears it. To you to take the (non)pace of (no) sense [*le pas de sens*]. There is no chance to decide, no chance to be decided, in whatever language it may be, what comes in *come*. No semantic exploration, no logico-grammatical analysis that, once led to its end, if that is possible, does not remain on the threshold, here, of this *come*. It is not the sense of the statement [*énoncé*], of the act of enunciation and other similar things that thwarts the closure of language, but indeed the *pas de sens*, the (non)pace of (no) sense, which takes place *here* in the *pas alone, by itself* (writing as the trace of a movement without origin, without end, without language, without . . .).

—Here, you say? Where? In *Death Sentence*, in *The One Who Was Standing Apart from Me*, in *Awaiting Oblivion*? Here in general, in every part [*partout*]?

—Come: here, wherever you'd like, in those parts [*parages*] wherever you'll be able to "be there" and to give what comes,[26] in your name but nameless. Come, each time the unique, but at the same time the copy [*exemplaire*]. Whence the "immeasurable" unhappiness and gladness [*réjouissance*] of the double affirmation, of what twice gives the *pas*. And if the fragments of the *récits* are already some exemplary citations, the unique power of *these récits* is that the unscathed possibility of the unique (we will call that, later, the *save/safe* [*le* sauf]) remains in the reserve from which "I would emerge" ("to say to one of them—but only to one—'Come,' for it to cry out its name, and right away I would emerge from that reserve . . . "): she/it holds [*elle vaut*] then for all, in every part, in general.

She/it to whom *come*, if it comes, would address itself, is not yet named at this instant. She/it is still nameless; she/it is the pronoun of a nameless one.

—Why she/it, then, and not he/it? Why I?

—At the moment when the *come* comes (I should not nominalize this "Come" and cannot describe its coming [*sa venue*] by any verb imposed on it and that does not come from it), the unique addressee (still nameless or without memory of its name: how would I be able to inscribe it in sexual difference?) is not there; nothing nor anyone has arrived that can be named already or receive a name.

And yet *come*, if it comes, is of/from the other, as you [*tu*] of course agreed. What has not yet taken place therefore must have happened already. Even when I cite "Come" as an eventuality to come, without premises—first "word" ["*mot*"] (whence its capital-letter appearance) or language event that escapes all the semantic or logico-grammatical analyses, that escapes indeed the order of language, designating thus all that overflows [*déborde*] it—even when I remain at the bottom of the reserve, I can call the eventuality of the "Come" only if it is no longer an eventuality, the probability to come of an event, if what has not yet occurred, will perhaps never occur, has, however, already taken place: already its monument, its vestige, its *pas*, trace of nothing, not even of self as of some identity, each time unique, according to a time that is not time, not the time of consciousness nor of perception, not of science, nor of philosophy.

—The time of the unconscious . . .

—Not even that is a sure step: the forgetting that he spoke [*parle*] to us about, which would be, beyond all our categories of forgetting, the forgetting of forgetting or the forgetting without forgetting, from this forgetting the apparatus of psychoanalysis—and psychoanalysis too—would get no more movement than it seems to arrest as science or practice, in its present state: for example, with everything that supposes an economy of repressions necessarily working toward protection. But if the name forgetting is retained for this forgetting completely other, if he always maintains the "old" names of the language, it is in order to attempt to give an account—in a way that is not simply nonscientific, nonphilosophical, and so on—of the *necessary* dissimulation of this completely other in the "old" name, in science or philosophy. The effects of this dissimulation are not fortuitous; a *pas d'autre*, a no/pace of other, is remarked there each time; and every revolution, whether scientific or political, must take this into account. This X (for example, the forgetting completely other) is *also* the same as the X that one thinks one is familiarly thinking in the current language, in science, or in philosophy, whatever the discrepancies [*écarts*] among these three languages. This can be said of each of his "words" ["*mots*"], *come*, for example, and each one, in the double *pas* that overlaps and cuts across it, comes round to crossing its own proper limit in remarking the generality of the proceeding [*procès*]: thus *le pas d*'oubli, the no/ pace of *forgetting*, describes, as one says of a trajectory, the *whole* path [*processus*] of the dissimulation, and so on.

This "terrifyingly ancient"[27] time therefore requires (the) *récit*; it makes of the thus determined *récit* the sole text that places us in (relationless) relation with this past of the *pas* that no concept, no poem either, as such, could even cite. Reciting therefore, since it can be a matter of nothing but that: of citing a *come* that has not yet called who is called, ever since a *come*, an *already* more ancient than time, an absolute crypt. This *récit* destroys the one that would claim to report, according to the current logic of these words, an event, but it does not do this in the name of the concept, as a philosophical gesture, rather in the name of another *récit* dissimulated, accorded to the other-event, to the *pas de concept*, the (non)pace of (no) concept. It "would be" the coming of this other-event called *come* if that *come* came about, arrived with a simple (non)pace. To say that the *récit* (of Blanchot) is not the relation of the event but the event itself would therefore not be enough. Rather, the *récit* "would have been" the labyrinthian and ensnared structure of the *pas d'événement*, the (non) pace of (no) event, the apparatus of a fascination as gentle as it is implacable: this desire of/for *paralysis* that never stops, that gives movement, and without measure. Nothing of "the '*pas*' of the completely passive" will have been read if this desire of paralysis, "desire of the without-desire,"[28] is thought as a simple dissolution, a regression toward the movement o. No analysis, if one understands thereby [*par là*] a regressive move [*démarche*] toward the first and undecomposable simplicity; no analysis can measure itself against *pas*: this chance of language, of a single language, will a historical analysis of its necessities reduce it? It—necessity, chance—still marks chance, risk: let the other of the language come to pass in the pace (not) beyond language. Not *its* other, but the other without language.

If a science or a theory of the reading of these *récits* had to constitute itself and come to its name, I would call it *paralys* [*la* paralyse]. This would also be the science and the practice of his/its writing, of what he/it does in writing. He/it—paralys—writes [*Il—la paralyse—écrit*], describes the desirable trap of a *come*. Since the analysis of what the "coming" [*la "venue"*] means (come [*venir*], gait [*allure*] of going-coming, and so on)—an analysis necessarily descriptive or, let us say in another code, for convenience, constative—since that analysis cannot give an account of what "comes to pass" with *come*, we are not very far along to say what this *récit* "is." To approach [*aborder*] the coming from a *come* that does not yet know what it says (neither approach nor appropriation), has no describable sense, does not constitute a present imperative, gives place [*donne lieu*] to no order, to no presentable present, a *come* without law, without hierarchy, without anything yet nameable that may be desired, asked, required from a lack; to approach the coming of a *come* that crosses language in an indirection without return, toward a beyond of language no longer reassured in traditional metalinguistic thought but no more allowed to be folded back, like all modernity, within language; to approach the coming of a *come* that may be a *récit*—that is the impossible, the unpresentable obscenity that will no longer let go of us, like the Thing that, he says in some part, "*remembers us.*"[29]

To approach in his/its approach [*aborder en son abord*] this terrifyingly ancient, more ancient than time, in which the presence of the present paralyzes itself, the gait [*allure*] of what is going—in which it was always going—to come about (you see that these words are no longer allowed to be subjected to the tenses/times of our grammar, and that "terrifyingly" comes to the position not of the accessory adverb but of the very "subject" of the experience in which nothing presents itself, save for the obscene [*fors l'obscène*], say, a certain augurality)—that is what awaits us still, very far in front of us, before us [*devant nous, avant nous*]. But as forgetting.

To approach time, what you still call time from this *pas de temps*, from this (non)pace of (no) time that is not [*pas*] its absence, but an other eternity ("A hurried, eternal *pas*" [*AO* 39/*AtOu* 77]), will this be to come to it from some space? *Pas* is not a part of space anymore. The topical figures that we have recognized in it/him (distance according to the trap, the labyrinth, room, so many structures of the *pas*) are not images; rather, one is going to see them disappear, effacements of the figure, figures without figure; they are not places *in* space. Nevertheless they have in common, whence the attribution of the spatial horizon, a certain horizontality, just so. There are also the abyss—the sea's [*mer*]—and the stairway. They would form some figures of *pas*, of no/pace, if they weren't straightaway made to disappear in the most high or the awfully low, higher or lower than height in general. Rather than accompanying such a text with a commentary it does without [*dont il se passe*] (as completely other) as surely as it requires it, I will read it slowly, underlining here or there a word [*mot*], a passage, a *moment*, a *movement*. Another reading, another time, will underline otherwise. The stairway is a stairway: all the stairways, all the winding ladders resemble it and are described here, with the most rigorous and economic of realisms, the most essential realism as well. But in order for this stairway, this stairway structure, not to be a metaphor and on the contrary render account of the *tropic* power of the stairway, it remains infinitely distant from—and thereby even infinitely near—every perceptible, presentable, familiar stairway. Also like the labyrinth, the trap, the room it "is." ("Of course it was a room, but all the same so little a room" one reads in *When the Time Comes*, in the passage of the "wild statement that has no rights" sprung "from the living memory of her name" [8/*AMV* 22–23].) Here then is one of the stairway paralys's, in *The One Who Was Standing Apart from Me* [32–35/*CQN* 62–69]: "*There was no movement I could have made. Where I was*, without turning around, I could see the *steps* [marches]; there were six or seven before one reached the sort of *vault*, rather low and heavy, under which the staircase *made a turn*. Now, the perception of what I saw brought a response to my companion. The figure [*la figure*] was *over there*, I saw it *motionless*, almost turned away, as it seemed to me, and I had the feeling that at the moment my eyes were fixed on it, it [*elle*] *was preparing to climb the last steps and disappear. This movement, which was not carried out, gave that presence a new truth, and the whole distance that separated us, measuring a few paces, made it astonishingly close, closer than a short time before when, as I realized [*je m'en rendais compte*], what made its insane proximity apparent was the distress of its distance.* But the strangest thing was that in the space at that confined spot—and the form was, I say, almost leaning against the wall—even though it couldn't see me and probably knew nothing of me, it was nevertheless stopped and suspended under my gaze, as though the fact that my gaze was riveted to it had, in fact, riveted it to that point. There was something odd, absolutely unhappy about that, and I was so shaken by it that the background of strangeness against which this scene was unfolding [*s'affirmait*] was transformed. Probably, affected by my disturbance, I must have moved slightly: now I saw the staircase from a steeper perspective, rising abruptly toward *the figure* I was still staring at, which *revealed itself more*, so that the impression I had was that of someone *larger than I had thought*; yes, it was this feeling that struck me then, of someone *a little larger than he should have been*, and I don't know why this singularity was like a disconcerting summons to my eyes, an insistence that *maddened my gaze and prevented its grasping anything*. It seems to me that I was *prepared to approach even closer*, perhaps to bring this instant back to life, to allow it to reconquer itself; but what *came about* and what *I could have foreseen*, actually struck me as unexpected—I believe I had *never forgotten him to this degree before*—and, when he asked me: 'Do you see him at this *moment?*' I, in my surprise and also because of a sort of pain that I felt spring up in me, faced with this speech, which sought to encroach on me and participate in a guarded [*réservé*] instant, did not answer, no doubt incapable. Shortly after, *from very far away, from the distance [*lointain*] that was made of my resistance and my disavowal*, I hear him murmur:

"'You know, there's no one there.'

"I don't know if I welcomed the remark at that *moment*, but at that *moment*, with *my* [*mon*] extreme *emotion*, I saw the figure visibly move a little, I saw it *slowly climb a step [*marche*], approach the turn, and enter the area of shadow*.

"Among all the impressions I had, I think the strongest was this: that the evidence of reality had never been as pressing as in this *slip toward disappearance; in this movement, something had been revealed that was an allusion to an event, to its intimacy, as though, for this figure, to disappear was its most human truth and also the truth closest to me*. And the other feeling I had was the *counterpart* of such a certainty: the disheartening but also radiant emptiness expressed for me by this disappearance, *an event I was not even tempted to ascribe [*rapporter*] directly* to what my companion had said. I won't say I saw no connection between these two signs, but I sensed a deeper, more imposing interdependence, that of two spheres that didn't know each other, *two moments in time perhaps entirely foreign to each other and coming together within their shared foreignness. Which had come before* the other? He had now uttered that remark, but 'now' had perhaps already happened in the past, was repeating itself, was taking place again—again? but it couldn't take place again, and everything returned to being *[redevenait]* empty and lifeless. This feeling expressed, at that point, the desperate movement I was making and that perspicacity could only cause to be infinite. Yes, it had already taken place, and the question of knowing just when was a futile one, the certainty of remembering a matter of indifference, for it seemed to me that I belonged, not *[n'appartenais pas]* to the order of things that happen and that one remembers with joy or sadness, but to the element of hunger and emptiness where what does not take place, because of that, begins again and again without any beginning or any respite.

"I did not deny that I would have done anything, given up anything, to be able to get out of *[passer]* there . . . connected by this disappearance, connected ever more closely to it, of being called, sworn to sustain it, make it more real, more true and, at the same time, push it farther, *always farther, to a point truth can no longer reach, where possibility ceases.* . . . but the fall was infinite, at each moment *of the fall the reflection formed again under my paces [sous mes pas], indestructible.* . . . this demand was the bond that joined me to myself, to the one who had lived in the small room. . . . What was he expecting? I did not know. Could it have been that the strange distance established between us, through which, as I clearly saw, entered the infinite torment that was my space and my air and my days, could it have been that this distance *[lointain]*, interior. . . . Yes, I said to myself, my part is the best—for my part, I am here, I'm staying here.

"Which he did not fail to answer:

"'But you have all the time in the world.'"

Each time, I underlined *moment*, the moment but also the *word* "moment" [*le* mot *"moment"*], *movimentum*, which would come to carry the day; then in the word, each letter, each syllable—mo/ment; then the implied sentence [*le mot ment*: the word lies], deceptive effect of language between words morcellated or entire. Whole and part, form and sense, *moment* (when the moment comes, at the right moment [*au moment voulu*], a passed moment) is regularly insistent in his text, remarked by the cadences or terms [*échéances*] of the double *pas*, of the double no/pace. The *citation* of the *récit* sets—the word *citation* indicates this—in *moment*.

The double *pas* that in advance and from before time, beyond all time, resounds in *come*, you [*tu*] can certainly understand it as a walking pace [*un pas de marche*], but on the condition of the stairway. Its taking place, so unusual and so familiar nevertheless, *turns* according to a stairway scene without truth, without visibility, without figure that disappears in it, without representation. Some stairway steps [*marches*] according to which it comes near, de-distances itself, with an excessive force, sufficient to defeat the *pas*'s of negation, denegation, of "disavowal," of "resistance." No limit either toward the high or the low, only the tropic of an infinite ascension or fall. The stairway turns in effect on itself, without advancing but without every coming back on itself. And if it is not turning, it distances according to immobile steps that are not, in their structure, keeping pace, underfoot, but not (under) themselves.[30] Each (non)pace, each step repeats the same, completely otherwise. Neither ground nor sky is part of them. The stairway-steps. Come . . .

—But this "desperate movement," this "movement, which was not carried out," paralys . . .

—This paralys prohibits nothing; it causes movement, the false movement that proceeds according to desire's need-not-pace [*faut-pas*] and crosses the limit: that latter, "inasmuch as uncrossable, summons to cross, affirms the desire (the false step, the *faux pas*) that has always already, through an unforeseeable movement, crossed the line." Apropos dying: "something accomplishes itself there, in every absence and by default, which does not accomplish itself, something that would be the 'pace/not/beyond' that is not part of duration, that repeats itself endlessly and that separates us" (*The Step Not Beyond* [24, 105/*PAD* 38, 145]).

—But if you do not manage to get to (say), *come*,[31] will it/she be the only one to lose the power to call itself, to pronounce itself (on), to "cry out its name"?

—This counterpart, this counterpath?

—The one who says *I* in the *récit* will also be dependent, by his very name, in his identity, on the possibility of saying *come* or on the terrifyingly ancient event of another *come*, the same nevertheless. So that the drowned man, the drowned in itself, would be the one who says *I* and sees them—*elles*—"coming to meet him" [*OW* 76/*CQN* 144], these drowned bodies. Isn't that right?

    —I do(es) not exist before *come*—upsurging alone, before you or me, without origin and without end, without subject or complement—is raised, hoisted, like the word or death ("reared up" "in the room"[32]) that appeals to itself. Recall: "It goes toward that to which it appeals." Then it appeals to itself, *come*, since her/it to whom he/it says, appealing to her/it, *come*. "But does it make something come? Only that which asks to come in the appeal. But is it an appeal that questions [*interpelle*]? It responds by appealing" (*Awaiting Oblivion* [64/*AtOu* 122]). We had just recognized this equivalence: it is also death [*la mort*] and the word "*mort* (death/dead)" that are called [*s'appelle*] in the *come*: *I*—call—*myself*—dead—I begin here to speak and to work/walk [*marcher*] in my name. When death has come about, always from/of the other, *I myself* is no longer possible. But without what forces itself with added force in *come*, the call of death preceding *me, I myself* (am affected by my name) is not yet possible. I is always called *I dead*. And like *her/it*, he/it is without name before *come*, before responding to what he/it calls.[33]

    —Like she/it [*elle*], like them [*elles*], like me?

    —It is necessary, now, to specify these *elles*—they are not what are called women. In *Death Sentence*, *elle*, she/it to whom "I say eternally, 'Come,' and eternally she/it is there" [*DS* 80/*AM* 147], is "thought," the thought, a thought, "that *thought*," written in italic, which is very rare, another discretion accumulating violence. The excessive force is "that thought": "As for me, I have not been the unfortunate messenger of a thought stronger than I, nor its plaything, nor its victim, because that *thought*, if it has conquered me, has only conquered through me, and in the end has always been equal to me. I have loved it and I have loved only it. . . . " Above is named "the summons of the all-powerful affirmation that is united with me" and "a mysterious command, which came from me, and which is the voice that is always being reborn in me, and it is vigilant too . . . " [*DS* 79–80/*AM* 145–46].

    This time, in *The One Who Was Standing Apart from Me* [77/*CQN*

145], it is to some "words" ["*paroles*"] that "it would be enough for me to say" "'Come.'"

Reread at least the sequence that begins in this way: "I listen to this. Whom is he addressing? Who is involved here? who is speaking? who is listening? who could answer such a distance? this comes from so far away and it doesn't even come . . . " [*OW* 66/ *CQN* 125]. Nothing I could say to you here can measure up to this. What he then calls "*paroles*" are not some *mots*, words, some discourse, or a figured designation of who would converse and pronounce some words [*mots*] in the proximity of his thought or his voice, nor anything of what one thinks one recognizes under these words [*mots*]: *paroles*, *mots*, discourse, utterance or enunciation, and so on. Nor are they some things that we could oppose to words [*paroles*] or acts. Heard from the *come* they hear and emit, seeing that only "starting from" *come* could they cry out their name, they are part of the nameless. And yet, what marks and neutralizes at once sexual difference is that the anonymous, improper name (*thought, word*) given to the nameless is chosen so that its gender in French is feminine and its pronoun always *elle*. The whole transfer of the code (for example, "*je l'ai aimée et n'ai aimé qu'elle*" / "I have loved and only loved her/it") laterally causes, as in a silent accompaniment of the language, her/it—*la pensée* "thought" or elsewhere *la parole* "word"—to press toward, lean toward the feminine side; it is literally a *movimentum*, a feminine moment; it announces by unconscious pressure sexual difference before every other determination, every other identification. And as it—*elle*—is determined, called only starting from the *come* that it *launches and sends back*, the distance of the *come* instructs the (non)pace of sexual difference.

Since "thought" "word" emits the appeal that it [*elle*] receives in order to cry out its name, she/it—*elle*—is also on the other side, counterpart or counterpath, of sexual difference: faux pas of the *il*, the he/it—that does not accompany me, that stands apart from me. This neuter is the affirmation of the *come*, the repeated affirmation, the nuptial alliance (yes, yes), the annulus of the *récit*. The whole conclusion of *Death Sentence*, before the *come*, also describes the unique possibility of this *récit* in its event as *récit* [*en son événement de récit*], vigilance [*jalousie*] linking the affirmation to its repetition, which will have had to be this bond without pact and without debt (" . . . it was not important to know if things had really happened that way. But I must say [*affirmer*] that for me it seems that it did happen that way, setting aside the question of dates, since everything could have happened at a much earlier time [*moment*]. But the truth is not contained in these facts. I can imagine suppressing these particular ones. But if they did not happen [*n'ont pas eu lieu*], others happen [*arrivent*] in their place, and answering the summons [*l'appel*] of the all-powerful affirmation that is united with me, they take on the same meaning and the story [*l'histoire*] is the same. It could be that N., in talking to me about the 'plan,' wanted only to tear apart with a vigilant hand the pretenses we were living under. It may be that she was tired of seeing me persevere with a kind of faith in my role as man of the 'world,' and that she used this story to recall me abruptly to my true condition and point out to me where my place was. It may also be that she herself was obeying a mysterious command, which came from me, and which is the voice that is always being reborn in me, and it is vigilant [*jalouse*] too, the voice of a feeling that cannot disappear. Who can say: this happened [*est arrivé*] because certain events allowed it to happen? This occurred [*s'est passé*] because, at a certain moment, the facts became misleading and because of their strange juxtaposition entitled the truth to take possession of them? As for me, I have not been the unfortunate messenger of a thought stronger than I, nor its plaything, nor its victim, because that *thought*..." [*DS* 78–79/*AM* 145–46]), and as for the *come* of *The One Who Was Standing Apart from Me*, it upsurges in the sequence of an "I think I have to write" [68/*CQN* 128] relaunched, farther on, with "In this way I understood better why this was what it was, to write: I understood it, I mean this word [*ce mot*] became completely other . . . " [71/*CQN* 134].

She/it, *elle*—thought, word [*parole*]—is not therefore thought or word, but just as well not what, each time, we dissimulate under these words [*mots*] as their terrifying, essential evidence, their very dissimulation. And keeping an old name, the same one, in order to proceed toward this dissimulation, you [*tu*] do not just clarify, you do not unveil according to a continuous gesture: you cross over—toward the completely other—the semantic line, the line of the semantic, the line that, in the paleonym, arrests dissimulation. And, of course, you do this with/in a pace (not) beyond that still makes a laughing stock of the opposition between a clarification and a cut. For the shameless violence that may be the most unbridled today, for me, only shies away [*se dérobe*]—in other words, only shows off with an apparently untenable discretion—in this thought, right before bursting out laughing. Without ever leaving a word, above all not the last one, to the prosopopeia of the law that would still come to condemn in a sentence the blind and the deaf, those who, frightened, hasten to resist, to deny, caught in the trap of the dress, the neutral, or discretion. But this trap belongs to no one, and no one can escape it. Dressed, the thing is undermined [*La chose est sapée*].

—But paralys—for he's thought about the Medusa, whom he names in some part—is good too, isn't it [*n'est-ce pas*], for laughter and the obscene?

—With its double band logic, it arrests laughter and shamelessness when they shield themselves against anguish, against affirmation too. But however rigorous, however fine the difference of quality between the laughs and the violations, contamination is inevitable. Denegation's no/pace beyond is never a simple, decidable, voluntary gesture. Those who believe it is are more sheltered than others. The whole logic of denegation and disavowal is displaced in *The Step Not Beyond*. But (no)-(pace-of)-denegation [*pas-de-dénégation*] does not mean that the apotropaic movement can ever be suspended. It bends everything to its double *pas*, and first of all its contrary; it keeps the fall from falling itself, up to oblivion. Perhaps because of that he often says the "double fall" [*SNB* 110/*PAD* 151] or the "fragile fall" [*SNB* 1, 15, 135/*PAD* 8, 24, 184]. He perverts up to the limit between perversion and its other.

Here is a word [*une parole*]. Some words rather, he always insists on their uniqueness but also—and at the same time—on their plurality and then the strangeness of their being-together. He/it speaks (about) some words [*Il parle des paroles*]: " . . . they have no relations with me. . . . I live close to them, and perhaps I must live because of them, perhaps because of them I am sustained in myself, but I am also somehow separated from that proximity; it is in that separation that we are close, there they remain, there they pass, and they respond to no one.

" . . . I forget nothing; it is in this respect that I am part of forgetfulness.

"They're always together. No doubt this means I can only see them together, together even though unconnected, motionless around me though wandering" (*The One Who Was Standing Apart from Me* [75/*CQN* 141–42]). No word [*mot*] is ever advanced that is not immediately taken away, withdrawn, undermined [*sapé*] ("but," "although," "though"), replaced by its apparent contrary, without (it is the strange syntax of the *without* that we will patiently have to interrogate) any trace of *pas* becoming altogether *annulled* or *established* in this postulated double negation. Here then is a word, some words that are not understood, that derange the order of time and of discourse we say the word is part of, that take their essenceless place in the gait [*allure*] of an "errant coming and going" [*OW* 52, 72/*CQN* 99, 136]. It is a matter, for it/him, of *saving* them, as if from drowning, a matter of interpellating in them, in calling rather on *save* to speak [*lui donnant plutôt la parole, le* sauf]. (While/by/in) saying *come* [*viens*] to them, *tutoieing* them so that they call themselves. For them, "I sacrificed my right to summon another person and say 'you' [*toi*] to him" [*OW* 72/*CQN* 137]. I am again going to cite without any right to do so, and without any right above all to underline or omit. It is a matter then of some words the *come* would address: "the risk was the pivot around which what was threat turned immediately into hope, and I myself turned around myself, given up to every appeal of this place where all I could do was wander.

"To say that I understand these words [*ces paroles*] would *not* be to explain to myself the dangerous peculiarity [*l'étrangeté*] of my relations with them. Do I understand them? I do *not* understand them, properly speaking, and they too who partake of the depth of concealment [*dissimulation*] remain without understanding. But they don't need that understanding in order to be uttered, they do *not* speak, they are *not* interior, they are, on the contrary, without intimacy, being altogether outside, and what they designate engages me in this 'outside' of all speech [*parole*], apparently more secret and more interior than the speech of the innermost heart [*for intérieur*], but, here, the outside is empty, the secret is *without* depth, what is repeated is the emptiness of repetition, it does*n't* speak and yet it has always been said already. I couldn't compare them to an echo, or rather, in this place, the echo repeated in advance: it was prophetic in *the absence of time*.

"The fact that they were deprived of intimacy to this degree was, it seems to me, what associated me, in the course of their wandering, their coming and going [*au cours de leur va-et-vient errant*], with a feeling of infinite unhappiness, with the chill of the greatest distress I had ever had to endure, a distress that immediately reverberated in an endless gaiety that made him ask me: 'Why are you laughing'—which I could not answer except to say: 'Because I'm not alone,' a phrase [*parole*] that, in its turn, flew off dangerously through the house. Perhaps the idea that I must save them from this lack of intimacy also belongs [*appartient-elle*] to the project of writing, an idea I could have had at an earlier time, an idea to which, no doubt uselessly, I sacrificed my right to summon another person and say 'you' to him. But this is only an idea from an earlier time . . . " [*OW* 7/*CQN* 135–37].

—It is always a matter of words, isn't it, those that *come* addresses . . .

—Yes, but "it doesn't speak" and remains a name for the nameless. To one of them he/it will say *come* "for it to cry out its name."

—And it is a matter of saving them? How peculiar. And from what? From themselves, or rather from the "lack of intimacy," the outside, from an outside that is not even proper to them. What does *save* [*sauf*] mean?

—It is a powerful and secret [*dérobé*] word [*mot*], more or less than a word, neither adjective nor preposition, one and the other, nearly a noun/name at times [*parfois*], except for the language too that uses it a great deal and fascinates starting from it.

In forming as an enveloped sentence, barely suspended, the unity of a great syntagmatic articulation capable of everything, the immense ascetic skeleton walking (and working) in every sense and direction and beyond [*marchant dans tous les sens et au-delà du sens*], *sans/pas/sauf/without/non-pace/save-safe* would give the illusion of dominating or gathering together the totality of the corpus if each one of the notions or oppositions I have just advanced could ever itself arrive [*s'arriver*] at itself, could ever itself happen to itself, if each one did not crumble or collapse on its brink [*bord*]; and if each false term of this powerful formalization precluded the set from understanding itself in itself, disarticulating the law of/from the sentence and breaking the identity of the other term that already overlaps [*se recoupe*] and remarks itself. Yes, nothing saved save from the outside to which they are doomed. Nothing *save* the outside. Even at that this salvage [*de sauvetage*] project is part of the writing project "from an earlier time": the one then that would have tried to save from within, the inside, to reappropriate in a protective custody [*la garde de l'abri*], in the assimilating interiority of mastery. It is true that the inside can also be terrible and that the compulsion toward the outside sometimes organizes the defense: safe/save the outside, all safe/save the outside. Let it remain safe/save without us. The pace/not beyond no longer leaves intact the slightest opposition of inside and outside. The inviolate word saves [*la parole sauve*], here, responds nevertheless to the project from an earlier time: "But this is only an idea from an earlier time, I can't hope to give them what I myself have been deprived of, I don't even want to, they often please me extraordinarily this way (which is another aspect of the danger): they beguile me by this busy lack of work [*désoeuvrement*] . . . " [*OW* 72–73/*CQN* 137]. *From an earlier time* does not refer to a date, to the past of an event, rather to the structure of the relation to it, the word, to them. The *moment* . . .

—He/it will have said *come*, then, to a unique word, somewhat plural (a singular safe/save for being plural), or rather it "would be enough" for him/it "to say . . . 'Come'" [*OW* 77/*CQN* 145] to that word, *tutoieing* her/it then, and to it he will have sacrificed his "right to summon another person and say 'you' to him" [*OW* 72/*CQN* 137].

—But from them silently comes the appeal (*come*). From you [*toi*] the desire to write, you are the first [*la première*] to have said to me *come*, and you describe here, in me, on me . . .

—Come, you said to me in order to approach [*aborder*] me in the night of this enclosed and transparent space. This word was yours. But hers/its, too, isn't it, or mine. The diabolism of this (dis)approach [*démarche*] . . .

—No, the diabolical duplicity works with mastery in mind; it exempts itself with the presumption of escaping its very own trap; it still believes that the maze, the labyrinth, the staircase are a space in which to set its traps, and not the very spacing of its pace/not, of it very own pace/not.

—In that case I understand better what you [*vous*] were saying to me about the transparent clarity of his prose, and what he himself says about Lautréamont; and that this pace/not goes beyond the nihilist impasse, that this singular materiality of the pace/not goes beyond some "materialist theses" that today still mark time [*piétinent*] in metaphysics, which never goes without political consequence. Thus: "Where in a work lies the beginning of the instant when the words [*mots*] become stronger than their meaning and the meaning more physical than the word? . . . At what instant, in this labyrinth of order, in this maze of clarity, did meaning stray from the path? At what turning [*détour*] did reason become aware that it had stopped 'following,' that something else was continuing, progressing, concluding in its place, something like it in every way, something reason thought it recognized as itself, until the moment it woke up and discovered this other that had taken its place? But if reason now retraces its steps [*revient-il sur ses pas*] in order to denounce the intruder, the illusion immediately vanishes into thin air, reason finds only itself there, the prose is prose again, so that reason starts off again and loses its way again, allowing a sickening physical substance to replace it, something like a walking staircase [*un escalier qui marche*], a corridor that unfolds ahead. . . . *Each moment* has the clarity of a beautiful language being spoken, but the work as a whole has the opaque meaning of a thing that is being eaten and that is also eating, that is devouring, being swallowed up, and re-creating itself in a vain effort to change itself into nothing" (*La part du feu* [323/ *WF* 335–36]).

This word nevertheless was yours. The diabolism, this double of sovereignty, would not be what it is if its trap could not take on all the forms of the sovereign, up to repudiation [*méconnaissance*] and forgetting without remains. The sovereign traps the devil, declares him thus (in the) right, and risks leaving him the last word [*mot*]. This word [*parole*] was nevertheless yours because each moment, in effect . . .

—The word [*parole*], here (but here makes us attentive to an everywhere: "Everywhere I go, they are there" [*OW* 74/ *CQN* 139]), in order not to be a figure of a word [*mot*], or a discourse, or some utterance's origin or subject, is not however some thing, according to the dissimulating determination of that word [*mot*] (but perhaps the Thing that comes back [*souvient*], the Other-Thing), nor even some already nameable addressee.

Without saying it, the word—*la parole*—can cry out its name rather than say it, on the condition of a *come* that it receives but that it first [*d'abord*] gives, as if it was its very name, barely the crypt of its name, above a hole that lacks nothing. Previously she/it lives nowhere [*nulle part*]; she/it has no place, has not taken place, or only in what comes before the name and places itself in the place of every proper name (the Thing, the pronoun, the forename). Booked in the space of this anonymity, the word's *tutoieing* is a sign of discretion addressed to the unknown that denies itself in the name-less; it breaks with indiscreet familiarity, with appropriation in proximity. This *tutoieing* does not succumb, despite some appearances, to what certain individuals, with as much assurance as ignorance, denounce as negative theology. *Tutoieing* describes negative theology's law, its motivation, its jurisdiction [*ressort*], and even its perversion. Theological discourse, he says in some part, is the most perverse.

These values ceaselessly pass one into the other: both the value and the value-less that does not lack value. He has not [*pas*] yet *tutoied* them, moreover, and he does not say "*tutoie*" in this case, but "say you [*dire toi*]," which is closer, because verb-less, to this absence of order, of request, of prayer, of desire itself, absence yet of a (non)pace that we are all discussing. I could *tutoie* without saying you [*toi*]. And, a possibility even odder, I could say you [*toi*] without *tutoieing*. He has not yet *tutoied* them when he evoked the *come*. Thus, when he said, "I sacrificed [in order to save the words by my project of writing such as in an earlier time . . . , etc.] my right to summon another person and say 'you' to him" [*OW* 72/*CQN* 137], one would be inclined to think that the word [*parole*] is another [*autrui*], provided that both word and another are thought otherwise, as is the double since the *come* beyond all the philosophical or psychoanalytical categories.

The drowning does not become a simple figure always to be dragged into the abyss of this other word (the "confidence," you recall, and a "loyalty" without law are due to him [*OW* 70, 76/*CQN* 131, 143]). Nor the devouring-one-another that follows. The word also follows another form of drowning at the beginning of *Thomas the Obscure*, the abyss of the word [*parole*] having an *oral* form, we would say if we knew what we are saying in speaking of the mouth before this abyss (it is the [hi]story of *ra* or of the *rat*, of which he doesn't know, as of the *water* [*eau*], if it "really" was a rat:

"bitten or struck, he could not tell which, by what seemed to him to be a word [*mot*], but resembled rather a gigantic rat" [*TO* 28/*Thlo* 32]). I take up again my citation: " . . . they beguile [*séduisent*] me by this busy lack of work [*désoeuvrement*], this torment that is a kind of laughter, this presence in which I am never 'me' for them nor they 'you' for me, a presence that is no doubt disabling [*effrayante*], for I'm not able to deal [*frayer*] with anything in them, disabling but attractive, an enigma there is no need to elucidate, the key word to the enigma is this enigma, capable not of devouring me, but of associating me with its devouring avidity.

" . . . And no doubt what they may ask of me has no relation to the idea of writing; it is rather they who want to be inscribed in me as though to allow me to read on myself, as on my gravestone, the word [*mot*] of the end, and it is true that, during these nocturnal moments, I have the feeling of being able to read myself that way, read in a dangerous way, well beyond myself, to the point where I am no longer there, but someone is there" (*The One Who Was Standing Apart from Me* [73–74/*CQN* 137–39]).

He is riveted to them by a fascinated look [*regard*], by fascination itself. He looks at them, them who are neither subjects nor things; they are therefore visible in some fashion, or rather they are the visibility that does not see itself, even if it gives to be seen, which gives nothing to be looked after, even if everything in it looks at them. They do not look at him; indifference is de rigueur on both parts. You [*tu*] have to understand what indifference must comprise fascination, this *admiration* (wrest this word [*mot*] from its easy circulation; when he uses this word, it is to say the "wonderful progress" [*TO* 105/*Thlo* 124] of the *pace/not beyond*[34]) for the gift without law and without authority. They do not look at him, and the origin of his look for them is unassignable. " . . . I could try to find out at what moment they first attracted my gaze [*regard*], they turned me in their direction to the point that all things are visible to me through their transparent presence and they hold me in the fixedness of their appearance. When did this happen [*arrivé*]? A vain question, it has always been happening; but I didn't perceive it, which says a good deal about my blindness, I didn't see them as an obstacle, I didn't see them, whereas now, I am looking at them: as though they have risen from their graves" [*OW* 75/*CQN* 141].

A little farther on, the fascination having become, necessarily, reciprocal because it has always been so ("In return, and because, in a way I don't understand, I fascinate them, I have to remain [*demeurer*] within their fascination" [*OW* 76/*CQN* 143]), it is the scene of water/o [*eau*], drowning, and the eventuality of *come*.

—You always come back to the water/o [*Vous revenez toujours à l'eau*], without my ever knowing what you are talking [*parlez*] about, what you are pronouncing or designating (*o* sign of nothing, the letter, the cry, the syllable, the words [*mots*], the names, the thing [*chose*]); and as for the thing, is it the water [*eau*] of the "drink" [*OW* 58/*CQN* 110], of the "beverage" [*OW* 93 "drink"/*CQN* 174], the chance of a jackpot [*lot*], the water of the "glass of water" that often comes up again in *The One Who Was Standing Apart from Me* [*OW* 15, 51, 58/*CQN* 33, 96, 110], seawater, or some other thing that would signify—*rebus*—a morsel [*morceau*] or a moment of a word [*mot*], *mo*, for example, or *ot*, or *mor*, *mors* [bit], *mort* [death, dead man, dummy], or the proper forename affecting indeed bre/oaching to the nearest point, ceaselessly accompanying, but as a stranger, the one who . . .

—Yes, yes, I always come back (see what he says about coming back and about "everything comes again" in *The Step Not Beyond* [15–16, 22–23/ *PAD* 26–27, 35–36]), and I would like to cite several times, as these *récits* demand, just what I should not cite, subject to never [*sauf à ne jamais*] turning it aside from its unique course.

The *eau* [water/o], what I designate in the same way *rebus*, is not, by reason of all the resources you have just [*tu viens de*] recalled, a theme, sense, or signifier. This has to be said, for the same reason, about the orality of *rat*, of *pas, sans*, or *sauf*, and consequently of all that they mark and that advances or distances itself in these *récits*. They are *récits* in that, by that, and are no longer some discourses or (hi)stories, narrations, or poems.

If I write, for example: *l'eau sans eau*, the water without water, what comes to pass? Or still, a response without response? The same word [*mot*] and the same thing seem robbed of themselves, withdrawn from their reference and their identity, while going on letting themselves be traversed, in their old bodies, toward a completely other dissimulated in them. But no [*pas*] more than in "*pas*," this operation does not consist in simply depriving or denying—far from it—and forms the trace or the no/pace of the completely other that acts (on) itself there, the with-drawal [*re-trait*] of the (non)pace, and of the pace without pace (not without not). In its syntax, this with-drawal plays, between two apparently identical words [*mots*]: "it expresses without expressing," "that death without death," "survival that is not a survival" ("Literature and the Right to Death" [*WF* 340; *PF* 327]); "death without death," "dead person but without death," "the origin of that which has no origin," "air without air," "thought without thought" (*Thomas the Obscure* [108, 37, 97, 93/*Thlo* 129, 41, 112, 105]); "speechless . . . speech [*parole sans parole*]," "resemblance . . . without resemblance" (*The One Who Was Standing Apart from Me* [51, 91/*CQN* 97, 170]); "being without being," "anew, without novelty," "place without a place," "distance without there being any distance" (*The Infinite Conversation* [47, 271, 385, 386/*EI* 67, 405, 565, 566]); "the approach had no approach," "'waiting and without waiting,'" "spaced without space," "'Restless rest'" (*Awaiting Oblivion* [56, 20, 82, 78/*AtOu* 107, 43, 155, 149]); "secret (without secret)" (*Friendship* [173/*A* 196]); "The other, in his attraction without attraction," "the name without name," "another unhappiness, unhappiness without unhappiness," "the end (without end) of books" (*The Step Not Beyond* [126, 118, 127, 57/*PAD* 173, 162, 173, 81]); "me without selfhood [*moi sans moi*]," "destroyed without destruction" ("Discourse on patience"), "To live without a lifetime—likewise, to die forsaken by death. . . . To write elicits such enigmatic propositions" ("A primal scene"), "the *alètheia*, as it is thought of without being thought" (*The Writing of the Disaster* [19, 21–22, 136, 95/*ED* 37, 40, 206, 148]). *Sans* [without, -less] plays like a strange spring, neither a force [*énergie*] nor a function [*fonctionnement*]. X *without* X no longer seems to function. But if it does, it is otherwise than one believes. Doubtless it [*ça*] no longer functions, it no longer works [*ça ne marche plus*], it no longer means to say anything and rejoins a degree *o* of the thesis, discourse, and sense. It means to say *o*, and yet there is no *o* [*il n'y a pas* o]. There remains a remnantless remnant of this passage (there is—pace/not—nothing, a text, a *récit*, already).[35] That is why none of these "words" (without word in their turn), of these old words of natural language, parted [*écartés*] from themselves, can be replaced by a conventional X. A certain formalization of this is impossible, in any case always limited. The *without* will have walked and worked [*Le sans aura marché*].

Pas de sans. No/pace/of/without. And it will have invested the paleonym with a completely other—archi-ancient, more than ancient, sheltered by the paleonym but without relation with it. *Sans—trace de pas.* Without—trace/track of no/pace.

It remarks the same X (X *without* X), without annulling it, of the completely other that parts it from itself. Absolutely, up to making it lose all memory of self, all relation to self, "self without self [*moi sans moi*]," all looking after self: up to forgetting without memory, in other words, gift without knowing, the sole possible, the impossible. It neutralizes without negativity, while affecting the neutral with an absolute heterogeneity, and from first approach regarding what, in the language thus neutralized, could have riveted it to the negative of the "neither one nor the other." This springless spring, this with-drawal [*re-trait*] leaves everything intact (safe, unharmed) on the surface, the language, the discourse, consciousness, body, etc., the very instant when it has let take place in silence an absolute *ravage*, an abduction [*rapt*], an instantaneous erasure.

But this absolute rapidity is that of an affirmation, of a redoubled affirmation: double no/pace of the *without* that forms the *récit* of the *récit*. Double no/pace, "a hurried, eternal *pas*." And if the abduction is absolutely rapid, if it leaves no time, in the dispossession (skidding out of control [*dérapage*], in other words), it is because the same is exhibited there affecting itself, affected rather than affecting itself, by the absolutely heterogeneous that deprives it of nothing save its identity to self, of what would prevent it from distancing itself from self: absolute rarefaction without the least lack.

—I hear no more than some *rats*, the word or the syllable that comes to rasp in the bottom of the throat, death or enjoyment [*jouissance*] resisting themselves in the rattle. The figure of the *rat*, in his bestiary, and of the rat in the mouth, all these words in *ra* in *Thomas the Obscure* and elsewhere . . .

—No/pace of negativity in this withdrawal, no/pace of negation of denegation in this neutralization. The *without* (of) Blanchot has to work [*opérer*], but it does not; it lets come back again what has always been dissimulated as the completely other and can only be dissimulated. It has to work without the negativity with which *without* is charged in so-called natural language, in formal or dialectical logic. And in this passive labor [*travail*], etymology, as such, is of no help to us. According to a singular (dis)approach [*démarche*], the most untimely, the one we are perhaps the least prepared to follow or recognize, we his so-called contemporaries or readers; according to what would have the form of an advance only in the order of an oriented (hi)story and no longer be in current use as soon as this advanceless advance occurs there (try to read "*mes pas sans but* [my aimless paces/no's]" in *The One Who Was Standing Apart from Me* [28/*CQN* 55]), the *without* auto-affects itself by the completely other (*without without without . . .*). It is then infinitely passive with regard to the completely other that affects or approaches [*aborde*] it. That's how he writes and initials *without*, rather lets it cover over his signature, neutralize sense, language, discourse, writing, etc., all the words or watchwords of our "modernity." He does not work against [*joue contre*] them; he has, on the contrary, without reserve, always written for them, but without them, beyond them, in the course of the most discreet and fascinating traversal. How does this *without*, distant from his signature, mix itself with the water [*eau*]? and with what water? Within sight of what shore [*rive*]? in what waters [*parages*]?

Near a depthless abyss, in this presentation of "Come" (*The One Who Was Standing Apart from Me*), it is the water of the ocean. The water is, from first approach, the ocean [*mer*].

This is not the sole marine locale of the *récits*. Someone recently put forward a remarkable reading of the "undecidable border" (I am citing the reader)[36] that opens and closes, on the ocean, *Thomas the Obscure*. I cannot name here . . .

—"Then I remarked with some incoherence:
"'You mean there shouldn't be any name between us?'
"'Yes, that's it'" (*The One Who Was Standing Apart from Me* [21/*CQN* 43]).

—But you are not very coherent. You have already named anyway . . .

—Some absent ones only, who no longer read or write. Here the name no longer returns to them, is no longer theirs, from then on. I cannot name therefore all those who, for some years, dare, before the singular dissimulation of the immense text, not to break the fascination (why and how would one want to? And isn't the wanting still an effect, disavowed or denied, of fascination? I read him in fascination, I love and desire fascination; is there any desire without it?

You [*Tu*] fascinate me, I love you. The fascination that he describes, don't forget, that he ceaselessly analyzes, explicates, and produces too, is not his, or rather, he fascinates from the moment he too is under fascination [like the *I* of *The One Who Was Standing Apart from Me*]. It is not him, it is fascination that fascinates, its fascination [it is always the other's fascination, from which he takes fascination as an object even though it still looks at him]. There is no [*pas*] non-fascination to be opposed to fascination, only some differences of force within it, some no/paces in order to de-distance itself from it, a force to be deferred in difference [*à différer*]. *Come* would be the word of this fascination, of this attraction without attraction, of this identification without identity. Not [*Pas*] a word but the fascination that defers in difference what it does), not to break with it, therefore, but to dare, so that yet another dissimulation won't come . . .

—Why would it still be necessary that it not come? what if it had, as you've said, to come necessarily, anyway? Doesn't one write for it? Doesn't one always clear up, deforming only the borders, one dissimulation within sight of another? Then you [*vous*] are even less justified in not citing his "readers," because the distinction between a "first" text and its "commentary" or its accompaniment is scored by what you have just called, yielding for the first time to praise, the immense text.

—*Immense*, without measure, should not increase the value of, qualify, elevate, dissimulate the neutral and, in the worst misreading [*méconnaissance*] of *this* text, hand it over to the market, to the hierarchy, with the dominant effects tied to the name and to the law, etc.

—Yet that always comes about [*advient*], whether you want it or not, and it is necessary to give an accounting of/for it. There are always some benefits of mastery for sovereign renunciation, and the gift itself never forgets itself, nor the forgetting.

—Yes. I must renounce justifying anything (above all not myself) of what I let be advanced here. For example, not to cite the "readers" is as illegitimate as the sampling of extracts over the immense corpus. I feel this as useless, ridiculously so, according to the cold rigor that the structure of the text imposes. Desire to tell you [*te*]: read, reread, endlessly, without the help of anyone, not even him, without me. Here then I obey, very badly and very confusedly, erroneously, some purely external constraints.

—That [*Ça*] exists? I was thinking that what you [*vous*] said about the edge or border [*bord*], here or elsewhere . . .

—Let's say: it lacks any [*il en faut*]—to center the thing, to say or do something that may be limited by its beyond, by the immense that always leads back to the water. From the first approach, in these waters [*parages*], the sea's.

I would like to return [*revenir*] with you to that beach, at night, when the edge of the sea is a more indistinct line. So that you [*tu*] remember. Remember by your name that I pronounced when *come*, between us, was said just once, with the desire to drive toward the sea.

—The sea or the edge of the sea?

—All the paradoxes of the limit, of the march or of the margin are multiplied when one determines them as *borders* [bords]. This word [*mot*] often comes up again in his writings.

—Does he love the thing or the word? And the border, is it ever a thing? Or rather the *without* that cuts out the thing and abducts it from itself? And *starting* from [à partir *de*] what does one love a word? Why does he come back to it ceaselessly, without ever using it up or wearing it down, without the uniqueness of each usage, each time, ever bre/oaching it? Can one love a thing other than self, than its name, in its name, in every part that it grows detached from itself in order to re(-)present itself again, up to being able to omit itself there [*s'y omettre*]? What affinity, what magnetization between *border* and the signer that is held there, in love, calls itself far off in the distance up to disappearing into oblivion? In *Death Sentence*, the proper names . . .

—It is on the border [*bord*] that everything arrives or just misses arriving, happens or just misses happening [*arriver*], one could at times say misses the brink of happening [*le bord d'arriver*]. There is no border in (it)self [*pas de bord en soi*], no border (pace) that does not mark the limit of/with a drawing near [*approche*], that is, of/with a de-distancing, of/with a (non)pace. And just as every arrival [*toute venue*] (of event, advent, of future [*avenir*], of going-to-come, etc.) causes its "coming" ["*venir*"] to occur "only starting from" a *come* [*viens*], so too the border does not occur before what "lands" or "lands at itself" ["*aborde*" *ou* "*s'aborde*"] (again in saying *come*, say, you've seen this, in saying it to itself to another, from the place of another, etc.). To land, to approach is the strange slowness of a movement of drawing near, between gesture and discourse, that does not yet touch/tamper with the end [*bout*], does not yet attain the goal [*but*]—here the shore—does not yet arrive, has not yet arrived, has not yet happened. As movement (or non/pace), it does not yet have any contact with the border, which remains a border for it only inasmuch as one does not touch/tamper with it or as the contiguity does not totally efface the distinct or the distant. To land, to approach is to interpellate or beckon from afar; it is thus to call (for) distance from/at a distance and depends on the initiative and the place of the other that, in order to be provoked, does not necessarily let itself be approached. Come: in this suspense of the de-distancing proximity, the border of the approach [*abord*] (or to come back to the sea, of the coming alongside [*abordage*] for boarding [*arraisonnement*] for identification) dissimulates itself without however presenting itself elsewhere.

The One Who Was Standing Apart from Me begins with an event *of approach first* [d'abord] that is not an event and not a beginning since nothing has, properly, taken place: "I sought, this time, to approach [*aborder*] him." The approach [*abord*] is not an originary event [*événement originel*], and the *récit* begins with this false beginning or this *faux-pas* of beginning. The approach is still less an originary event (I take these words in their current sense) when no one, above all, approaches no one, but tries, without being sure of getting there [*y arriver*], to approach; does not try but says (recites), now, that he tried, in the past, to succeed in approaching [*à arriver à aborder*]. To try to succeed in approaching, in landing, to try to find the bank of a border is the insistence of de-distancing.

And yet, there is *récit*, irreplaceably. Approaching has not taken place, but this non-place is produced "this time," a unique time, then, marked by a simple past. The desire to touch/tamper with the border has taken place: "I sought, this time, to approach him." What is it for a *faux pas* to have taken place? It has taken place, toward the other, in the past. Now this past, the unique time of an approach that has not taken place, has not arrived at its term, its shore, its margin or its border, its bank [*berge*] (if you like rather to understand this word *berge* as from what looks after [*garde*] and finds shelter, for example, against a fall or a drowning) but which, as the movement of approach, has however taken place, this past is reprised, without being able to be reprised, in the strange present, the unlimited present of the *récit*: "I sought, this time, to approach him. I mean I tried to make him understand that, if I was there, still I couldn't go any farther, and that I, in turn, had exhausted my resources. The truth was that for a long time now I had felt I was at the end of my strength.

"'But you're not,' he pointed out.

"About this, I had to admit he was right. For my part, I was not [*Pour ma part, je ne l'étais pas*]" [*OW* 1/*CQN* 7].

I was not. What? At the end. Feeling of being at the end of my strength, at the apparent beginning [*début*] of a *récit* that begins only to mark that the origin of the *récit* (I) does not arrive at the goal or end of [*au but ou au bout de*] its movement. In this immediate context, that signifies then a feeling of not being able to go farther, a sort of paralysis. To go farther in view of what? Of the other, of the other's drawing near to approach him finally. To be at the end of one's strength: not able to go farther in order to go nearer, neither farther nor nearer. And yet, in the eyes of the other, of the one who remarks, I was not at the end of my strength. In a state of going neither farther nor nearer, of not being able to approach him, I was not. No/pace of distancing possible. The not [*ne-pas*] does not cause the negation to bear on a position or a negation but on the singular undecidability of the approach of the other: not able to go either farther or closer. That is what would suffice to disable every traditional dialectical schema, even if the *not* was in accordance with what we understand of its grammaticality, if it was a negation. The pace/not toward the other (no/pace of de-distancing) does not find its place there or rather does not admit of finding its place there. That, so long as one reads the knot [*noeud*] of this not [*pas*] that overlaps and cuts across itself in the *récit* such as Blanchot . . .

—You mean as only in the *récits* signed with this name . . .

—No, but it is necessary perhaps, through this reading, through what is given to be read there, to transform the possibility of this question.

Two apparently incompatible certitudes cross there. The chain of these *récits* is unique, and each one of the *récits* is unique in its turn, opening a possibility till then prohibited, in its narrow margin, by the greatest force; opening it in an inaugural and unanticipatable way with/of a faux pas—signed in the name of Maurice Blanchot. And yet this unique snatches from its dissimulation, this time in an exemplary way, the *récit* of the *récit*, the (hi)story against which his writing has worked from the start, the truth and sense that he causes to tremble on first approach [*d'abord*], with all its consequence, sexual, economic, political . . .

—To cause to tremble on (first) approach [*Faire trembler d'abord*]: I sometimes feel that he—not he, but you [*vous*], with him, as if you are using his force—you try to frighten, to frighten me. And in view of what? And why less in beginning with causing to tremble on (first) approach [*d'abord*], than in causing to tremble with the approach of the approach [*l'abord de l'abord*], with the beginning, *to tremble on first approach,* denying fear (in order to frighten still more) the least possibility of self-arriving, of recognizing a beginning, of taking a presentable marker, of touching whatever it may be, of appearing to itself from a border. Pure fright, without life, without phenomenon, without relation to self. In view of what and from what fright a fascination so organized . . .

—So little organized, in the end [*au bout du compte*], that it can be exercised only starting from what (the one who) renounces using it, mastering it, dominating it; undergoes it; and would not know how to sign its effects or organon. Whence the difficulty I was talking about earlier. The *I*, like the proper name of the signer, signs its own proper withdrawal [*retrait*], effaces (without remains) its own proper signature, withdraws its withdrawal, and itself—*pas d'insistance,* no/pace of insistence—distances itself on first approach. What I have just called the "*pas-d'insistance,*" he will have described very early, in this text apparently still very Hegelian, according to the era, but at that time already being self-evidently far from a certain Hegel: "Speaking man exercises at once the negation of the existent of which he speaks and of his own existence, and this negation is exercised *starting from* his power to *distance himself from self*, to be other than his being."[37] The example that he then gives of this, on several occasions, is not only "I say a flower!" but "I say, 'This woman.' Hölderlin, Mallarmé, and all poets whose theme is the essence of poetry have felt that the act of naming is disquieting and marvelous. A word [*mot*] may give me its meaning, but first it suppresses it. . . . Of course my language does not kill anyone. And yet, when I say, 'This woman,' real death has been announced and is already present in my language . . . my language essentially signifies the possibility of this destruction. . . . My language does not kill anyone. But if this woman were not really capable of dying, if she were not threatened by death at every moment of her life, bound and joined to death by an essential bond, I would not be able to carry out that ideal negation, that deferred assassination that is what my language is" [*WF* 322–23/*PF* 312–13]. Literature supposes this double death, but of course [*mais si*] "it does not stop here" [*WF* 326/*PF* 315]; it is powerless to efface itself *as death*: "If it were to become as mute as a stone, as passive as the corpse enclosed behind that stone, its decision to lose the capacity for speech [*parole*] would still be legible on the stone and would be enough to wake that *bogus corpse* [*ce* faux mort]" [*WF* 329/*PF* 317–18]. " . . . inexorable affirmation, without beginning or end—death as the impossibility of dying" ("Literature and the Right to Death") [*WF* 328/*PF* 317]. My emphasis.

Death's *faux pas*, starting from the distancing from self: the effacement should no longer even efface itself. To remain close by self in its effacement, to sign it still, to remain in its absence as remnant, that is the impossible, death as the impossibility of dying starting from which is announced deathless death. The no-longer-effaced remnantless remnant of this effacement is perhaps what there is, by chance, but what *is* not or what is *not* [*qui n'est pas ou qui est* pas]: that's *pas* under the name of *forgetting* such as he uses it, such as it can no longer be thought, thought "starting from" a thought-of-being. If "being is yet another word [*nom*] for forgetting" [*AO* 35/*AtOu* 69], it names a forgetting of forgetting, which it violently places in a crypt, and not a synonym of forgetting, and is exchanged with forgetting as its equivalent, giving it to be thought. Naming it, being rather (un)names it, makes it disappear under its name. This *thought* that is no longer of being or of the presence of the present, this *thought* of forgetting tells us perhaps what it was necessary to hear under this name (*thought*)—you [*tu*] remember this—that named, without declaring its name, she/it to whom *Death Sentence* was saying "eternally, 'Come,' and eternally she/it is there"; or the unique *word* [*parole*] to which, in *The One Who Was Standing Apart from Me*, *come* is said so that she/it can cry out its name. "When I say, 'This woman' . . . "

It is you, your name for you. Not yours, but the name for you, the one that is given to you in the call, without it ever being a part of you or possessing you. The *to* of the apostrophe or of the address, when I call you . . .

—One of my names, it seems to me, for you [*vous*] do not cease to show how they exchange themselves (forgetting, thought, word, *pas*, come, etc.). My name is unique, and you hide it, you forget it.

—*Come* is unique, it is said "to one of them—but only to one." Each time. And in absolute forgetting. In the dissemination that does not play, as would be too easily believed, with the plural, the dispersed, the apart [*épars*], not [*pas*] between multiplicity and unity, but between the unique, the unique and itself.

On condition of this forgetting, of its signature effacing itself still, it will have given, without even looking after the memory, neither conscious nor unconscious, of giving.

—What will it have given? A word [*parole*]? Some unique words? Some names? My name? You [*vous*] still hide it.

—Nothing, save the gift itself, which gives itself here, reaffirmed, recited, but this time, to you [*toi*], *come*.

Through [*Par*] a self without self, in doubly banded desire, as you cry out your name and become again, immediately and just by that, anonymous, no longer even looking after our bank [*berge*].

He [*Il*] does not give, since to give it is necessary that he forget up to what he gives, and that he gives, and that he is the one who gives, without having self [*s'avoir*].³⁸

It gives [*Ça donne*], forgetting, it gives being, that perhaps is how being is a name, a name of forgetting for forgetting. It gives being (*Es gibt Sein*, Heidegger gives to be thought), it (*ça*) names being, forgetting. And this *there is* [*il y a*] enjoins itself *come*. The gift *come* is, gives rather, gives itself in forgetting itself beyond being: pace/not beyond being. In one stroke, with one cup. But the gift stroke or cup needs, since it needs forgetting, to re-affirm itself ceaselessly.³⁹ Eternally, the word that requires a thought very new or more than ancient. Now in this necessary repetition of the gift, forgetting has to look after itself again—the bank [*berge*] again—and contamination poisons it. To give two times, however unique they were in the alliance of the *pas*, is the necessity of the gift that transforms it into poison, in the same word [*mot*], with and without play (*gift-Gift*). The "beverage" of *The One Who Was Standing Apart from Me*: "wasn't it I who took the beverage?" [93/*CQN* 174]. Therefore gift: a pace of the gift allows for no gift, again, (no) more gift. The bank and its border. Take, drink.⁴⁰

—"... slight but infinite laugh.... This laugh ran along the border of space, without crossing it, but also seemed to be that space, and this gaiety, though foreign to me, nevertheless passed by where I thought I was, dispersed me, dispersed my decision about the serious things.... the storeroom where I was in danger of falling was not far from there, I turned away, and what immediately seized me again was the desire to drink, I was thirsty, that thirst led me back the way I had come.

"'Give me a glass of water,' I said in a low voice. I could barely hear the words. Yet he answered distinctly:

"'I can't give it to you. You know I can't do anything.'

"... Perhaps I didn't understand anything, perhaps I was calling 'speech' [*parole*] something that was speechless, but here, what was speechless was already a speech, what was not understood was expressed. I should have gone farther..." (*The One Who Was Standing Apart from Me* [50–51/*CQN* 96–97]).

—You [*tu*] must then be able to reject the gift, vomit what calls you to say *come*, to have said it before it, in order to cry out your name. You then want to forget in order to reject the poison and not keep [*garder*] the gift. You want to escape this closed and transparent place, then the stairway, the room where neither the gift stroke or cup nor the contamination ever ends. You still remember that.

—She says: "'I know who you are and I don't give a damn about you.'

"She started shouting again [*crier*], and yet her voice still came to my ears with a sad and self-important calmness. I heard words [*mots*] and more words; they went past and left no other trace than mockery, indecency, desecration, the sad and cold truth of her face next to mine. 'I have no use for your feelings.' She was repeating that now, she repeated it with a pointless rage, as if whole days had passed with nothing other than this fettered language being produced. 'I'll lock you up like a dog. No one will know anything about you, no one other than me will have seen you.'

"'Let me speak,' she screamed [*cria*] again, pushing her face even closer to mine—and I took in her breath, I fathomed its odor, which was that of a plant coming out of the ground.

"'I expect nothing from you. I've asked for nothing. I've lived without being concerned with your life. You should know that I have never, ever implored or begged you. I have never said: come, come, come!'

"She let out a terrible cry: suddenly the black, abject tide came out of her and overwhelmed me. Her hair covered me, her body flowed over mine. I couldn't tell if everything was happening with words [*en paroles*], or if, with her saliva and moist limbs, she was really drawing me into a corner of the room, into the street, into these always saturated and inundated places. My mouth was dripping. I felt her stuck against me, a foreign flesh, a dead, liquefying flesh; and the more I pushed it away, the more it collapsed and curled around me. I think in the end I spat in her face; my whole body was expiring, but she too spat in my eyes, on my cheeks, wordlessly, and I sensed the triumph in the incredible cry coming from her throat" (*The Most High* [238–39/ *TH* 228–29]).

—Then (I interrupt) the cry, the cry of triumph snatched from the fettered language (here by "come," there against "come") continues on, "alone" beyond its disappearance from her/it. And up to the fact that it may still be interrupted by "the strong and authoritarian voice of a loudspeaker [that] came from the street" and was "still addressing anyone from the depths of death, searching for an undiscoverable and anonymous someone incapable of hearing or understanding it" [*MH* 239/ *TH* 229].

—But you would have spoken to me on first approach [*vous m'auriez parlé d'abord*] . . .

—"I sought, this time, to approach [*aborder*] him." In what follows this strange onset without purchase, the assurance (that of negation, for example, and of dialectics or of negative theology) is thwarted by the unpresentable time of the *récit*. In the unlimited, elementary medium of a floating present without authority, breathless after the completely other past that no longer even has the form of a present past, of a past that would still resemble it, of a presentable or representable past keeping some common measure with the quasi-now of the *récit*, the event adrift abducts its simple past ("I sought, this time . . . ") from an indefinite background of repetition or habitus. Background without background indicated by the imperfects of state or recurrence: "I mean I tried to make him understand that, if I was there, still I couldn't go any farther, and that I, in turn, had exhausted my resources. The truth was that for a long time now I had felt I was at the end of my strength.

"'But you're not,' he pointed out.

"About this, I had to admit he was right. For my part, I was not. But the thought that perhaps I did not have 'my part' in mind made it a bitter consolation. I tried to put it another way.

"'I would like to be.' A manner of speaking that he avoided taking seriously; at least, he took it without the seriousness that I wanted to put into it" (*The One Who Was Standing Apart from Me* [1/ *CQN* 7]).

In this sequence on *abord*, on first approach [*d'abord*] (approach [*abord*] of the *récit* in the *récit* of the approach that does not get aboard [*aborde*]: a-board without privation) whose citation I always interrupt very arbitrarily (this logic of abortive interruption—clipping, bordering, violence of cropping—brings both of us closer together here, from one border to the other; it is this logic of *part* and *parti[cipa]tion* that interests both of us), in this sequence on first approach, nearly four tenses affect one another, among which an imperfect that never has the same value. The imperfect of "he pointed out [*remarquait-il*]" evasively implies the indefinite repetition of similar events; the others, a lasting and continuing state ("I had felt," "I . . . had exhausted," "I was not," etc.). The whole dislocation of tangled temporal chains does not even stray [*s'écarte*] from any fixed frame of reference; it is engaged above the abyss hollowed out in the very presence of the narrator who seems only to speak in the present of his presence but in order to say, "if I was there" (" . . . I tried to make him understand that, if [*si*] I was there, still I couldn't go any farther . . . ").[41]

Apparently homogeneous with the other imperfects (insofar as I was there: if it is true, agreed, that I was there), this imperfect lets itself be contaminated, in a not very determinable way, one would say vague—floating—in these waters [*parages*], by the conditional suspense: if one could think that I was there, supposing that I was there. The decision is not only suspended in it but insinuated, I definitely say insinuated [*sous-entendue*], between two readings, as always.

—*Si*, in the French language, isn't it, also, to a question of the negative form, a sort of reaffirmation?

—*Si*, yes. One more time, yes [*oui*]. If you [*tu*] ask me: weren't you there, you [*vous*], in order to approach me in saying *come*, I can respond to this interrogative *not*, leaving out in my intonation all unreadable punctuation, writing slowly, with a regular pace [*d'un pas égal*], with a blank voice [*d'une voix blanche*]: *si-j'étais-là*, if/yes-I-was-there. You will have been able to hear it in at least three ways.

It will have been necessary to hold your breath or a sigh from the *if*, continuously, up to the singular upsurge of the *save* on the following page, up to the syntactic suspense of this word [*mot*]: " . . . without the seriousness I wanted to put into it. It probably seemed to him to deserve more than a wish. I continued to reflect on what 'I wanted.' I had noticed that he was interested in facts, he became more exacting and perhaps more sincere when it was possible to speak to him in the language everyone spoke, and that language certainly seemed to be the language of facts. Yet the obstacle was that—just then—events seemed to have receded extraordinarily. He came to my assistance in his own way.

"'It seems to me,' I said, 'that in a sense I have everything, save . . . '

"'Save?'

"I had the impression he was more attentive now, even though that

attention was not directed at me, but was, instead, a silent direction, a hope for himself, a sort of daybreak that, finally, revealed nothing more than the word 'save.' A little more, nevertheless, for I was induced to add:
"'Save that I would like to be rid of it'" [*OW* 1–2/*CQN* 7–8].

I am following—elsewhere—the inner rhythm of *save*, the law of its multiplication and its contamination, always unharmed and always altered, its pulse reverberating throughout the immense corpus: attribute without subject, preposition prepositive to nothing, word [*mot*] of exception, word without word, without a language. More than a decade after *The One Who Was Standing Apart from Me*, the same suspensive dash that also seems to let the other speak: " . . . *'who holds the place of me?'* and the answer, *joyful, infinite*: him, him, him.

"◆ *The thought that had led him to the edge of awakening: nothing was forbidden to him, ruses, frauds, habits, lies, truths, save (another one of those words on which he was used to relying), save—. And he was not fooled, even this law could turn around, leaving it intact, safe, it also.*

"◆ *'We would give them a name'*—*'They would have one.'*—*'The name we would give them would not be their real name.'*—*'All the same, able to name them.'*—*'Able to make it known that, the day they would recognize that they were ready, there would be a name for their name.'*— . . . " (*The Step Not Beyond* [7–8/*PAD* 16]).

It is necessary (to): leave unharmed, do not leave unharmed. What? Everything, safe/save—the save that it is necessary to leave unharmed, not to leave unharmed. What? The law, unharmed from the moment it is necessary to leave nothing unharmed, save—it is necessary—not/pace—otherwise [*sans quoi*]—if, etc. "'The prohibition remains intact [*sauve*]: one does not die in the present.'—'It remains intact. But, inasmuch as it is the present that pronounces it and in which the transgression is unaccomplished in a future-past time, removed from any affirmation of presence, the transgression has always already withdrawn the present time of its pronouncement from the prohibition: has prevented it or prohibited it in dislocating it'" (*The Step Not Beyond* [107–8/*PAD* 148].

Elsewhere, in the same book: " . . . this limit that none of us passes alive—save in speech" [129/*PAD* 177].

The edge [*bord*], "*the thought that had led him to the edge of awakening*": leaving the edge and remaining on the brink [*quitter le bord et rester au bord*], in *The One Who Was Standing Apart from Me*, from the moment "I sought, this time, to approach him," a statement that is repeated and displaced constantly, comes back near the border. The paralys of the border . . .

—"The edge of the bed" also, of the "large bed" ("I was standing a few feet away from a vast, excessively wide bed . . . ,'" "'At this moment, I am sitting on the edge of a bed . . . ,'" "It is true that I am only on the edge of the real posture . . . ,'" "The fall is endless . . . I'm not even falling, I'm only sitting on the edge of a bed, while there plunges into the distance the slight derision of a murmur: 'Are you writing, are you writing at this moment?'" [*OW* 50, 61, 62/*CQN* 95, 115–16, 117]). Yes, the edge [*bord*] prohibits the fall that it provokes; it guards (against) just what it carries along in the fall, the "fragile fall," therefore, as he often says. The edge provides safe harbor [*héberge*]. And again: "it collides, as against itself, against the truth of appearance that shows me sitting on the edge of the bed or not sitting, but perhaps lying down, or not even lying down, incapable of doing anything but wandering" [*OW* 64/*CQN* 120].

—The border edge [*bord*] that he leaves without leaving, approaches without approaching, in and as *The One Who Was Standing Apart from Me*, is also a seacoast [*bord de mer*]. A hidden vicinity. The indeterminate proximity, the undecided direction that one names, in the course of drawing near, *parages* (waters, these parts). The water [*eau*] here is seawater [*eau-de-la-mer*]. Beyond her [*elle*], the coast, everywhere [*le bord, partout*]. It is also a lake. Beyond the coast, water [*elle*]: everywhere. She surrounds an island. In her, one no longer walks, the pace is not possible. In other words, the *pas* accomplishes itself in its very impossibility, it frees itself from itself. The sea's *faux-pas*. No two paces [*pas deux pas*] in the seawater.

Some five pages[42] after the scene on first approach, the errancy of distancing follows a marine discourse: " . . . this deflection. I could recall, as an intoxicating navigation, the motion that had more than once driven me toward a goal, toward a land that I did not know and was not trying to reach, and I did not complain that in the end there was neither land nor goal, because, in the meantime, by this very motion, I had lost my memory of the land. . . . " And the same sequence leads to "randomness," to "the day" being at one's disposal, "this day," "in part forgotten," "the sun of forgetfulness" [*OW* 7/*CQN* 18–19].

—Since you [*vous*] pretend to talk to me, here at length, there briefly, opening or closing your mouth, everything that you pronounce *o*—like zero, *eau* (water), *faut* (necessary/lack), *faux* (false), *fors* (except), *fort* (strong/very), *mot* (word), moment, *mort* (death/dead man/dummy), now border, coast, in a short time *dehors* (outside)—aren't you, with this policing overzealousness, once more going to decipher some identities, spin out there a signature, the concern (Sorge[43] hides *or* in its body, in *The Most High*, Dorte also, the other character; and next, in the same novel, there are Louise and Roste, and then elsewhere, if he never chooses his names fortuitously, there is Thomas; and then again so much *o, om, mo* at work or sleeping in his titles), the insistent preoccupation with his name? the dissimulation, more or less anagrammatic, of his entire signature, in any case of its borders (*maur/chot, m': o*)? Would you seek to catch everything, as in a raid or a dragnet, with a zeal also ready to unmask the absence of name, the (pace-of)-(no)-name, *le pas-de-nom*; are you going to say again, playing even from page to page with the name name, *le nom de nom*, with the letters in the name in French (*n, o, m*), from right to left, and why not the *non de pas*, the no of no/pace, since you have already remarked the reduplicated *a*'s and *pa*'s of his titles (*Faux pas, Celui qui ne m'accompagnait pas, La part du feu, L'espace littéraire . . .*, etc.)? Isn't this also a bit easy? Too narrow? Where would all these letters be missing in the words of our language? In Me? In the Other? And the concern, his, isn't it also the forgetting of the name and the false name of forgetting? Yes, why, since you pretend to talk to me . . .

—Neither here nor elsewhere has such a derivation seemed to me, in its very principle, possible, I mean such a genealogical derivation of the text from the matrix of the patronymic proper name. The very structure of a text and of a name, of a signature too, is enough to complicate, in a fashion already completely preliminary, the premises of such an inquiry, when it rushes toward the assured mastery of a filiation, whether conscious or not, zealous, that is, jealous or not.

You [*tu*] interrupted me while I was stressing that *border edge* as the *sea*coast under the "sun of forgetfulness." His first book opens at the seacoast ("Thomas sat down and looked at the sea."), also opens out onto the sea. His whole text is surrounded, perhaps, by the sea. She surrounds it, on all its coasts (since there would be only coasts), like an island. Coasts of an island, under the sun that is lavish with forgetfulness, nearly in the middle of the sea. "Edges of a bed," a moment ago, in the anonymous room. Archipelago, rather, with isthmuses and straits, canals or channels [*passes*], narrow corridors, tight passages opening all at once onto the immense. From his first book. And in his latest book, he remarks and leaves intact the fascinating ellipsis of what leaves the sea, relates to or with one dash opposes the sea (sea-it). Take this, read.

—"♦ From where does it come, this power of uprooting, of destruction or change, in the first words [*mots*] written facing the sky, in the solitude of the sky, words by themselves without prospect or pretense: '*it—the sea*'?

"It is certainly satisfying (too satisfying) to think that, by the mere fact that something like these words, '*it—the sea*' is written, with the demand that results from them and from which they also result, that somewhere the possibility of a radical transformation is inscribed, be it for a single one—the possibility, that is, of its suppression as a personal existence. Possibility: nothing more.

"Do not draw any consequences from these words written one day (which were, or could have been, at once and just as well, some other words), nor even from the demand to write, to suppose that this had been entrusted to you, as you [*tu*] persuade yourself and sometimes dissuade yourself that it had. . . . Do not hope, if there lies your hope—and one must suspect it—to unify your existence, to introduce into it, in the past, some coherence, by way of the writing that disunifies. . . .

". . . That happened [*se passait*] 'at night.' During the day there were the daytime acts. . . . The certainty that in writing he was putting between parentheses precisely this certainty, including the certainty of himself as the subject of writing, led him slowly, though right away, into an empty space whose void (the barred zero, heraldic) in no way prevented the turns and detours of a very long process" (*The Step Not Beyond* [1–2/*PAD* 8–9]).

How can we read everything? And even if one could read everything here, cite "in full" once more, everything, the whole would still be lacking ... I turn some three pages and read again: "♦ he/it: at the border of writing" [*SNB* 6/*PAD* 13].

He/it—paralys. Is that the blazon of his name, this "barred zero, heraldic"? of his nameless name (*pas de Sans-Nom*, [pace of] no Name-Less, that is still too much), or as well of an anonymous island, bordered on all parts, like the borders of the *o* or the *o* of the border, aboard, without any other quality or determination, white or black island, white water/black water, degree zero of appearance, from the first pace/no or the first word [*mot*], when it [*ça*] begins to walk or work or speak, to hoist itself onto self or to raise its voice. The white and the black are becoming as well to this *o* of the nameless name. The water [*eau*], white or black, the *o*, clear or obscure, day/night, isn't this the double zero, this "equal power of the o and the 2 in the unmarked and unmeasurable distance of their difference" [*SNB* 30/*PAD* 45], this equal power that the Eternal Return does not permit to identify, or gather together, or exclude each other? Thinking about the *o*, I let myself drift thus toward what he says of the o/2 in *The Step Not Beyond* or of the "hole-word" in *The Infinite Conversation* ("a hole-word, hollowed out in its center by a hole, the hole in which all the other words should have been buried": at the time he is citing Marguerite Duras, and the *he/it* is this hole-word, "immense, endless, an empty gong," *he/it* is the "narrative voice" [385/*EI* 565]), but there is also as it were a similar hole in all the names, in all the words, in his name, in his words in *o* hollowed out in the center of themselves—border, coast, mouth, word, *le mort* (the dead man), hole, *nom* (name), no, moment. The double color (white/black) of the *o*, the opposition day/night is effaced without confusion in the night remarked in this way: "All that which Anne ... loved ... was called night. All that which Anne hated ... was also called night.[44] Absolute night where there were no longer any contradictory terms, where those who suffered were happy, where white found a common substance with black. And yet, night without confusion...." I am reading this in *Thomas the Obscure* [76/*Thlo* 82], which you described, from the moment in which on first approach, from the first word [*mot*], "Thomas sat down and looked at the sea," as a genesis of color, from the "absolute night," "where white found a common substance with black. And yet, night without confusion ..."

—We are trying out here only a preface—barely, running aground in front of *Thomas the Obscure*—"to the pages entitled *Thomas the Obscure* begun in 1932 ... " (Foreword to *Thomas the Obscure*).

—Did you [*vous*] say *come* to me for that, a preface to the foreword of a first *récit*?

—Listen when I say *come*. I scream and hold back a murmur that no one will have heard, this unique time, in the closed and transparent place. My cry is very imperious and very gentle, it obeys you, it responds to you. Its urgency leaves you eternity to give me, the first, the affirmation that I repeat once again, the unique time. *Come*—speaks and utters nothing, cries out but yet, patiently, silently, on each of our bodies, is written. You hear it here, now, yourself, close by yourself, as if you had just pronounced it, but you remembered it, and you will remember it eternally, in the very forgetfulness in which it will have left us, when what, finally, will have reached the other . . . [45]

—What you [*vous*] were calling: death, the other name of *come*—which reaches then only the other . . .

—You [*toi*].

—The citation wounds me, eternally. I always have the feeling that you [*vous*] are speaking to me of his/its name, from his/its name, in his/its name. If you say, for example . . .

—I love you [*t'*].

—Yes, if you [*vous*] say that to me, what are you calling me, will it be I, the unique?

—You [*te*] have to forget. Leave these *pas*'s behind. "Sometimes I say to myself:
"'Don't look at that, let it decide between you and him, let the decision leave you, don't go back [*ne reviens pas en arrière*].'" Read the following in *The One Who Was Standing Apart from Me*; follow the word "decision" up to the "point of truth that makes it smile" and to "I must not free myself of it," and to what "fascinates it" [92/*CQN* 172]. You have to forget. Forget this question; it is *come* that you have to love, uniquely, it, the unique, the coming to come of *come* that is not an impersonal infinitive, not a name but it, *il*/he/it: *come* . . .

—Neither you nor I, he/it? Like a work or like a lost infant? In the night? Still without a name? Stillborn? She/it, I? I the to come t*here* [*moi l'à venir*]? a woman nevertheless . . .

—. . . in the night "without confusion," says *Thomas the Obscure*. I give you [*te*] some words [*mots*] or *syllables* from this book. When we bind them together, life will not be enough for that. "Thomas sat down and looked at the sea. . . . and slipped among the currents, which quickly immersed him. The sea was calm. . . . he had chosen a new route. The fog hid the shore. . . . The conviction that there was, in fact, no water. . . . everything was already destroyed. Thomas sought to free himself from the insipid flood that was invading him. A piercing cold paralyzed his arms. The water swirled in whirlpools. Was it actually water? One moment the foam leapt before his eyes in whitish flakes, the next the absence of water . . . " [7/*Thlo* 9–10].

—These words, *blanchâtre* "*whitish*" near *l'eau* "*water*' (I hear there the silent, dissimulated displacement of a *cachalot*, sperm-whale[46]), all near one another, and the turbulent absence of water [*eau*] that is therefore no longer a thing but a vocable, you cite them still in order to read his name, to call him/it, violently, softly [*doucement*], to gather it in the economy of a *syllable* like *The One Who Was Standing Apart from Me*, on the (next to) last page: " . . . distancing [*écarte*] once again? No, don't distance him, don't push him away, draw him to you instead, lead him to you, clear the way for him, call him, call him softly by his name. By his name? but I mustn't call him, and at this moment I couldn't. You can't? at this moment? But it is the only moment, it is urgently necessary, you haven't said everything to him, the essential part is missing, the description must be completed, 'It must be. Now! Now!' What have I forgotten? why doesn't everything disappear? why is it someone else who is entering the sphere? then, who is the one involved here? wasn't it I who took the drink? was it he? was it everyone?" [*OW* 93/*CQN* 173–74].[47]

—Friendship does not give or take the name; it repays with anonymity. Not [*Pas*] with another name. If friendship is possible, it gives anonymity in the name. It harbors and hands over the nameless name. Those words that you just detached (for example, *blanchâtre* or *eau*), without any right, can indeed resemble some *elements* of his name: as much (indivisible) parts of the name as its (indivisible) elementary environs. But the element is also infinitely divisible, anonymous, in(to) things and syllables. The name no more consists of its elements than it is dispersed in them like foam "before his eyes" or drown in the watery absence of the anonymous sea. If there was one, the signature, the anagrammatic more than anything else, would lose the name in the infinite measure of its keeping. *Plus de nom.* (No) more name. Not only because the name we know him by can serve as a *hiding place*, in his eyes or in ours, for a completely other name working (over) his text in silence, using even his text as hiding place (literature can always play this role), for insisting in due course and throwing the most ingenious, thus the most naive readings off the track into the complacency of a police investigation. And then, again, in signing, whether he does it with his unscathed and entire name, safe/save [*sauf*], at the top or the bottom of the text, on the border or outside it, or whether he abandons its seeds [*semences*] in the language, to the state of dispersion or magnetization, he keeps and loses at once the name, he signs without signing. And the more he keeps, the more he loses. In both cases, anonymity is the effect: by effacement or monumentalization. This double band is the structure of the name said to be proper, before every decision on it, on the subject, before every subject. In any case, he will have been drowned in the waters [*eaux,* o's] of his name with his name, in which everything is engulfed: that's *plus-de-nom* or *pas-de-nom*, (no)-more-name or (pace-of)-(no)-name. The gift of the name (to give a name to the other or to give oneself a name) is corrupted in advance in(to) the *pas-de-nom*. According to this syntagm, this false syntagm, the *pas* crosses the line, toward the name to be posited, or toward the transgression of the name, beyond the anonymous or beyond the name; but the *pas* immediately folds back before itself, this side of itself, the *pas* of negation having marked the withdrawal. *Pas* does not (*pas*) pace beyond, does not surpass:[48] what takes place in the language but beyond it and leaves the fold of this folding back, this refolding, in the *pas* that you hear here but will never be able to grasp, surprise, comprehend [*prendre, surprendre, comprendre*]. *Pas-de*[49] (*[no]-pace-of*) is ungraspable, impregnable, but . . .

—The fact that it remains, therefore, which astonishes me . . .

—(Not even) *pas* itself [*Pas même*].

—But then what are you [*vous*] doing with his name? Do you want to give it to him or help him, push him right up to losing it? Where, in which of these two cases, (no) more friendship . . .

—Read *The One Who Was Standing Apart from Me* . . .

—"'You would like to give me a name?'
"'Yes, at this moment I would like to.' And when he did not answer: 'Wouldn't that make things easier. Don't we have to come to that?'
"But he still seemed to be dwelling on his question:
"'Give me a name? But why?'
"'I don't know exactly: maybe to lose my own'" [21/*CQN* 42–43].

—You [*tu*] are speaking. Is it in order to lose my name that I have called you to speak to me finally, and "to protect" you "against the nameless," as it is said farther on [68/*CQN* 127]?

—The other can never believe this. The response "maybe to lose my own" makes him smile: "Which, strangely enough, caused him to recover his good humor:
"'Oh, you won't get out of it that way!'" But the other's vigilance, because it is vigilant, can also remain lulled by this: you truly want, perhaps, to lose your name and, for a completely other calculus, you do not want to get out of it ("'But I don't want to get out of it'").

—But the other, that too he knew. We have to read the following and everything that is said about "the vain struggle for the anonymous" in *The Step Not Beyond*; and around "We write to forget your[50] name, wanting it, not wanting it . . . " up to the "inscription that effaces itself on an absent tomb." At stake is this "Friendship for the demand to write that excludes all friendship" [34–36/*PAD* 51–53].

—In saying *come*, haven't you [*vous*] therefore spoken to me about him/it, called me in his/its name? And in the course of this preface to a forewarning or foreword (by this declared discretion you reserve everything for yourself), accompanying only, without arriving there, three or four words (*sans, pas, sauf, si*), some syllables that are not even words perhaps, and not so numerous, a single one at the most, unique element . . .

—(Not even) *pas* itself.

I was beginning to read to you [*te*], to read for you those syllables in the waters off [*parages de*] *Thomas the Obscure* from the first pages: " . . . the next [moment] the absence of water took hold of his body and drew it along violently. His breathing became slower; for a few moments he held in his mouth the liquid that the squalls drove against his head: a tepid sweetness, strange brew of a man deprived of the sense of taste. . . . the same sense of foreignness as the water in which they were tossed. . . . reverie in which he confused himself with the sea [*mer*]. The intoxication of leaving himself, of slipping into the void, of dispersing himself in the thought of water, made him forget every discomfort. And even when this ideal sea [*mer*] that he was becoming ever . . . " [7–8/ *Thlo* 10–11].

—It is your ideal sea, the true sea. To love, for you [*vous*], his text, to drown yourself in it, now, to have loved it, as the original first name . . .

—" . . . more intimately had in turn become the real sea, in which he was virtually drowned, he was not moved as he should have been . . . his endless journey, with an absence of organism in an absence of sea. The illusion did not last. He was forced to roll from one side [*bord*] to the other, like a boat adrift, in the water that gave him a body to swim. What escape was there? To struggle in order not to be carried away by the wave that was his arm? To go under? To drown himself bitterly in himself? That would surely have been the moment to stop, but a hope remained; he went on swimming as if, deep within the restored core of his being, he had discovered a new possibility. He swam, a monster without fins. . . . so perfectly resuited[51] to him. . . .

" . . . he tried to tell in which direction he had gone [*éloigné*]. . . . he discovered a man who was swimming far off. . . . the swimmer was always escaping him. He would see him, then lose sight of him, though he had the feeling that he was following his every move: not only perceiving him clearly all the time, but being brought near him in a completely intimate way, such that no other sort of contact could have brought him closer" [*TO* 8–9/ *Thlo* 11–13].

Pace Not(s)   101

This is read in the first chapter. The second, as you know, begins like this: "He nevertheless decided to turn his back to the sea..." [*TO* 13/ *Thlo* 14].

Here it is, at the end of the last chapter, the twelfth, in the waters [*parages*] of an hour that is the most distant from the other, from the first: "Could the world be more beautiful? The ideal of color spread out across the fields.... an immense sea spread out at his feet. He walked [*marchait*].... The man immersed in the waves piled up by the absence of flood spoke to his horse in a dialogue consisting of a single voice.... Thomas still went forward. Like a shepherd he led the flock of the constellations, the tide of star-men toward the first night. Their procession [*La marche*] was solemn and noble, but toward what goal, and in what form? They thought they were still captives within a soul whose borders [*limites*] they wished to cross.... But little by little forgetfulness came.... Some who proudly plunged their glance into the sea, others who clung with determination to their name, lost the memory of speech [*parole*], while they repeated Thomas's empty word [*mot*].... the guardian of the impossible seized them, and they were engulfed in the shipwreck [*naufrage*]. A prolonged... fall.... the monsters that had terrified them when they were men came near them, they looked on them with indifference, saw nothing, and, leaning over the crypt, remained there in a profound inertia, waiting mysteriously for the tongue whose birth every prophet has felt deep in his throat to come forth from the sea and force the impossible words [*mots*] into their mouths.... they all recognized the ocean, and they perceived a glance whose immensity and sweetness awoke in them unbearable desires. Becoming men again for an instant, they saw in the infinite an image they grasped [*jouissaient*] and, giving in to a last temptation, they stripped themselves voluptuously in the water" [*TO* 113–17/ *Thlo* 131–37].

. . . .

—Come.

—Yes, yes.

Note: The first version of this text was published in English in a work entitled *Deconstruction and Criticism* (The Seabury Press, New York, 1979). It is perhaps not pointless to say here a few words about this work, or rather about the situation that explains, in a certain measure, its publication, composition, and form. Around 1975, people were beginning to talk about a new school of literary criticism or philosophy gathered at Yale (*Yale group, Yale school*).[1] There would be much to say on the presumed reality, on the overdetermined diversity or complexity of said phenomenon. My intention is not to tackle [*aborder*] these problems here, only to recall the circumstances: an editor proposed to the supposed supporters of this "school" (my friends and colleagues Harold Bloom, Paul de Man, Geoffrey H. Hartman, J. Hillis Miller, and myself) to set out what was called their "method," their project, or their axioms in a volume in common and on one example of their choice. In sum, a presentation of their own work! With a conviction unequal, no doubt, but sufficiently shared [*partagée*], we thought we had to accept the proposition as an impossible wager [*gageure*]. In order to bring out its character as bet or gamble, we decided at that time to give ourselves a very artificial rule (it was that way for me above all, of course): to treat of Shelley's long poem *The Triumph of Life*. I will limit myself to these summary indications. They will explain perhaps to the French reader certain traits of this text. Under the title "Living On / Border Lines," it was translated by James Hulbert, to whom I want to state here all my gratitude.

Living On

Translated by James Hulbert

But who's talking about living?
In other words on living?
This time, "in other words" does not put the same thing *into other words*, does not clarify an ambiguous expression, does not function like an "i.e." It amasses the powers of indecision and adds to the foregoing utterance its capacity for *skidding*. Under the pretext of commenting upon a terribly indeterminate, shifting statement, a statement difficult to *pin down* [*arrêter*], it gives a reading or version of it that is all the less satisfactory, controllable, unequivocal, for being more "powerful" than what it comments upon or translates. The supposed "commentary" of the "i.e." or "in other words" has furnished only a textual supplement that calls in turn for an overdetermining "in other words," and so on and so forth.

In other words on living? This time it sounds to you more surely like a citation. This is its second occurrence in what you have every

---

BORDER LINES. *10 November 1977.* Dedicate "Living On" to the memory of my friend Jacques Ehrmann. Recall that it was in response to his invitation, and to see him, that I first came to Yale in 1968. He had the good fortune to sign J. E. when he wrote his initials. This permitted him to inscribe my copy of his book *"Textes" suivi de "La mort de la littérature,"* published anonymously (L'Herne, 1971), as follows: "To J. D. in friendly remembrance of this '10 November' on which JE called [*téléphonait*] you." The obvious quotation marks around this date recall that it cites *"La mort de la littérature"* (on page 99,

reason to suppose is a common context, although you have no absolute guarantee of it. If it is a sort of citation, a sort of "mention," as the theoreticians of *speech acts*² feel justified in saying, we must understand the entire performance "in other words on living?" as having quotation marks around it. But once quotation marks demand to appear, they don't know where to stop. Especially here [*surtout pas ici*], where they are not content merely to surround the performance "in other words on living": they divide it, rework its body and its insides, until it is distended, diverted, out of joint, then reset member by member, word by word, realigned in the most diverse configurations (like a garment spread out on a clothesline with clothespins). For example, several pairs of quotation marks may enclose one or two words: "living on" ["*survivre*"], "on" living ["*sur*" *vivre*], "on" "living," on "living," producing each time a different semantic and syntactic effect; I still have not exhausted the list, nor have I brought the hyphen into play. Translating (almost, in other words) the Latin *dē*, the French *de*, or the English "of," "on" immediately comes to contaminate what it translates with meanings that it imports in turn, those other meanings that rework "surviving" or "on" living or "living" "on" (*super, hyper,* "over," *über,* and even *above* and *beyond*).³ It would be superficial to attribute this contamination to contingency, contiguity, or contagion. At least, chance [*aléa*] makes sense, and that's what interests me here.

Be alert to these invisible quotation marks, already, even within a word: *survivre,* living on. Following the triumphal procession of an "on," they trail more than one language behind them.

Forever unable to saturate a context, what reading will ever master the "on" of living on? For we have not exhausted its ambiguity: each of the meanings we have listed above can be divided further (e.g., living on can mean a reprieve or an afterlife, "life after life" or life after death, *more*

---

which reproduces a page from a pocket-calendar). J. E. are also the last letters of these "texts," at the end of the last paragraph, i.e., their final paraph [*paraphe*, also "initials"]: " . . . first letters of the name that, combined, compose (pure chance? no one's said that) the first-person pronoun [the letters that spell *je*, "I"]—it is a matter of inventing the first person that is pointed out here last: J.E." Untranslatable signature. Signed: unreadable. *24–31 December 1977.* Here, economy, the law of the *oikos* (house, room, tomb, crypt), the law of reserves, reserving, savings, saving: inversion, reversion, revolution of val-

life *still* or *more than* life, *and better*; the state of suspension in which it's over—*and* over again [*plus-de-vie*], and you'll never have done with that suspension itself) and the triumph *of* life can also triumph *over* life and reverse the procession of the genitive. I shall demonstrate shortly that this is not wordplay, not on your life. What tack shall we take [*depuis quel bord*; lit., "from what side," "edge," "border," "shore" . . .] to translate the ambiguity of an *in-other-words*? I know, I am already in some sort of untranslatability. But I'll wager that that will not stop the procession of one language into another, the massive movement of this procession, this *cortège*, over the border [*rive*] of another language, into the language of the other.

(In fact, the hymen or the alliance *in the language of the other*, this strange vow by which we are committed in a language that is not our mother tongue, is what I wish to speak of here. I wish to commit myself with this vow, following the coupled pretexts of *The Triumph of Life* and *L'arrêt de mort*. But thus far the commitment is my own; it is still necessary that you be committed, already, to translating it.)

And to go write-on-living? If that were possible, would the writer have to be dead already, or be living on? Is this an alternative?

Will it be possible for us to ask whoever asked the initial question, "But who's talking about living?", what inflection governs his or her question? By definition, the statement [*énoncé*] "But who's talking about living?", like every other statement, does not require the presence or assistance of any party, male or female. The statement survives them a priori, lives on after them. Hence no context is saturable any more. No one inflection enjoys any absolute privilege; no meaning can be fixed or decided upon. No border is guaranteed, inside or out. Try it. For example:

(1) "But *who's* talking about living?": the question stresses the identity of the speaker, without ruling out the possibility (a further complica-

---

ues [*valeurs*, also "securities," "meanings"]—or of the course of the sun—in the law of the *oikos* (*Heimlichkeit/Unheimlichkeit*). That makes three languages I'm writing in already, and this is to appear, supposedly, in a fourth. A question to the translators, a translator's note that I sign in advance: What is translation? Here, economy. To write in a *telegraphic* style, for the sake of economy. But also, *from afar*, in order to get down to what *é-loignement, Entfernung*, "de-distance," *mean* in writing and in the voice. Telegraphics [*téléscription*] and telephonics, that's the theme. My desire to take charge of the

tion) that it refers to the subject of the question "But who's talking about living?", and so forth.

(2) "But who's *talking about living*?": in other words, who can really speak about living? Who is in a position to? Who is already on the other side [*bord*], little enough not about one life, nor even about life, but about living, the immediate, present, even impersonal process of an act of living that nevertheless guarantees even the spoken word that it conveys and that it thus defies to *speak on living*: it is impossible to use living speech to speak of living—unless it is possible only with living speech, which would make the aporia even more paralyzing. Is this the point at which the aporia of a triumphant procession fails to finish itself off? "'Then, what is Life?' I said...." The structure of this line, very close to the end (the end of the poem *and* Shelley's end), the "I said" and the self-citation are perhaps not so foreign to the canonical question of the supposed "unfinished" quality of a "*Triumph*."

(3) "But who's talking about '*living*'?": an implicit citation of "living," a "mention" of the word or the concept, which is not the same thing and doubles the possibilities. In other words: who is saying what about "living," the word or the thing, the signifier or the concept, if we suppose that in this case these oppositions are pertinent in the least, and that *living*, precisely, does not go beyond their bounds?

(4) In French, the language, "my" language, which I am speaking here but which you are already translating, a context governed by the everyday nature of oral exchange would, *in most cases*, put the principal accent on the following intended meaning, which I translate in an approximate way like this: Is it really a question of living? In other words, who said that we *had* to live? But who's talking about living? Must we live, really? Can "living," "live," be taken as an imperative, an order, a

---

Translators' Note myself. Let them also read this band as a telegram or a film for developing (a film *to be processed*, in English?): a procession underneath the other one, and going past it *in silence*, as if it did not see it, as if it had nothing to do with it, a double band, a *double bind*, and a blindly jealous double ... what Hillis Miller would call a "double blind" ("double blind-alley" in "The Mirror's Secret"). Double proceedings, double cortege, double triumph. *The Triumph of Life / L'arrêt de mort* (how will they have translated this title? Better to leave it in "French," assuming that it belongs to a deter-

necessity? Where do you get this axiomatic, valuational certainty that we (or *you*) must live? Who says that living is worth all the trouble? That it's better to live than to die? And that living is something other than dying? That, since we've started, we have to keep on living? In other words living on? (The sentence in the second line has put in for a transfer and brought about its displacement.) In other words, then, what is life ("'Then, what is Life?' I said. . . . "), a *cited* question that, for want of a saturating context, we can always understand as having two meanings, at least: (a) the meaning of meaning or of value (Does life have meaning, sense? Does it have the slightest value? Is it worth living? Who's talking about living?—and so forth); (b) the ontological sense (What is the essence of life? What is Life? What is the living-ness [*l'être-vivant*] of life?—and so forth). These two meanings (at least two) inhabit *The Triumph of Life* and rework its supposedly "unfinished" edge. *The Triumph* talks about living. But what does it say about it? A great deal, far too many things, but this much at least, in its writing-on-living: it is, itself, the poem, and it gives itself a name, *The Triumph of Life*. In a sense still to be determined, it lives-on. But—I must say it in the syntax of my language to defy the translators to decide, at each moment—*au nom de qui ou de quoi, in/after whose name, or the name of what*, does it live on? Does it live on in/after Shelley's name? This deserves a translators' note explaining both *survivre au nom de* and what happens in French when *triomphe de la vie* (triumph of life) is transformed into *triompher de la vie* (to triumph over life). This is not playing with language, as one might easily suspect. I maintain, not without delaying the proof a bit longer, that this is a question of what takes place *in* the poem and of what *remains* of it, beyond any opposition between finished and unfinished, whether we mean the end of the last poem or that of the man who drowned "off Lerici" on 8 July 1822, "writing *The Triumph of Life*" (as

---

minable language; but then in what language will this text appear?), each "triumph" (there are two triumphs) forming the double band or *double bind* of double proceedings. This would be a good place for a translator's note, for example, about *everything* that has been said elsewhere on the subject of the *double bind*, the double band, the double procession, and so forth (a citation in extenso, among others, of *Glas*, which itself . . . and so forth): this, as a measure of the impossible. How can one text, assuming its unity, give or present another to be read, without touching it, without saying anything about it,

is said in one account of *Shelley's Life,* with a chronological table in five divisions, "Dates," "Events," "Residence," "Finance," "Chief Works").

"Who's talking about living?" I am treating this sentence as a citation; there can be no doubt about it now. And you may even have the feeling that all I've been doing is commenting on this *incipit* that came, with no quotation marks, from who knows where. But wasn't this attack already a citation? I was apparently the one who decided to write that, without asking for anyone's authorization, not taking it out of any well-defined corpus, not indicating any *copyright*.[4] But I immediately began to reconstitute all sorts of corpora or contexts from which I might have taken it. One of the most general or broadest of the categories that might limit such a corpus would be something like the language called French, or a family of languages more or less susceptible of translation of or into French. This reconstitution is far from finished. I set down here as an axiom and as that which is to be proved (*demonstrandum*), that the reconstitution cannot be finished. This is my starting point: no meaning can be determined out of context, but no context permits saturation. What I am referring to here is not richness of substance, semantic fertility, but rather structure: the structure of the remnant [*reste*] or of iteration. But I have given this structure many other names, and what matters here is the secondary aspect of nomination. Nomination is important, but it is constantly caught up in a process that it does not control.

Since I began, and since you read the question "Who's talking about living?" (wherever it came from), the word *bord* [edge, brink, verge, border, boundary, bound, limit, shore] has imposed itself more than once.

If we are to approach [*aborder*] a text, for example, it must have a *bord,* an edge. Take this text. What is its upper edge? Its title (" Living On")? But when do you start reading it? What if you started reading it af-

---

practically without even referring to it? How can two "triumphs" read each other, each one *and* the other, without even knowing each other, at a distance? At a distance and without knowing each other, like the two "women" in *L'arrêt de mort.* What I will call farther on the *mad hypothesis,* the manic *hubris* of a reading toward which the other procession (what happens [*se passe*], or not, between the two women, one of whom he imagines—if only to rule out the notion—to have drowned herself) is directed, *obviously* has nothing to do with Shelley's drowning, or even with the event thus recorded in

ter the first sentence (another upper edge), which functions as its first reading head but which itself in turn folds its outer edges back over onto inner edges whose mobility—multilayered, citational, displaced from meaning [*portée*] to meaning—prohibits you from making out a shoreline? There is a regular submerging of the shore.

When a text cites and recites, with or without quotation marks, when it is written on the brink, you start, or indeed have already started, to lose your footing. You lose sight of any line of demarcation between a text and what is outside it.

(This is where my scenario breaks off, unfinished—it would have related, *on the one hand*, all the "triumphs of death" of the Italian quattrocento, the ironical or antithetical citation of a genre by *The Triumph of Life*, the supposed unfinished quality at the apparent lower edge of a poem by Shelley at the moment when, in greatest proximity to the signature, at the apparent lower edge of the poem, the signatory is drowned, loses his footing, loses sight of the shore, and, *on the other hand*, all the drownings in Blanchot's *récits*, the drownings that I recited in "*Pace* Not(*s*)" as well as the others, all the representations [*mises en scène*] of a shoreline that disappears or is overrun at the edge of *Thomas the Obscure*, a book that is *remarkable*—and *re-marked*—from its *incipit* on:

Thomas sat down and looked at the sea. He remained motionless for a time, as if he had come there to follow the movements of the other swimmers and, although the fog prevented him from seeing very far, he stayed there, obstinately, his eyes fixed on the bodies floating with difficulty. Then, when a more powerful wave reached him, he went down onto the sloping sand and slipped among the currents, which quickly immersed him. [New version (*TO* 7/ *ThIo* 9)]

or

---

one chronology: "*Date*: 1816, December *Events*: Harriet found drowned. Shelley marries Mary." Or with "glu de l'étang lait de ma mort noyé" ["glue of the pool milk of my drowned death"] (in *Glas*[a]), which I would like to have translated here. Beyond all this grand phantasmic organization and these real or fictitious events, I wish to pose the question of the *bord*, the edge, the border, and the *bord de mer*, the shore.[b] (*The Triumph of Life* was written in the sea, at its edge, between land and sea, in the waters off, *dans les parages*, but that doesn't matter.) The question of the borderline precedes, as it were,

I sought, this time, to approach [*aborder*] him. I mean I tried to make him understand that, though I was there, still I couldn't go any farther, and that I, in turn, had exhausted my resources. In truth, I had long had the impression that I was at the end of my rope.

"But you're not," he pointed out.

[These are the "first" words of *The One Who Was Standing Apart from Me* (1/*CQN* 7).] You may ask what I mean by that: do Blanchot's *récits* treat, in their own way, *The Triumph of Life*, and even the supposed unfinished quality that separates it from its ending, and even what separates it from its supposed signatory and his drowning? For now, I shall not answer this question, but ask one of my own: What is to say that the supposed signatory of a piece of writing must answer for it, and answer at every turn [*moment*] the questions of this person or that, telling them "exactly" what the "story" is?)

If we are to approach a text, it must have an edge. The question of the text, as it has been elaborated and transformed in the last dozen or so years, has not merely "touched" "shore," *le bord* (scandalously tampering, changing, as in Mallarmé's declaration, "On a touché au vers"), all those boundaries that form the running border of what used to be called a text, of what we once thought this word could identify, i.e., the supposed end and beginning of a work, the unity of a corpus, the title, the margins, the signatures, the referential realm outside the frame, and so forth. What has happened, if it has happened, is a sort of overrun [*débordement*] that spoils all these boundaries and divisions and forces us to extend the accredited concept, the dominant notion of a "text," of what I still call a "text," for strategic reasons, in part—a "text" that is henceforth no longer a finished corpus of writing, some content enclosed in a book or its margins, but a differential network, a fabric of traces referring endlessly to something other than itself, to other differential traces. Thus the text overruns all the

---

the determination of all the parti(cipa)tions that I have just mentioned: between a fantasy and a "reality," an event and a non-event, a fiction and a reality, one corpus and another, and so forth. Here, from week to week in this pocket-calendar or these minutes [*procès-verbal*], I shall perhaps endeavor to create an effect of *superimposing*, of superimprinting one text on the other. Now, each of the two "triumphs" writes (on [*sur*]) textual superimprinting. What about this *on*, this *sur*, and its surface? An effect of superimposing: one procession is superimposed on the other, accompanying it without accompa-

limits assigned to it so far (not submerging or drowning them in an undifferentiated homogeneity, but rather making them more complex, dividing and multiplying strokes and lines)—all the limits, everything that was to be set up in opposition to writing (speech, life, the world, the real, history, and what not, every field of reference—to body or mind, conscious or unconscious, politics, economics, and so forth). Whatever the (demonstrated) necessity of such an overrun, such a *dé-bordement*, it still will have come as a shock, producing endless efforts to dam up, resist, rebuild the old partitions, to blame what could no longer be thought without confusion, to blame difference *as* wrongful *confusion*! All this has taken place in nonreading, with no work on what was thus being demonstrated, with no realization that it was never our wish to extend the reassuring notion of the text to a whole extra-textual realm [*à tout un hors-texte*] and to transform the world into a library by doing away with all boundaries, all framework, all sharp edges (all *arêtes*: this is the word that I am speaking of tonight), but that we sought rather to work out the "theoretical and practical system" of these margins, these borders, once more, from the ground up. I shall not go into detail. Documentation of all this is readily available to anyone committed to breaking down the various structures of resistance, his own resistance as such or as primarily [*d'abord*] the ramparts that bolster a system (be it theoretical, cultural, institutional, political, or whatever). What are the borderlines of a text? How do they come about? I shall not approach the question directly, frontally, in the most general way. I prefer, within the limits that we have here, a more indirect, narrower channel, one that is more concrete as well: at the edge of the *récit*, of the text *as récit*. The word is *récit*, a story, a narrative, and not *narration*, narration. The reworking of a textual problematic has affected this aspect of the text as narrative (*récit* of an event, the event of *récit*, *récit* as the structure of an event) by placing it in the foreground.

---

nying it (Blanchot, *Celui qui ne m'accompagnait pas* [*The One Who Was Standing Apart from Me*]). This operation would never be considered legitimate on the part of a teacher, who must give his references and tell what he's talking about, giving it its recognizable title. You can't give a course on Shelley without ever mentioning him, pretending to deal with Blanchot, and more than a few others. And your transitions have to be readable, that is, in accordance with criteria of readability very firmly established, and long since. At the beginning of *L'arrêt de mort*, the superimposing of the two "images," the image

(I note parenthetically that *The Triumph of Life*, which it is not my intention to discuss here, belongs in many ways to the category of the *récit*, in the disappearance or overrun that takes place the moment we wish to close its case after citing it, calling it forth, commanding it to appear.

(1) *There is* the *récit* of double affirmation,[5] the *yes, yes* that must be cited, must recite itself to bring about the alliance [*alliance*, also "wedding band"] of affirmation with itself, to bring about its ring. It remains to be seen whether the double affirmation is *triumphant*, whether the triumph is affirmative or a paradoxical phase in the work of mourning.

(2) *There is* the double *récit*, the *récit* of the *vision* enclosed in the general *récit* carried on by the same narrator. The line that separates the enclosed *récit* from the other—

. . . .
And then a Vision on my brain was rolled.

. . . .

—marks the upper edge of a space that will never be closed. What is the *topos* of the *I* who cites himself in a *récit* [of a dream, a vision, or a hallucination] within a *récit*, including, in addition to all his ghosts, his *hallucinations of ghosts*, still other visions within visions [e.g., "a new Vision never seen before"]? What is his *topos* when he cites, in the present, a past question formulated in another sort of present [" . . . 'Then, what is Life?' I said. . . . "] and that he recounts as something that presented itself in a vision, and so on?

(3) *There is* also the ironic, antithetical, underlying re-citation of the *triumphs of death* that adds another level of coding to the poem. What are we doing when, to practice a "genre," we cite a genre, represent it, stage it, expose the *law of genre*, analyze it practically? Are we still practicing the

---

of Christ and, "behind the figure of Christ," Veronica, "the features of a woman's face—extremely beautiful, even magnificent"—this superimposing is readable "on the wall of [a doctor's] office" and on a "photograph" [*DS* 9/ *AM* 21]. Inscription and reimprinting, reimpression, of light in both texts. *La folie du jour*. The course of the sun, day, year, anniversary, double revolution, the palindrome and the anagrammatic version or reversion of *écrit*, *récit*, and *série*. The series (*écrit*, *récit*, *série*, etc.). Note to the translators: How are you going to translate that, *récit* for example? Not as *nouvelle*, "novella," nor as

genre? Does the "work" still belong to the genre it re-cites? But inversely, how could we make a genre work without referring to it [quasi-] citationally, indicating at some point, "See, this is a work of such-and-such a genre"? Such a mark does not belong to the genre and makes the declaration of belonging an ironical exercise. It interrupts the very belonging of which it is the condition. I must abandon this question for the moment; it's capable of disrupting more than one system of poetics, more than one literary pact.)

What is a *récit*—this thing that we call a *récit*? Does it take place? Where and when? What might the taking-place or the event of a *récit* be?

I hasten to say that it is not my intention here, nor do I claim, nor do I have the means, to answer these questions. At most, in repeating them, I would like to begin a minute displacement, the most discreet of transformations: I suggest, for example, that we replace what might be called *the question of récit* ("What is a *récit*?") with *the demand for récit*. When I say *demande* I mean something closer to the English "demand" than to a mere request: inquisitorial insistence, an order, a formal demand [*mise en demeure*], a petition. To know (before we know) what *récit* is, the being-*récit* of *récit*, the narrativity of narrative, we should perhaps first recount, return to the scene of one origin of *récit*, to the *récit* of one origin of *récit* (will that still be *récit*, a narrative?), to that scene that mobilizes various forces, or if you prefer various agencies or "subjects," some of which *demand* the *récit* of the other, seek to extort it from him, like a secret-less secret, something that they call the truth about what has taken place: "Tell us '*just* exactly' what happened."⁶ The *récit* must have begun with this demand, but will we still call the *mise en scène* [representation, staging] that relates or rather repeats this demand a *récit*? And will we even still call it *mise en "scène,"* since that origin of the *récit* concerns *the eyes* [*touche aux yeux*] (as we shall see), the invisible ori-

---

"short story."ᶜ Perhaps it will be better to leave the "French" word *récit*. It is already hard enough to understand, in Blanchot's text, in French. An essential question for the translator. The *sur*, "on," "super-," and so forth, that is my theme above, *also* designates the figure of a passage by *trans*-lation, the movement in *trans*- of an *Übersetzung*. Version [*version*; also "translation into one's own language"], transference, and translation. *Übertragung*. The simultaneous transgression and reappropriation of a language [*langue*], its law, its economy? How will you translate *langue*? Let us suppose then that here, at the foot

gin of visibility, the origin of origin, the birth of what, as we say in French, "sees the light of day" [*voit le jour*, is born] when the present leads to presence, presentation, or representation? "'Oh, I see the day [*je vois le jour*], oh God,'" says a voice in *La folie du jour*,[7] a "*récit*" (?) by Maurice Blanchot. (This title, *La folie du jour*, appears only in what would be called, according to a certain convention, the "second version," in book form this time [1973], of a "*récit*" first published in a literary magazine [*Empédocle* No. 2, May 1949] under the title "*Un récit?*" Is it the *same* text, except for the title? Or are these two versions of the same *écrit* [piece of writing], the same "*récit*"? Usually, from one version to the next, the title remains the same. What is a version? What is a title? What borderline questions are posed here? I am here seeking merely to establish the necessity of this whole problematic of judicial framing and of the jurisdiction of frames. This problematic, I feel, has not been explored, at least not adequately, by the institution of literary studies in the university. And there are essential reasons for that: this is an institution built on the possibility of that very system of framing. In the case of *La folie du jour*, the matter is even more complicated, as we shall see little by little, and this complication involves a certain "*sur*" ["on," "super-," etc.], or what I have called elsewhere, in *Dissemination*, a certain "overcasting" [*surjet*]. For now, let us point out that the question mark [in "*Un récit?*"] appears as an integral part of the title only on the cover of the review *Empédocle*, under the general heading "Sommaire" ["contents"]. Under the same heading, on the inside of the review, on a sort of flyleaf [*page de garde*] before the text itself, the question mark disappears. This disappearance is confirmed on the first page of the *récit*, where the title is repeated: "*Un récit.*" Whether this variation, which Andrzej Warminski pointed out to me, is deliberate or not, it managed to construct its own *récit* of variation, in its relative specificity, only by means

---

of the other text, I address a translatable message, in the style of a telegram, to the translators of every country. Who is to say in what language, *exactly* what language, if we assume that the translation has been prepared, the above text will appear? It is not untranslatable, but, without being opaque, it presents at every turn [*pas*], I know, something to stop [*arrêter*] the translation: it forces the translator to transform the language into which s/he is translating or the "receiver medium," to deform the initial contract, itself in constant deformation, in the language of the other. I anticipated this difficulty of translation,

of such *protective* structures [*structures de* garde] and institutions as the registering of copyright, the Library of Congress or the Bibliothèque Nationale, or something like a flyleaf.) Thus a voice says, "'Oh, I see the day, oh God!'" in *La folie du jour*, a "*récit*" (?) by Maurice Blanchot, a *récit* whose title runs wild and drives the reader mad, (*s'*)*affole* in every sense of the word and in every direction: *la folie du jour*, the madness of today, of the day today, which leads to the madness that comes from the day, is born of it, as well as the madness of the day itself, itself mad (another genitive): the madness of the *jour* in the sense of *dies, day*, and in the sense of light, brightness. The title seems to refer at times to the "I went mad," "only my innermost being was mad" [*MD* 6/*FJ* 11], of the "narrator" (an impossible narrator, though, incapable of responding to the demand for *récit*, mad for light: "and if seeing would infect me with madness, I madly wanted that madness" [*MD* 12/*FJ* 23–24]), at times to the madness of a "character" following the narrator on the street ("a strange sort of lunatic" [*MD* 8/*FJ* 16]), at times, in another genitive, to "the madness of the day" itself, in a phrase that is a homonym of the title and is taken from or grafted onto the body of the story ("In the end I grew convinced that I was face-to-face with the madness of the day. That was the truth: the light was going mad, the brightness had lost all reason" [*MD* 11/*FJ* 22]). In a dissemination as glorious as it is fleeting, the seme *jour*, the "same" *jour*, the other, is both *ajouré* and *ajourné* ["perforated" and "adjourned, postponed"; derived from the two senses of *jour*]—in itself, so to speak, in the precarious instability of its title. The madness of the day, of this moment, is momentary. The abyss that carries it away is expressed (for example) when a voice says, "Oh, I see the day [*jour*], oh God." It is not the narrator's voice but a feminine one [i.e., referred to by the pronoun *elle*] that discreetly sets free (by means of a sort of game that tires the narrator, he says) all the powers of an idiom

---

if only up to a certain point, but I did not calculate it or deliberately increase it. I just did nothing to avoid it. On the contrary, I shall try here, in this short steno-telegraphic band, for the greatest translatability possible. Such will be the proposed contract. For the problems that I wished to formalize above have an irreducible relationship to the enigma, or in other words the *récit*, of translation. I have sought to present these problems [*les mettre en scène*] practically, and in a sense *performatively*, in accordance with a notion of the performative that I feel must be dissociated, by an act of deconstruction, from the

EMPÉDOCLE
REVUE LITTÉRAIRE MENSUELLE

PREMIÈRE ANNÉE

SOMMAIRE

BRICE PARAIN
Notes sur le style

RENÉ CHAR
Rougeur des Matinaux

MAURICE BLANCHOT
Un récit ?

R. M. RILKE
A Hœlderlin

SIMONE WEIL
Les deux grandeurs

JEAN BLOCH-MICHEL
Vanité de l'expérience

ANDRÉ PLATONOV
La famille Ivanov

AUJOURD HUI
PIERRE BLANCHET ✱ JACQUES DUPIN

CHRONIQUES
ALBERT BÉGUIN : LES LETTRES ✱ CHRISTINE CARENNAC : LA PEINTURE

MAI 1949

EMPÉDOCLE
REVUE LITTÉRAIRE MENSUELLE

SOMMAIRE

BRICE PARAIN
    Notes sur le style 3
RENÉ CHAR
    Rougeur des Matinaux 11
MAURICE BLANCHOT
    Un récit 13
R. M. RILKE
    A Hœlderlin 23
SIMONE WEIL
    Les deux grandeurs 25
JEAN BLOCH-MICHEL
    Vanité de l'expérience 41
ANDRÉ PLATONOV
    La famille Ivanov 48

AUJOURD'HUI

PIERRE BLANCHET
    Les belles années 79
JACQUES DUPIN
    Comment dire 93

CHRONIQUES

ALBERT BÉGUIN : *Les Lettres*
    Actualité d'Homère 96
CHRISTINE CARENNAC : *Les Arts*
    Tendances de la jeune peinture 101
    Correspondance 104

1ere ANNÉE   N° 2   MAI 1949

UN RÉCIT

par

MAURICE BLANCHOT

Je ne suis ni savant ni ignorant. J'ai connu des joies. C'est trop peu dire : je vis, et cette vie me fait le plaisir le plus grand. Alors, la mort ? Quand je mourrai (peut-être tout à l'heure), je connaîtrai un plaisir immense. Je ne parle pas de l'avant-goût de la mort qui est fade et souvent désagréable. Souffrir est abrutissant. Mais telle est la vérité remarquable dont je suis sûr : j'éprouve à vivre un plaisir sans limites et j'aurai à mourir une satisfaction sans limites.

J'ai erré, j'ai passé d'endroit en endroit. Stable, j'ai demeuré dans une seule chambre. J'ai été pauvre, puis plus riche, puis plus pauvre que beaucoup. Enfant, j'avais de grandes passions, et tout ce que je désirais, je l'obtenais. Mon enfance a disparu, ma jeunesse est sur les routes. Il n'importe : ce qui a été, j'en suis heureux, ce qui est me plaît, ce qui vient me convient.

Mon existence est-elle meilleure que celle de tous ? Il se peut. J'ai un toit, beaucoup n'en ont pas. Je n'ai pas la lèpre, je ne suis pas aveugle, je vois le monde, bonheur extraordinaire. Je le vois, ce jour hors duquel il n'est rien. Qui pourrait m'enlever cela ? Et ce jour s'effaçant, je m'effacerai avec lui, pensée, certitude qui me transporte.

J'ai aimé des êtres, je les ai perdus. Je suis devenu fou quand ce coup m'a frappé, car c'est un enfer. Mais ma folie est restée sans témoin, mon égarement n'apparaissait pas, mon intimité seule était folle. Quelquefois, je devenais furieux. On me disait : Pourquoi êtes-vous si calme ? Or, j'étais brûlé des pieds à la tête ; la nuit, je courais les rues, je hurlais ; le jour, je travaillais tranquillement.

Page from *Empédocle*. Maurice Blanchot, "Un récit," later reprinted in *La folie du jour* © Éditions Gallimard.

by making it apparently untranslatable: "Suddenly, she [*elle*] cried out, 'Oh, I see the day, oh God,' etc. I protested that this game was tiring me out enormously, but she was insatiably intent upon my glory" [*MD* 17/*FJ* 34]. The game did not consist solely or surely in wordplay. But language is involved from the first. The feminine voice that says "I see the day"—insatiable for the "glory" of the one who says *I* in the *récit*, for his triumph—this voice is spoken, is translated by language: *I am born* (*voir le jour also* means *to be born* in French), but also *I see* (things) and, what's more, *I see* light, glory, the element of visibility, the visibility of that which is visible, the phenomenality of the phenomenon; thus I see vision, both eyesight and what it can see, the stage [*scène*] and the possibility of representation [*scène*], the scene of visibility, a *primal scene*, I might say, quoting the title of a very short text [i.e., "Une scene primitive"], of a "broken windowpane"[8] by Blanchot, a text whose powerful enigma I do not wish to touch on here. Visibility should not be visible. According to an old, omnipotent logic that has reigned since Plato, that which enables us to see should remain invisible: black, blinding. *La folie du jour* is a story of madness [*histoire de la folie*], of that madness that consists in seeing the light, vision or visibility, from an experience of blindness. If from *life* we appeal to *light*,[9] from *vie* to *vision*, we can speak here of *survie*, of living on in a life-after-life or a life-after-death, as *sur-vision*, "seeing on" in a vision-beyond-vision. To see sight or vision or visibility, to see beyond what is visible, is not merely *to have a vision* in the usual sense of the word, but to see-beyond-sight, to see-sight-beyond-sight. As in Ponge's "Le soleil placé en abîme," the story of glory engulfs or clouds over a sort of paternal figure, placing it in an abyss-structure, in vision-beyond-vision. The story obscures the sun ("the sun their father," says *The Triumph of Life*) with a blinding light. (Thus perhaps the mother lives on, and on, as a ghost—phantom or revenant—an absolute figurant, a walk-on who walks on and on, in accor-

---

notion of presence with which it is generally linked. The maximal translatability of this band: impoverishment by univocality. Economy and formalization, but in the opposite sense to that of what takes place in the upper band: there, too, are economy and formalization, but by semantic accumulation and overloading, until the point when the logic of the undecidable *arrêt de mort* brings and opens polysemy (and its economy) in the direction of dissemination. Why have I chosen to stress the translation-effect here? (1) Effects of transference, of superimposing, of textual superimprinting between the

dance with the "obsequent logic" to which I referred in *Glas*. I am my father who is dead and my mother who is alive, announces Nietzsche at the midpoint of his life, in *Ecce Homo*, after passing through blindness.) To see vision, to see on beyond sight: this abyss-like madness of an utterly primal scene, the scene of scenes, stages, representation, is simulated and dissimulated in the *récit* in the reassuring form (for those who want to be reassured) of spectacles [*spectacles*] within bounds, determinate "visions" or "scenes" that come in a way to allegorize the abyss and contain the madness. The word "vision" itself is ambiguous enough to make this economy possible.

The feminine voice that says, "Oh, I see the day, oh God," is, as we have said, insatiable for the "glory" of the speaker who says *I* in *La folie du jour*. This speaker has supposedly triumphed over blindness. I do not know whether it is possible to consider the "glories" of *The Triumph of Life* and those of *La folie du jour* as translating one another, and if so, which translating which, and in what ways. If we are not restricted to literal recurrences of the word *glory*, then that translation can go every which way, can pass through the tropics, through the Meridian, Celan would say. Its detours become both endless and inevitable. Let us say that I interrupt them here. I stop [*Je m'arrête*]. Thus I shall not cite "Outdoors, I had a brief vision" from *La folie du jour* [18/*MD* 10], at the hinge of the text, to give it the resonance of an echo translating "And then a Vision on my brain was rolled," which is at once the linking point and the opening of the *récit* in *The Triumph of Life*. After the "brief vision," before the traumatic accident in which "I nearly lost my sight, because someone crushed glass in my eyes" [*MD* 11/*FJ* 21], the accident that left him at first with his eyes bandaged (to be translated, I suppose, by "eyes banded" or by "banded eyes" as in lines 100 and 103 of *The Triumph of Life*), the beginning of the end is there for us to read. The beginning of the end describes in an abyss-structure [i.e., in an inserted miniature representing the whole] the

---

two "triumphs" or the two "*arrêts*" *and* within each of them. Both are written in a certain (arrested [*arrêté*]) relationship of translation. (2) The hymen (alliance, wedding-band, reaffirmation, "Yes, yes," "Come," and so forth) is related, in *L'arrêt de mort*, thematically related, to what commits [*engage*] us "in the language of the other." (3) Above all, by making manifest the limits of the prevalent concept of translation (I do not say of translatability in general), we touch on multiple problems said to be of "method," of reading and teaching. The line that I seek to recognize within translatability, between two transla-

structure of *un récit?* entitled *La folie du jour*. This *récit seems* indeed to *begin* with a certain sentence that will subsequently be cited toward the end as part of the *récit*, unless the first sentence cites in advance the one that comes at the end and that relates the first words of a *récit*. I shall return to this structure, which deprives the text of any beginning and of any decidable edge or border, of any *heading* or *letterhead* [en-tête]. (*Entête* is the word with which Chouraqui translates the beginning of Genesis:

ENTÊTE [in-head] Elohim created heaven and earth.
The earth was in shambles,
darkness upon the face of the abyss,
the breath of Elohim moving upon the face of the waters.

Elohim says:
    "There will be light."
      And there is light.
Elohim sees the   light: Oh, the good,
Elohim separates the   light from the darkness.
Elohim cries to the   light: "Day."
To the darkness, he cries: "Night."

And it is evening and it is morning:
day, unique.)

After the "brief vision," before the injury from which "I nearly lost my sight," he tells himself that this brief vision, in mid-*récit*, marks the beginning of the end:

This brief scene excited me to the point of delirium. I was undoubtedly not able to explain it to myself fully and yet I was sure of it, that I had seized the moment when the day, having stumbled against a real event, would begin hurrying to its end. Here it comes, I said to myself, the end is coming;

---

tions, one governed by the classical model of transportable univocality or of formalizable polysemy, and the other, which goes over the edge into dissemination—this line also passes between the *critical* and the *deconstructive*. A politico-institutional problem of the university: it, like all teaching in its traditional form, and perhaps all teaching whatever, has as its ideal, with exhaustive translatability, the effacement of language [*la langue*]. The deconstruction of a pedagogical institution and all that it implies. What this institution cannot bear, is for anyone to tamper with [*toucher à*; also "touch,"

something is happening, the end is beginning. I was seized by joy. [*MD* 10/ *FJ* 19–20][10]

What is judiciously called the *question*-of-*récit* covers, with a certain modesty, a *demand* for *récit*, a violent putting-to-the-question, an instrument of torture working to wring the *récit* out of one as if it were a terrible secret, in ways that can go from the most archaic police methods to refinements for making (and even letting) one talk that are unsurpassed in neutrality and politeness, that are most respectfully medical, psychiatric, and even psychoanalytic. For reasons that should be obvious by now, I shall not say that Blanchot offers a representation, a *mise en scène*, of this demand for the *récit*, in *La folie du jour*: it would be better to say that it is there to be read, "to the point of de*lire*ium," as it throws the reader off the track. For the same reasons, I do not know whether the text can be classified as being of the genre (or Genette would say: the "mode") "*récit*," a word that Blanchot has repeatedly insisted upon and contested, reclaimed and rejected, set down and (then) erased, and so forth. In addition to these general reasons there is a singular trait, involving precisely the (internal and external) *boundaries* or *edges* of this text. The boundary from which we believe we approach *La folie du jour*, its "first word" ("I"), opens with a paragraph that *affirms* a sort of triumph of life at the edge of death. The triumph must be excessive (in accordance with the "boundlessness" of *hubris*) and very close to what it triumphs over. This paragraph begins [*entame*] a *récit*, it seems, but does not yet recount anything. The narrator introduces himself in that simplest of performances, an "I am," or more precisely an "I am not . . . not . . . ," which immediately removes the performance from presence. The end of this paragraph notes especially the double excess of every triumph *of* life: i.e., the excessive double affirmation, *of* triumphant life, of death that triumphs *over* life.

"change," "concern oneself with"] language, meaning *both* the *national* language *and*, paradoxically, an ideal of translatability that neutralizes this national language. Nationalism and universalism—indissociables. What this institution cannot bear is a transformation that leaves intact neither of these two complementary poles. It can bear more readily the most apparently revolutionary ideological sorts of "content," if only that content does not touch the borders of language [*la langue*] and of all the juridico-political contracts that it guarantees. It is this "intolerable" something that concerns me here. It

I am not learned; I am not ignorant. I have known joys. That is saying too little: I am alive, and this life gives me the greatest pleasure. And what about death? When I die (perhaps any minute now), I will feel immense pleasure. I am not talking about the foretaste of death, which is stale and often disagreeable. Suffering dulls the senses. But this is the remarkable truth, and I am sure of it: I experience boundless pleasure in living, and I will take boundless satisfaction in dying. [*MD* 5/ *FJ* 9]

A number of signs make it possible to recognize a man in the first-person speaker. But in the *double* affirmation seen (remarked upon) in the syntax of triumph as *triomphe-de*, triumph *of* and triumph *over*, the narrator comes close to seeing a trait that is particularly feminine, a trait of feminine beauty, even.

Men want to escape from death, strange beings that they are. And some of them cry out "Die, die" because they want to escape life. "What a life. I'll kill myself. I'll give in." That is lamentable and strange; it is a mistake.

Yet I have met people who have never said to life, "Quiet!", who have never said to death, "Go away!" Almost always women, beautiful creatures. [*MD* 7/ *FJ* 12–13]

Later, on the next-to-last page, we learn that this opening paragraph (the upper edge of *La folie du jour*) corresponds in its content and form, if not in its occurrence, to the beginning of the *récit* that the narrator tries to take up [*aborder*] in response to the pressing demand of his interrogators. This creates an exceedingly strange space: what appeared to be the beginning and the upper edge of a discourse *will have been* merely part of a *récit* that forms a part of the discourse in that it *recounts* how an attempt was made—in vain!—to force a *récit* out of the narrator. The starting edge will have been the citation (at first not recognizable as such) of a narrative fragment that in turn will merely be citing its citation. For all these cita-

---

is related in an essential way to that which, as it is written above, brings out the limits of the concept of translation on which the university is built, particularly when it makes the teaching of language, even literatures, and even "comparative literature," its principal theme. *Questions of method* run throughout this book (here, a translators' note: I have published a text that is untranslatable, starting with its title, "Pas [*Pace* Not(*s*)]," and in "The Double Session," referring to "dissemination in the folds [*repli*] of the *hymen*": "Its steps allow for (no) *method* [*pas de* méthode] for it: no path leads around in a circle

tions, citations of re-citations with no original performance, there is no *speech act*[11] not already the iteration of another, no circle and no quotation marks to reassure us about the identity, opposition, or distinction of speech events. The part is always greater than the whole, the edge *of* the set [*ensemble*] is a fold [*pli*] *in* the set ("'Happy those for whom the fold / Of . . . ,'" *The Triumph of Life*), but as *La folie du jour* unfolds, explains itself [*s'explique*] without ever giving up its "fold" to another discourse not already its own, it is better if I cite. If I cite, for example, these last two pages:

I had been asked: Tell us "*just* exactly" what happened. A *récit?* I began: I am not learned; I am not ignorant. I have known joys. That is saying too little. I told them the whole story and they listened, it seems to me with interest, at least in the beginning. But the end was a surprise to all of us. "That was the beginning," they said. "Now get down to the facts." How so? The *récit* was over!

I had to acknowledge that I was not capable of forming a *récit* out of these events. I had lost the sense of the story [*histoire*]: that happens in a good many illnesses. But this explanation only made them more insistent. Then I noticed for the first time that there were two of them and that this distortion of the traditional method, even though it was explained by the fact that one of them was an eye doctor, the other a specialist in mental illness, constantly gave our conversation the character of an authoritarian interrogation, overseen and controlled by a strict set of rules. Of course neither of them was the chief of police. But because there were two of them, there were three, and this third remained firmly convinced, I am sure, that a writer, a man who speaks and who reasons with distinction, is always capable of recounting the facts that he remembers.

A *récit?* No. No *récit* [*pas de récit*], never again. [*MD* 18/ *FJ* 36–38]

By definition, there is no end to a discourse that would seek to describe the invaginated structure of *La folie du jour*. *Invagination* is the inward refolding of *la gaine* [sheath, girdle], the inverted reapplication of the

---

toward a first pace, nor proceeds from the simple to the complex, nor leads from a beginning to an end ['a book neither begins nor ends: at most it pretends to' . . .]. 'All method is a fiction.' . . . We here note a point/lack of method [*point de méthode*]: this does not rule out a certain marching order [*une certaine marche à suivre*]."[d] The translators will not be able to translate this *pas* and this *point*. Will they have to indicate that this reminder is to be related to what is called the "unfinished" quality of Shelley's *Triumph* and the impossibility of fixing [*arrêter*] the opening and closing boundaries of *L'arrêt*

outer edge to the inside of a form where the outside then opens a pocket. Such an invagination is possible from the first trace on. This is why there is no "first" trace. We have just seen, on the basis of this example refined to the point of madness, how "the whole story [to which] they listened" is the one (the same but another at the same time) that, like *La folie du jour*, begins "I am not learned; I am not ignorant. . . . " But this "whole story," which corresponds to the totality of the "book," is also only a part of the book, the *récit* that is demanded, attempted, impossible, and so forth. Its end, which comes before the end, does not respond to the request of the authorities, the authorities who demand an *author*, or even a narrator, an *I* capable of organizing a narrative sequence, of remembering and telling the truth: "'*just* exactly' what happened," "recounting facts that he remembers," in other words saying *I* (I am the same as the one to whom these things happened, I keep the memory of myself, I keep myself, *I* keeps itself in memory, and so on). Saying *I*, an I would be able to assure the unity or identity of narratee, as well as of reader. Such is the demand for the *récit*, for narrative, the demand that society, the law [*droit*] that governs literary and artistic works, medicine, the police, and so forth, claim to constitute. This demand for truth is itself recounted and swept along in the endless process of invagination. Because I cannot pursue this analysis here, I merely situate the place, the locus, in which *double invagination* comes about, the place where the invagination of the upper edge on its outer face (the supposed beginning of *La folie du jour*), which is folded back "inside" to form a pocket and an inner edge, comes to extend beyond (or encroach on) the invagination of the lower edge, on its inner face (the supposed end of *La folie du jour*), which is folded back "inside" to form a pocket and an outer edge. Indeed the "middle" sequence ("I had been asked: Tell us '*just* exactly' what happened. A *récit*? I began: I am not learned; I am not ignorant. I have known joys. That is saying too little. I told them the whole

---

de mort, all problems treated, in another mode, in the procession above? Will they relate this untranslatable *pas* to the *double knot* [*le double noeud*] of *double invagination*, a central motif of that text, or, along with its entire semantic family, to all the occurrences of "path," "past," "pass" in Shelley's *Triumph*?). If the question of teaching (not only the teaching of literature and the humanities) also runs throughout this book, if my participation is possible only with supplementary interpreting by the translators (active, interested, inscribed in a politico-institutional field of drives, and so forth), if we are not

story and they listened, it seems to me with interest, at least in the beginning. But the end was a surprise to all of us. 'That was the beginning,' they said. 'Now get down to the facts.' How so? The *récit* was over!"), this antepenultimate paragraph, recalls, subsumes, recites without quotation marks the first sentences of *La folie du jour* ("I am not learned . . . ," etc.), including in itself the entire book, *including itself,* but only after anticipating, by citing it in advance, the question that will form the lower edge or the final boundary of *La folie du jour*—or *almost* final, to accentuate the dissymmetry of effects. The question "A *récit?*", posed as a question *in response to* the demand (Do they demand a story, a *récit,* of me?) in the antepenultimate paragraph, will be taken up again in the final sequence ("A *récit?* No. No *récit,* never again."), but again, just as in the previous instance, this repetition does not follow (chronologically or logically) what nevertheless seems to come before it in the first line, in the immediate linearity of reading. We cannot even speak here of a future perfect tense, if this still presumes a regular modification of the present into its instances of a present in the past, a present in the present, and a present in the future. In this re-citation [*ré*-citation] of the *récit,* intensified or reinforced here by the re-citation of the *word* "*récit,*" it is impossible to say which one cites the other, and above all which one forms the border of the other. Each *includes* the other, *comprehends* the other, which is to say that *neither comprehends the other.* Each "*récit*" (and each occurrence of the word "*récit,*" each "*récit*" in the *récit*) *is part* of the other, makes the other a part (of itself), each "*récit*" is at once larger and smaller than itself, includes itself without including (or comprehending) itself, identifies itself with itself even as it remains utterly different from its homonym. Of course, at intervals ranging from two to forty paragraphs, this structure of *crisscross double invagination* ("I am not learned; I am not. . . . A *récit?* I began: I am not learned; I am not. . . . The *récit* was over! . . . A *récit?* No. No *récit,* never again.") never ceases to re-

---

to pass over all these stakes and interests (what happens in this respect in the universities of the Western world, in the United States, at Yale, from department to department? How is one to step in? What is the *key* here for decoding? What am I doing here? What are they making me do? How are the boundaries of all these fields, titles, corpora, and so forth, laid out? Here I can only locate the necessity of all these questions), then we must pause to consider [*on devra s'arrêter sur*] translation. It brings the *arrêt* of everything, decides, suspends, and sets in motion . . . even in "my" language, within the

fold or *superpose* or *overemploy* itself in the meantime, and the description of this would be interminable. I must content myself for the moment with underscoring the supplementary trait of this structure: the chiasma of this *double invagination* is always possible, because of what I have called elsewhere the iterability of the mark. Now, if we have just seen a strikingly complex example of this in the case of a *récit*, using the word "*récit*" and re(-)citing both its possibility and its impossibility, double invagination can come about in any text, whether it is narrative in form or not, whether it is of the genre or mode "*récit*" or not, whether it speaks of it or not. Nevertheless—and this is the trait that interested me in the beginning—double invagination, wherever it comes about, has in itself the *structure of a récit in deconstruction*. Here the *récit* is irreducible. Even before it "concerns" a text in *récit* form, double invagination constitutes the *récit* of *récit*, the narrative of narrative, the *récit of deconstruction in deconstruction*: the apparently outer edge of an enclosure [*clôture*], far from being simple, simply external and circular, in accordance with the philosophical representation of philosophy, makes no sign beyond itself, toward what is utterly other, without becoming double or dual, without making itself be "represented," refolded, superposed, *re-marked* within the enclosure, at least in what the structure produces as an effect of interiority. But it is precisely this structure-effect that is being deconstructed here.

If "No. No *récit*, never again" belongs to *La folie du jour* as it is inscribed at its edge, at the edge of a text that recounts the demand for an impossible *récit*, a text that was first called "*Un récit*," and so on, the *récit* effaces itself from the *récit* by making itself more noticeable, by re-marking itself, with a "double exposure," a superimprinting. And the (hi)story of the *récit* or the *récit* of (hi)story is the *récit* of effacement *as* superimprinting, of all the logic of the *double bind*[12] or of double invagination that is reaffirmed in that story. It is not absolutely

---

presumed unity of what is called the corpus of a language. *9–16 January 1978.* What will remain unreadable for me, in any case, of this text, not to mention Shelley, of course, and everything that haunts his language [*langue*] and his writing. What will remain unreadable for me of this text, once it is translated, of course, still bearing my signature. But even in "my" language, to which it does not belong in a simple way. One never writes either in one's own language or in a foreign language. Derive all the consequences of this: they involve each element, each term of the preceding sentence. Hence the triumph

necessary that this superimprinting by effacement also stress the *word récit*, the name of the mode or genre, but it makes for a remarkable supplement ... especially if the "mention" "*récit*" is part of the title without being part of it, between the title and the rest. This is what happens with the first titles of *La folie du jour* and "in" the text that bears these titles, but it is also what happens between the two versions of *L'arrêt de mort*. The first one (1948) carries, beneath the title, if not as a subtitle, the mention "*récit.*" This disappears in the second version (1971), which also effaces the last two pages, an enigmatic epilogue that threatened to gather together, under the authority of a meta-*récit*, the two "*récits*," apparently independent and indeed in fact disparate, that precede it. Here we cannot go deeply into this event, this double effacement, which is a *récit* in itself: the two versions are part of the corpus registered at the Bibliothèque Nationale in the name of Maurice Blanchot. I allude to this institution to indicate with one reference all the problems that I cannot go into here, problems of the mark that superimposes by effacement (judicial, political problems and the like, involving the convention or the fiction that guarantees an author his due [*les "droits d'auteur,"* royalties; lit., an author's rights], the unity of an author's corpus, the presumption of the "real" author in his proper name as set down in the registry office, which distinguishes him from the narrator, and so on: I reserve all these questions under the title "du droit à la littérature" ["from law to literature" / "of the right to literature"]).

This double effacement, then, is a *récit* in itself, a *récit* of "*récit*," a "*récit*" of the *récit.* It is enough, in *La folie du jour*, to disrupt or unhinge the demand for the *récit*, to strike the instigators with impotence but also to sustain them as instigators on the basis of that impotence. As to the double version, it is no contingent accident: it is fated, even within what in "copy-

---

(necessarily double and equivocal, because it is also a phase of mourning). Hence the triumph as the triumph of translation. *Übersetzung* and "translation" overcome, equivocally, in the course of an equivocal combat, the loss of an object. A text lives only if it lives on [*sur-vit*], and it lives on only if it is *at once* translatable and untranslatable (always "at once ... and ...": *hama*, at the "same" time). Totally translatable, it disappears as a text, as writing, as a body of language [*langue*]. Totally untranslatable, even within what is believed to be *one* language, it dies immediately. Thus triumphant translation is

right" law is considered to be one and the same version. Like the meaning "genre" or "mode," or that of "corpus" or the unity of a "work," the meaning of version, and of the unity of a version, is overrun, exceeded, by this structure of invagination: not merely canceled or invalidated but exposed in the precariousness of its effect, the fragility of the conventional artifices that provisionally guarantee it, the set of historical fictions that certify its *carte d'identité*. Thus, on the basis of what happens to the *récit*, to "*récit*" from one version of *L'arrêt de mort* to another or even within what is considered a single "version" of *La folie du jour*—on the basis of what happens to the subtitle "*récit*" or the title "*Un récit* (?)" from one version of the two *récits* (?) to the other, we understand better how the unity of one version can be *encroached* [entamer] upon by an essential *unfinishedness* that cannot be reduced to an incompleteness or an inadequacy. I register, I record this remark on the waters off [*dans les parages de*] what is called the *unfinishedness* of *The Triumph of Life*, at the moment when Shelley is drowned. I do so without claiming to understand what people mean in this case by "unfinished," or to decide anything. I do so only to recall the immense procedures that should come before a statement about whether a work is finished or unfinished. Where are we to situate the event of Shelley's drowning? And who will decide the answer to this question? Who will form the *récit* of these borderline events [*événements de bord*]? At whose demand?

The Triumph of Life

Once we have accentuated the *question* of the *récit* as *demand* for *récit*, once the response to this demand undecidably invaginates every border, then this will affect all the questions with which I began: the question of *récit* (What is a *récit*?), that of *la Chose* (What is a thing and that thing

---

neither the life nor the death of the text, only or already its living on, its life after life, its life after death. The same thing will be said of what I call writing, mark, trace, and so on. It [*Ça*] neither lives nor dies; it lives on. And it "starts" only with living on (testament, iterability, remaining [*restance*], crypt, detachment that lifts the strictures [*déstructurant*] of the "living" *rectio* or direction of an "author" not drowned in the waters off his text). The relative synonymy or intertranslatability that I seek to open a passage for above between *arrêt de mort* and triumph of life. It also means that these two *titles* can

that is called a *récit* or that is called to from a *récit*? What is the demand for/of *la Chose*? And so on . . .), that of the place and of taking place, of the topics of the event, which will lead us to a certain "Come" ["*Viens*"] and a certain "*pas*" [pace, not] that open the door to the impossible possibility of what comes about [*arrive*] in its taking place.

Within the boundaries of this sketch, I shall propose a fragment, itself unfinished, detached from a more systematic reading of Shelley, a reading oriented by the problems of *récit* as *reaffirmation* (yes, yes) of life, in which the *yes*, which says nothing, describes nothing but itself, the performance of its own event of affirmation, repeats itself, *cites* itself, says *yes* to itself as (to an-) other in accordance with the ring, re(-)cites a commitment that would not take place outside this repetition of a performance without presence. This strange ring says *yes* to life only in the overdetermining ambiguity of the triumph *de* ["of," "over"] life, *sur* ["over," "on," etc.] life, the triumph marked in the *on* of living on [*le* sur *d'un survivre*].

All this syntax, almost untranslatable, is sealed in the French expression *l'arrêt de mort*.

In order that my fragmentary discourse may remain somewhat intelligible, concrete, coherent, I shall refer to the example of the former "*récit*" that has this title, *L'arrêt de mort*. In this text you will recognize the "narrative voice" that Blanchot, in *The Infinite Conversation*, distinguishes from the "narrating voice." The narrative voice, he says, is "a neutral voice that speaks the work from out of this place without a place, where the work is silent." The placeless place where the work is silent: a silent voice, then, withdrawn into its "aphony" [*IC* 385/*EI* 565]. This "aphony" distinguishes it from the "narrating voice," the voice that literary criticism or poetics or narratology strives to locate in the system of the *récit*, of the novel, or of the narration. The narrating voice is the voice of a subject recounting something, remembering an event or a historical sequence, knowing

---

always, in addition to or beyond any other possible reference, *designate* the very thing to which they *give a title*, that is, the text below, the writing of the "poem" or "*récit*" that *bears* the title. The triumph of life or *L'arrêt de mort* would be *the* text, this text, its element, its condition, its effect. This assumes a certain functioning of titles, and that we analyze its laws, its relationship to the law and to the judicial conventions of "literature." This schema is not its own *telos*, not self-mirroring or mere *mise en abyme*; at least the *double bind* that structures these titles, as I seek to demonstrate it, keeps this reflecting

who he is, where he is, and what he is talking about. It responds to some "police," a force of order or law ("What 'exactly' are you talking about?": the truth as adequation). In this sense, all organized narration is "a matter for the police," even before its genre (mystery novel, cop story) has been determined. The narrative voice, on the other hand, would surpass police investigation, if that were possible. In *La folie du jour*, we can say that the authoritarian demand puts pressure on a narrative voice to turn into a narrating voice and to *bring about* [donne lieu à] a *récit* that would be *identifiable*, gathered together, connected, in its subject and in its object. Now, the narrative voice (*I* or *he*, "third-person . . . that is neither a third person nor the simple cloak of impersonality" [*IC* 384/*EI* 563]) has no fixed [*arrêté*] place. It takes place place*lessly*, being both *a-topical*, mad, extravagant, and *hypertopical*, both placeless and over-placed. Blanchot speaks of that which "designates 'its' place as both the place from which it [*il*, the neuter "it" of the narrative voice]¹³ will always be missing and that will thus remain empty, but also as a surplus of place, a place that is always too many: hypertopia" ("L'absence de livre," in *L'entretien infini* 564n [*IC* 462 n2 of "The Narrative Voice"]). The neuter *il*, "it," of the narrative voice is not an "I," not an ego, even if it is represented in the *récit* by *I*, *he*, or *she*. We might wonder—and this is one of the questions that will run through my reading of this fragment—why the neuter of the *il* that is not an "I," not an ego, is represented in French, according to Blanchot, by a pronoun that privileges the affinity or apparently fortuitous and external resemblance between the masculine *il* ["he"] and the neuter *il* ["it"]. Why not *elle* ["she"]? And are we dealing with a simple, fortuitous homonymy between the *il* of the "I," of the masculine "subject," and the neuter *il*? Atopia, hypertopia, place-*less* place [*lieu* sans *lieu*], this narrative voice calls out to this "-less" [*sans*, without] syntax, which in Blanchot's text so often comes to neutralize (without positing, without negating) a word, a con-

---

representation from folding back upon itself or reproducing itself within itself in perfect self-correspondence [*adéquate à elle-même*], from dominating or including itself, tautologically, from translating itself into its own totality. Writing and triumph. Nietzsche: "*Writing in order to triumph.* Writing should always mark a triumph" (*Opinions et sentences mêlées*, aphorism 152; I cite from a French translation now in use but quite inadequate, precisely in its triumph. Nietzsche writes: "*Schreiben und Siegen-wollen.*—Schreiben sollte immer einen Sieg anzeigen . . . "). See what he says then of the triumph (*Überwin-*

cept, a term (x-*less* x): *without* (or "-less") without privation or negativity or lack ("without" without *without*, *less*-less "-less"), the necessity of which I have attempted to analyze in "The *Sans* of the Pure Cut"[14] and "*Pace* Not(*s*)." This "-less" syntax enters at least twice (and that's no accident) into the (definitionless) definition of the narrative voice. We have already read "place without a place," and now we come to "at a distance without there being any distance," in a passage that makes the ghost return [*fait revenir le revenant*], "ghostly," "phantom-like" *revenance* (the element of haunting that inundates, if you will, *The Triumph of Life*, its "ghosts," "phantoms," "ghostly shadows," and the like):

> The narrative voice that is inside only inasmuch as it is outside, at a distance without there being any distance, cannot be embodied. Although it may well borrow the voice of a judiciously chosen character, or even create the hybrid function of a mediator (the voice that ruins all mediation), it is always different from what utters it; it is that indifferent-difference that alters the personal voice. Let us (on a whim) [*par fantaisie*] call it spectral, ghostlike. . . .
> . . . The narrative voice bears the neutral [*porte le neutre*]. (565–66 [of *EI/ IC* 386])

The neutral and not neutrality, the neutral beyond dialectical contradiction and all opposition: such would be the possibility of a "narrative," a "*récit*," that would no longer be simply a form, a genre, or a literary mode, and that goes, that is borne, beyond the system of philosophical oppositions. The neutral cannot be governed by any of the terms involved in an opposition within philosophical language and natural language. And yet it is not outside of language: it is, for example, narrative voice. Despite the negative form that it takes on in grammar (*neuter*, neither-nor) and that betrays it, it surpasses negativity. It is linked rather to the double affirmation (*yes, yes, come, come*) that re-cites [*ré-cite*] itself and becomes involved in the *récit*.

---

dung) over oneself, i.e., he claims, without using force (*Gewalt*) on others. He opposes the triumph that he prescribes for literature, to that of "dyspeptics who write only at the very moment when they are unable to digest something, or from the moment that the morsel [*morceau*] sticks in their teeth. . . ."[f] The problem of the *mors* [literally "(bridle-) bit"] (how can *mors* be translated?), set forth in *Glas* and "Fors." Obviously (and this is the place to note [*marquer*] it, in this short telegraphic band addressed to the translators and that I am burying here underneath the other one), I can try for a

One text reads another. How can a reading be settled on [*arrêter*]? For example, we can say that *The Triumph of Life* reads, among other texts, *L'arrêt de mort*. And, among other texts, vice versa. Each text is a machine with multiple reading heads for other texts. To read *L'arrêt de mort*, starting with the title in its endless mobility, I can always be guided by another text—for example, in this case, by a certain passage from *The Step Not Beyond*, which, more than twenty years later (1973), also seems to provide a "commentary" for the title *L'arrêt de mort*:

♦ *Taking three paces, stopping, falling, and all of a sudden, becoming sure of himself in this fragile fall.*

♦ To survive, to live on: not to live or, not living, to maintain oneself, without life, in a state of pure supplement, movement of substitution for life, but rather to arrest [*arrêter*] dying, arrest [*l'arrêt*] that does not arrest, making it, on the contrary, last [durer]. "Speak on the edge [*l'arrête*]¹⁵—the line of instability—of speech." As if it attended the exhaustion of dying, as if the night, having started too early, at the earliest time of day, doubted that it would ever become night.

♦ It is almost certain that at certain moments we notice: speaking again—this survival of speech, sur-speech, speaking on—is a way of letting ourselves know that for a long time we have no longer spoken.

♦ Praise (of the far near) from the near to the far.

♦ *Come, come, come [*viens, viens, venez*], you for whom the injunction, the prayer, the wait [attente] could not be becoming [convenir]*. [*SNB* 135/ *PAD* 184–85]

In the first of these sequences that I have just cited, you will have noticed the shift to italic. This indicates quite uniformly the transition from a more assertive, theoretical, impersonal mode to a more fictional, narrative one. (The interweaving of these modes complicates this opposition

---

certain intertranslatability (*triumphant and arrested*) of *The Triumph of Life* and *L'arrêt de mort*, here, only on the basis of work undertaken elsewhere, the code of which cannot fail to enter into the translation. *Glas*, "Pas," "Fors," to limit myself to this sequence of hardly translatable titles, lead elsewhere, but I stress them more because in them the relationship to the work of mourning is more thematic, as is work on the Freudian concept of the work of mourning. Now, we know that according to Freud "triumph" corresponds to a phase, manic in type, in the process of mourning. All the difficulties recog-

even more, but let's not get into that here.) For example, *durer*, "last," already italicized, glides into [*amorce continument*] the serial interlacement. This *enduring, lasting, going on* stresses or insists *on* the *on* of a living on that bears the entire enigma of this supplementary logic. Survival and *revenance*, living on and returning from the dead: living on goes beyond both living and dying, supplementing each with a sudden surge and a certain surcease, deciding [*arrêtant*] life and death at once, ending them in a decisive *arrêt*, the *arrêt* that puts an end to something and the *arrêt* that condemns with a sentence [*sentence*], a statement, a spoken word or a word that goes on speaking. Now, the homonymy of "*arrête*," if we can call these words homonyms, the verb and the noun ("*arrêt qui ne l'arrête pas*," "arrest that does not arrest"; "Parle sur l'arrête," "*Speak on the arrête, edge*, the ridge, the arris, the 'arrist'"), is made complete by means of some tampering with spelling. This is rare in Blanchot's writing, but all the more significant. And we are further justified in paying attention to this by the fact that it is repeated elsewhere, thirty pages earlier [in the French, twenty-three in the English], when the noun *arête* (cutting edge, ridge, etc.) receives an extra *r* [in the context of a discussion of the words "I do not know"]: "'Not—I know' shows the double power of attack that these two terms maintain when isolated from one another: the decision of knowing, the cutting edge of the negative, the *arrête* (the edge at which we stop) that on either side impatiently puts an end to everything" [*SNB* 112/*PAD* 154]. *Arrête*, with two *r*'s, is thus indeed that which orders the *arrêt* (stopping/decision), but the *ar(r)ête*, as a noun, is also that sharp dividing line, that angle of instability on which it is impossible to settle, to *s'arrêter*. Thus this dividing line functions also *within* the word and traces in it a line of vacillation. This line runs within *L'arrêt de mort*, within what the *arrêt de mort* says, the expression "arrêt de mort," the title *L'arrêt de mort*—all of which are to be distinguished.

---

nized by Freud in "Trauer und Melancholia":[g] mania and melancholia have the same "content," and the states of "joy," "jubilation," and "triumph" (*Freude, Jubel, Triumph*) that characterize mania require the same "economic" conditions as melancholia, and so on. A movement from *Überwindung* to *Triumphieren*. Mania brings about phases of triumphant jubilation analogous to those that appear paradoxically in depression and in melancholic inhibition when the object seems to return. But in manic triumph, what the ego "has overcome and what it triumphs over" (*was es überwunden hat und*

Living On 135

How then is the title of the book to be read? First, is it readable? Its open polysemy plays with the language to the point of arresting any translation of it. In his introduction to (the translation by Lydia Davis of) a fragment of *L'arrêt de mort* (*Georgia Review*, Summer 1976), Geoffrey Hartman asks rightly: "Is *'arrêt de mort*,' then, 'death sentence' or 'suspension of death'?" (Which I shall play at translating into my language as follows: Does the *triumph of life* triumph over life [*triomphe de la vie*] or express the triumph of life [*le triomphe de la vie*]?) "Death Sentence," the title chosen for the fragment of the "novella" (*récit* is also untranslatable) presented under this title (this designation as a "novella") to the American reader, does translate one meaning of the expression *arrêt de mort*. In French an *arrêt* comes at the end of a trial, when the case has been argued and must be judged. The judgment that constitutes the *arrêt* closes the matter and renders a legal decision. It is a sentence. An *arrêt de mort* is a sentence that condemns someone to death. It is indeed a question of *une chose*, a thing, as case, *cause, causa,* and of a decision about *la chose*. As it happens, *la Chose* is here (as in Blanchot's text) Death, and the decision (verdict, sentence) of death concerns death as cause and as end. Death does not come *naturally*, just as *la Chose* does not. Death has an obscure relationship to decision, or more precisely to some sentence, some language that constitutes an *act* ("acts and deeds," "acts of a congress," action and archive) and leaves a trace. *L'arrêt de mort* makes death a decision. *I* bestow, *I* give [*donne*] death. *He, il,* gives death: the *Il* (who says *I,* who occupies the place of the narrating voice, the place of the narrator in the *récit*) gives death, after *declaring,* announcing, *signifying,* and then *suspending* it. And *he* (I) does indeed *give* death, both as a gift and as a murder. In French *donner la mort* means first of all "to kill."

Here, first of all, is the moment in which death is signified, announced, like a condemnation that calls forth death and calls J. to

---

worüber es triumphiert) is concealed from it. How is this dissimulation possible? Freud's dissatisfaction in this text, and in *Beyond the Pleasure Principle,* whose entire problematic should be introduced here. Speculations on the improbable death drive. Always one pace more [*un pas de plus*], and no thesis [*et pas de thèse*].[h] Freud is still—bereft of an answer, unable to kiss it good-bye [*faire son deuil de la réponse*]. Here, in "Trauer und Melancholie," the most difficult phase seems to concern the difference between normal *Überwindung* and "triumph." Of course, the mania must have "overcome" (*überwunden*)

death—assent, consent, that is also a sentence (J. is *condemned* in every sense of the word, given up and given over):

> After I spoke to the doctor, I told her, "He gives you another month."
>
> "Well, I'll tell that to the queen mother, who doesn't believe I'm really ill."
>
> I don't know whether she wanted to live or die. During the last few months, the disease she had been fighting for ten years had been making her life more limited every day, and now she cursed both the disease and life itself with all the violence she could rouse. Some time before, she had thought seriously of killing herself. One evening I advised her to do it. That same evening, after listening to me, unable to talk because of her shortness of breath, but sitting up at her table like a healthy person, she wrote down several sentences [*lignes*] that she wished to keep secret. I got these sentences from her, in the end, and I still have them. . . .
>
> No mention of me. I could see how bitter she had felt when she heard me agree to her suicide. When I think it over carefully, as I did afterward, I realize that this consent was hardly excusable, was even dishonest, since it vaguely rose from the thought that the disease would never get the better of her, she fought so. Normally, she should have been dead long ago, but not only was she not dead, she had continued to live, love, laugh, run around the city, like someone whom illness could not touch. Her doctor had told me that from 1936 on he had considered her dead. [*DS* 4–5/*AM* 13–14]¹⁶

Condemned (by the disease, the doctor, the "narrator"), J. should have been dead already. She thus lives on, more alive than ever, though. The disease has not got the better of her, *n'a pas eu* raison *d'elle*, another expression that is hard to translate: *avoir raison de* is here to overcome, to *triumph over*. Over life, to be precise, which does not give in to that *ratio* and of which it is difficult to give a reasoned account.

In truth it is also J. who makes the decision that condemns her to death: J., who will have to, will have had to die, should have died (but will we ever know whether she died, whether death came for her?), makes

---

the loss of the object or the mourning for this loss or the object itself. Hence the libidinal explosion of the manic, who, "famished," rushes to new cathexes, new objects. (During her "life after life" ["*sur-vie*"] or "resurrection," J., like the narrator, is surprisingly gay, and "she ate much more than I did" [*DS* 22/*AM* 45].) But if "normal" mourning does in fact "overcome" the loss of the object, how can we explain the fact that after it has run its course (*nach ihrem Ablaufe*) it gives no indication of anything that would provide the necessary economic conditions for a "phase of triumph"? After a long digression—

the decision, takes it upon herself to decide and enjoins the narrator from deciding. She orders him to kill her, to "give her death." She decides her death [*arrête sa mort*], takes up the decree of death herself. This is the penultimate page of the first part (which also forms an independent whole) of an erstwhile "*récit*" strangely cut up into two wholes and suspended around this undecidable *arrêt de mort*. The verb *arrêter*, made reflexive as *s'arrêter*, stopping (itself) [*s'arrrêtant*], twice marks a boundary that brings things to an end only to let them start or start over or start on again [*repartir*]. (The pulse "stopped [*s'arrêta*], then began to beat again. . . . What is extraordinary begins at the moment I stop [*je m'arrête*].") Here, she demands death, which he gives her; she gives it to herself [i.e., takes her own life] with the hand of the narrator. As we read this, we should remember that J. *was dead* before, since she had *returned* to life at the narrator's bidding, in response to his call. Having died once, she had already lived on. This double death is a triumph of life *and* of death. Here is the passage (my emphasis):

I never saw her more alive, nor more lucid. Maybe she was in the last instant of her agony [*agonie*], but even though she was incredibly beset by suffering, exhaustion and death, she seemed so alive to me that once again I was convinced that if she didn't want it, and if I didn't want it, nothing would ever get the better of her. While attack followed attack—but there was no more trace of coma nor any fatal symptoms—when the others were out of the room, her hand that was twitching on mine suddenly controlled itself and clasped mine with the greatest impatience and with all the affection and all the tenderness it could. At the same time she smiled at me in a natural way, even with amusement. Immediately afterward she said to me in a low and rapid voice, "Quick, a shot." (She had not asked for one during the night.) I took a large syringe, in it I mixed two doses of morphine and two of a sedative, four doses altogether of narcotics. The liquid was fairly slow in penetrating, but since she saw what I was doing she remained very calm. She did

---

namely, by way of "ambivalence" as one of the three necessary conditions for melancholia—Freud evokes the "regression of the libido toward narcissism" as the only effective factor. But he suddenly suspends, arrests the (dis)approach, calls a "halt," postpones, in a gesture for the sake of economy that concerns precisely economy. We must halt ("*Halt zu machen*"), he says in conclusion, until we know the "economic nature" of physical pain and of the mental pain that is "analogous" to it. Earlier, as he *often* does, he uses the judicial expression *Verdikt* (verdict, sentence, *arrêt*) to designate the operation

not move at any moment. Two or three minutes later, her pulse became irregular, it beat violently, *stopped*, then began to beat again, heavily, only to *stop* again, this happened many times, finally it became extremely rapid and light, and "scattered like sand."

I have no better way of describing it [*Je n'ai aucun moyen d'en écrire davantage*]. I could say that during those moments J. continued to look at me with the same affectionate and willing [*consentant*] look and that this look is still there, but unfortunately I'm not sure of that. As for *the rest*, I don't want to say anything. The difficulties with the doctor became a matter of indifference to me. I myself see nothing important in the fact that this young woman was dead, and returned to life at my bidding, but I see an astounding miracle in her fortitude, in her energy, which was great enough to make death powerless as long as she wanted. One thing must be understood: I have said nothing extraordinary or even surprising. What is extraordinary begins at the moment *I stop*. But I am no longer able to speak of it. [*DS* 29–30/*AM* 58–60]

This last sentence marks, if you will, the lower or final border of the "first" of the two "*récits*" entitled *L'arrêt de mort*. This outer edge or border can also be considered an inner fold. This fold is marked by indecision in more ways than one: not only because the "stopping" is an instance of a beginning or a new beginning but also because the temporality of "this young woman was dead" sinks into an indefinite past, and because "unfortunately" we are "not sure" of the sentence, of her "willing" "consent" to the death sentence. The reason for the interruption finally oscillates among three types of movement, at least ("I have no better way . . ."; "I could . . . but. . . . As for the rest, I don't want to say anything"; "But I am no longer able to speak of it").

Thus he/it stops, *s'arrête*, when it comes to the "rest."

As defined (indefinitely) in the passage from *The Step Not Beyond*, the *arrêt de mort* is not only the decision that determines [*arrêtant*] the undecid-

---

of Reality with respect to the lost object. Each time that we recall the lost object and the libido once linked to it returns, Reality gives its verdict, i.e., "that the object no longer exists." Then, if the ego does not want to be condemned to the same fate and if it values the narcissistic satisfactions that remain for it, it decides to break off its "tie" (*Bindung*) to the destroyed object. *23–30 January 1978.* In short, will it be possible to reduce the theme of double affirmation to the meaning of triumph, in the Freudian sense? The risk is that we may find the negativity of mourning, of economic resentment, and of

able: it also arrests death by suspending it, interrupting it, deferring it with a "start" [*sursaut*], the startling starting over, and starting on, of living on. But then what suspends or holds back death is the very thing that gives it all its power of undecidability—another false name, rather than a pseudonym, for differance. And this is the pulse of the "word" *arrêt*, the arrhythmic pulsation of its syntax in the expression *arrêt de mort*. *Arrêter*, in the sense of suspending, is suspending the *arrêt*, in the sense of decision. The *suspensive arrêt* suspends the *decisive arrêt*. The decisive *arrêt* arrests the suspensive *arrêt*. They are ahead of or lag behind one another. One marks delay; the other, haste. There are not merely two senses or two syntaxes of *arrêt* but, beyond a playful variability, the *antagony* [*antagonie*; cf. *agonie*, "death throes," and *antagonisme*] from one *arrêt* to the other. The antagony lasts from one to the other, one relieving the other in an *Aufhebung* that never lets up, *arrêt* arresting *arrêt*, both senses, both ways. The *arrêt* arrests *itself* [*s'arrête*]. The indecision of the *arrêt* intervenes not between two senses of the word *arrêt* but within each sense, so to speak. For the suspensive *arrêt* is undecided because what it decides, death, *la Chose*, the neuter, is the undecidable itself, installed by decision in its undecidability. Like death, the *arrêt* remains (rests, *s'arrête, s'arreste*, arrests itself) undecidable. Crisis: everything seems to begin in a period of crisis (1938, Munich, then "the end of 1940"), then with a "strange attack [*crise*]" when someone goes into "*râles*" ["breathing hoarsely" (tr. Davis); also "deathrattle"] after opening a closet where the "proof" [*DS* 3/*AM* 10–11] of the story was, perhaps, to be found, and so forth. Crisis is the urgency [*instance*, also "instance," "lawsuit," "tribunal"] of impossible decision, *krinein*, the "judgment" that it is impossible to reach, to *arrêter*, in the *arrêt de mort*. Since *arrêt* arrests *arrêt*, since the suspensive *arrêt* arrests the decisive *arrêt* and vice versa, the *arrêt de mort* arrests the *arrêt de mort*. Such is the arrhythmic pulsation of the title before it scatters like sand. The *arrêt* arrests *itself*, but in stopping itself [*s'arrêtant*] (as *arrêt*), it imparts movement,

---

melancholia as well, in the "yes, yes." Can it be avoided? But for Freud himself what he calls "triumph" is not clear, and all the rereading that I attempted of the athetic nature of *Beyond the Pleasure Principle* could be brought to bear here. What I have said elsewhere ("Ja, ou le faux-bond") about the *deuil du deuil* [i.e., "relinquishing mourning itself"], and of half-mourning. The *arrêt de mort* as *verdict*: it is obvious, and the translators must take this into account, that in "everyday" language, in "normal" conversation, the expression *arrêt de mort* is unambiguous. It means *death sentence*.[i] The syntax is clear: the

sets things in motion [*donne le mouvement*]. It makes them come and go, go and come again. It *gives* life; it *gives* death. And it gives them to itself, with a *consent* that "unfortunately" is not "sure," fortunately not sure. The *arrêt* arrests *itself.* It stands (but gets no foothold), stays (with no mainstay) on this unstable line, this ridge [*arête*] that relates it to itself (the *arrêt* arresting *itself*) without being able to constitute it in self-reflection and reappropriation of self. It remains [*reste*] on the *arête* of itself without remaining to itself, in itself, for itself. It *a-rests* (for) itself. No consciousness, no perception, no watchfulness can gather up this remnance, this *restance*; no attentiveness can make it present, no "I," no ego; hence its essential relationship to ghosts, fantasies, daydreams, to *Phantasieren* (Freud) or the "waking dream" (*The Triumph of Life*). This epochal [etym. *epokhē*, "pause"; in phenomenology, "bracketing"] suspension that retains the title and assures the compulsive pulsation of *L'arrêt de mort* is also an "ingenious" decision, one of those decisions that are made [*s'arrêtent*] only in a language, one language, and escape signature by any *I* or *ego*. But in the same way, linked to what is untranslatable in a language, this decision becomes *unreadable*. I maintain that this title is unreadable. If reading means making accessible a meaning that can be transmitted as such, in its own unequivocal, translatable identity, then this title is unreadable. But this unreadability does not arrest reading, does not leave it paralyzed in the face of an opaque surface: rather, it starts reading and writing and translation moving again. The unreadable is not the opposite of the readable but rather the ridge [*arête*] that also gives it the chance or force to start up again. "The impossibility of reading should not be taken too lightly" (Paul de Man).[17] If we say that the unreadable gives, presents, permits, yields something to be read [*l'illisible donne à lire*], this is not a compromise formula. Unreadability is no less radical and irreducible for all that—absolute, yes, you read me.

We had just read, in *L'arrêt de mort,* just before the end of the "first"

---

arrêt is a *verdict*, a decision that has been *arrêtée*, decided, determined, and that itself decides and determines, and its relationship to the object of the preposition (*de mort*) is, of course, the same as in *condamnation à mort*. But "literary" convention, the suspension of "normal" contexts, the context of everyday conversational usage or of writing legitimatized by law—starting with legislating writing or the body of laws that sets the norm for legal language itself—the functioning of the title, the transformation of its relationship to the context and of its referentiality (I locate here the necessity of a very "*récit*," just before the "central" ridge of the corpus, the *decisive arrêt de mort*, in which death is given and no longer deferred. True, this takes place in the course of an event that is hard to situate and about which we cannot be sure that it took place or that it was the effect of a consenting sentence. Here, now, is the *récit* of the *other arrêt de mort*, the *suspensive arrêt*, which gives respite, which gives an unexpected "start" to the dying J., or rather the dead J.: for this suspension is a resurrection. I extract this passage from the "first" "part" (neither part, nor whole, nor *pars totalis*, nor strictly speaking even first; no word is right anymore, not even the quotation marks) of *L'arrêt de mort*, from the "first" of the two "*récits*." I slice things up somewhat barbarously and illegitimately, as we always do, counting on an implicit contract, the impossible contract: that you read "everything" and that at every moment you know the "whole" "corpus" by heart, with a living heart that beats unceasingly [*sans arrêt*], without even a pulsation.

Shortly before, J. had asked her doctor for death, as one asks for a favor, and for life:

During that scene, J. said to him, "If you don't kill me, then you're a murderer." Later I came across a similar phrase, attributed to Kafka. Her sister, who would have been incapable of inventing something like that, reported it to me in that form and the doctor just about confirmed it. (He remembered her as saying, "If you don't kill me, you'll kill me.") [*DS* 15–16/*AM* 32]

The doctor, like the narrator, can receive this sentence only as a demand for what is impossible: a contradictory double demand, a double petition [*postulation*] to which the only possible response is to desist from granting it. This sentence [*sentence*] ("If you don't kill me, then you're a murderer") states, or rather produces, institutes, a law whose very structure

---

complex analysis: What does a title entitle, designate, delimit? Does it designate something other than what it entitles, i.e., the thing "entitled," the text or book? Or something other than itself? But who or what is it? And where? And how does it relate to self-citation? And so on and so forth.): all this forbids (prevents, inhibits, stops [*arrête*]) a translation of the title *L'arrêt de mort* by its "homonym" or by its synonym in everyday language, by *Death Sentence*.ʲ This translation, like any other, leaves something out, an untranslated remain(s).ᵏ It arrests movement. Illegitimately: for "literature" and in general

puts you in a position of fatal transgression. And yet, by the same token, you obey it even in the transgression that it will have defined. Because, in order not to be a murderer, I must kill, give death, *donner la mort*. Hence the infinite violence of what can strictly be called a *double bind*, double obligation, double demand. The disjunction allows of no respite, no hope for reconciliation; it is unceasing, *sans arrêt*. The narrator is subjected to the violence of this intractable law, like the demand for an impossible narrative. The same law, that of the *arrêt de mort*, relates this *double bind* and the double invagination described above. The narrator is here opposed to the doctor (as he is opposed to the doctors in *La folie du jour*), but he is also on the same side with respect to J.'s order. He "signifies," relates, decides [*arrête*], "gives" death, he is the "author" of death, but in all this he is only obeying a demand: a demand at once impossible to satisfy and satisfied the moment it is formulated, because it envisages its own transgression. This is how death is given, how one "gives" death to another or to oneself: oneself or another, it comes out the same. Murder is inevitable, and it is doubtless this uncompromising law of *arrêt* that the doctor's memory seeks to attenuate by transforming the sentence "If you don't kill me, then you're a murderer" into "If you don't kill me, you'll kill me." The *arrêt de mort* contains within itself this *double bind* that makes every death a crime, an event foreign to nature, related to law, *causa, la Chose*, and a law that can be posited only in its own transgression. In "On tue un enfant (fragmentaire)," Blanchot writes: "There is death and murder (words I defy anyone seriously to distinguish and that must nonetheless be separated). . . . It is an impersonal, inactive, irresponsible 'one' ['on'] that must answer for this death and this murder" (taken up in *The Writing of the Disaster* [71/ *ED* 115–16]). This fragment uses the vocabulary of the *arrêt* to designate the strange law that extends beyond the limits of (Hegelian) dialectic but still leaves a mark on it: "The result was perhaps, absurdly, that the experience that

---

"parasitism," the suspension of the "normal" context of everyday conversation or of "civilian" usage of the language, in short, everything that makes it possible to move from "death sentence" to "suspension of death" in the French expression *arrêt de mort, can always come about* (*de facto* and *de jure*) in "everyday" usage of the language, in language and in discourse. The dream of translation without remains, a metalanguage that would guarantee orderly flow between "entry language" and "exit language" (e.g., of a translating computer), between semantic radicals properly bordered (*arrêtés*). Who will dis-

initiates the movement of the dialectic—the experience that none experiences, the experience of death—arrested it right away, and that the entire subsequent process [*procès*] retained a sort of memory of this *arrêt*, as if of an aporia that always had still to be accounted for" [*WD* 68/*ED* 112]. This process is here first the one that goes from Hegel's "first philosophy"[18] to speculative idealism.

Thus there is a double *arrêt de mort*: "If you don't kill me, then you're a murderer." J. demands this morphine, this double-acting pharmaceutical drug, this death that *I* will in the end give her. But in the interval *I* will have arrested (suspended) death, this *arrêt de mort* in the interval will have given the interval, and that's the eventless event of this *arrêt de mort*. Before he is summoned, *from afar*, by a telephoned "Come [*Venez*]," before he is told, "Come, please come, J. is dying" (*J. se meurt*: this construction with the reflexive pronoun is familiar enough in French, but aside from a perceptible connotation from Bossuet's use of the expression in a famous funeral oration for a princess, this way of saying "she is dying" derives through repetition a literal element of reflexivity—*elle* SE *meurt*, she dies for herself, of herself, unto herself: her death sentence is decidedly her own)—before this "Come," or at least before he cites it, *I* mentions an exchange between the nurse, Dangerue (a proper name that recalls us to our projected systematic reading of all the names or initials of proper names in Blanchot's *récits*), and J., who "asked her, 'Have you ever seen death?'

"'I have seen dead people, Miss.'

"'No, death!' The nurse shook her head. 'Well, soon you will see it'" [*DS* 16–17/*AM* 34–35].

It is thus not a question of *one* death, one dead woman, a person who is dead or living on, between life and death—not *one* dead woman, *one* death, that is decided or undecided in this *arrêt de mort*, but *death*, LA

---

tinguish rigorously between these languages, here? Confusion of languages, of tongues. Shelley's activity as a translator: in the strictly linguistic sense, in which it was important, and in the "textual" sense, which cannot be separated from the other. Particularly in the case of *The Triumph of Life* (Dante, Milton, Rousseau, and so on, and all those whom Bloom calls the "precursors" in the triumphant course or procession, as well as "in the chariot-vision"). But he translates *himself*. The temptation, here, of an exhaustive reading, both of *The Triumph* and of everything else, beginning with all of

mort (*personne de mort*: no dead person, the person of death)—*la Chose*—itself as other. And *I*, who has just been summoned ("Come"), arrives like death, as death comes about, as death, almost dead [i.e., "dead on his feet"]. When someone says in French "*Je suis mort,*" he is playing with the word *mort*, *between* the noun ["death"] and the (masculine) adjective ["dead"], which can change everything (in what you would call a *sea change*¹⁹). The attribute *mort* leaves the *I* alive, otherwise, but the noun also puts him beyond the reach of the event that might happen to him, that might come about accidentally.

He is summoned—"Come"—by telephone. It was necessary to recount the exchange with the nurse before his arrival in order to suggest that the narrator and death are identical ("soon you will see it"). Now, the telephone had hardly been hung up, the nurse will tell him later, when "her pulse . . . scattered like sand" [*DS* 19/*AM* 39]: a sign of death, a death sentence, in an instant as elusive as the last grain of sand in the time of hourglasses, death also as the result of the dissemination of the rhythm of life with no finishing stroke [*coup d'arrêt*], unbordered and unbounded arrhythmia on a beach that is a continuation of the sea [*la mer*]. The unexpected expression (her pulse "scattered like sand") will be repeated, cited "in quotation marks" at the moment of the second death, on the last page [*DS* 30/*AM* 60], after the resurrection. This is the passage that I read earlier. J. appears dead; she died at the end of the telephone call, while the narrator was being told to "Come." She is dying; *elle "se meurt"* while the "Come" runs along the line and instantly reaches (comes to) the narrator. He is told to "Come," *and* she's dead. He arrives at the apartment, finds the door open, and J.'s death is announced to him with "vulgarity." This word recurs twice to describe the doctor [*DS* 17–18/*AM* 36], the one whose relationship to the identity of death is most secure and who is always more or less, as in *La folie du jour*, an expert in forensic medicine, a representa-

---

Shelley's *glas* [death-knells], "On Death," "Death," "Autumn: A Dirge," the fragment "The Death Knell Is Ringing," again "A Dirge," *Adonais*, etc., etc. The same temptation with Blanchot: beginning with *L'arrêt de mort*, a starting point chosen by chance *and* of necessity, to recognize a "logic" that would enable us to read *everything*, in *L'arrêt de mort* and elsewhere, down to the smallest element, the grain of sand, the letter, the space. . . . A wager: I feel at once its possibility and its impossibility, each equally essential. The same wager as that of translation, without remain(s) [*sans reste*], *du reste* ["after all"

tive of authority or social conventions, whose language he speaks ("It's a blessed release for the poor creatures"). (Vulgarity and foolishness are two values or non-values that, along with indiscretion, which is inseparable from them, are most reprehensible in Blanchot's view—or in the narrator's in any case. But since every value leads over into its opposite, this entails certain problems.) *I* arrives in the dead woman's room. The room is the privileged place of *la Chose* in all these *récits*, domestic but utterly foreign (*unheimlich*), left in the coldest anonymity, sealed off, usually a hotel room, in any case devoid of any other description, reduced to the most indispensable constants of Western habitation: a bed on the edge of which one sits, at times an armchair that one tries to reach, a door, a lock, and, in *L'arrêt de mort*, keys ("Yale" keys: "*du genre Yale*"); outside, corridors and stairways.

He ("I") arrives in this death-chamber, the dead woman's room.

I shall now read at great length, in the most neutral voice I can manage, and without stopping to make comments at every point, far from it. I stress only the instant of summons: J.'s first name makes her return to life, makes her be born, even, and makes her triumph over life, starting with a silent *come* [viens] that resonates with all the *come*'s that I have tried to recite in "*Pa*ce Not(*s*)." Then there will be the appearance of *la Chose* that does not appear, even though it is there, forbidding that it be spoken of, what, a little later, will be called the *event*. The reaffirmation, the *récit*, of life marks its discreet triumph in a "gaiety" (the words "gay" and "gaiety" recur five or six times [e.g., *DS* 20–22/*AM* 41–45]) the memory of which is terrifying, would "be enough to kill a man" [*DS* 22/*AM* 44]. Gaiety, reaffirmation, triumph *over* (triumph of the "on," "over," *sur, hyper* . . .): over life and of life, *sur-vie*, life after life and after death, at the same time between life and death in the crypt, more than life, when it's over (and over again), reprieve and hypervitality, a supplement of life that is *better*

/ "of the remain(s)"]. Everything that, in the text above, goes back to the dissemination of sand (beach, parti[cipa]tion, seaside, *parage*, hour-glass). The temptation to translate (turn over, transfer) Blanchot's hour-glass into Shelley's (" . . . and whose hour / Was drained to its last sand in weal or woe, / So that the trunk survived both fruit and flower." " . . . And suddenly my brain became as sand. . . . " Then comes the play of animal tracks [*traces*], "erased" or "visibly stamp[ed]," and the "burst" of the "new Vision."). *February 1978*. Patmos. Vision. Apocalypse. Revelation. The translators will have to return

than life *and better* than death, a triumph of life *and* of death; a living-on that is better than truth and that would be (if such living-on could ever be) *la Chose par excellence: sur-vérité*, truth beyond truth, truth beyond life and death. Here is the passage:

> ... and it dawned on me [*cette lumière me traversa*] that at a certain moment in the night she must have felt defeated, too weak to live until morning, when I would see her, and that she had asked the doctor's help in order to last a little longer, one minute longer, the one minute that she had so often demanded silently and in vain. This is what that poor fool mistook for anger, and doubtless he had given in to her by coming, but he was already too late: at a time when she could no longer do anything, he could do even less, and his only help had been to cooperate with that sweet and tranquil death he spoke of with such sickening familiarity. My grief began at that moment. [*DS* 18/ *AM* 37]

It dawns on the narrator that at one moment in the night, in that battle between life and death, which is also a battle between day and night, she was almost "defeated." Then she *triumphed*—like the day [*jour*]—by lasting until morning. *Triumph of life* as *triumph of light*: it is with the throes of death [*l'agonie*], the battle between life and death as between *light* and *night*,[20] that both *The Triumph of Life* and *L'arrêt de mort* are concerned. But this antagonism follows the syntax of a revolution. One spills over [*verse*] into the other; the ring makes one come back and come down to the other in a version or translation in which each word is committed and caught up in the language of the other, and inverted to become the opposite of itself. Thus the minute of living on is retained as a minute of truth beyond truth: almost nothing, a suspended moment, a "start" [*sursaut*], the time it takes to take someone's pulse and to turn over the hourglass.

He has entered the room "full of strangers."

---

again to the apocalyptic text of *Glas*. They should explain the necessary immodesty of these self-references and self-citations. I am writing here about self-citation, its necessity and its mirages. And then, all writing is triumphant. Writing is triumph (*Schreiber und Siegen-wollen*), manic life-after-life insurance. That is what makes it unbearable. Essentially indiscreet and exhibitionistic. Even if we read no "that's me there" in it. And the increase in discretion is only a surplus-value of triumph, a supplement of triumph—enough to make you sick [*vomir*]. This is what I am saying. I say it against Nietzsche,

I would have liked to understand why, after having resisted so stubbornly for so many interminable years, she had not found the strength to hold out for such a short time longer. Naively, I thought that interval had been a few minutes, and a few minutes was nothing. But for her those few minutes had been more than a lifetime, more than that eternity of life that they talk about, and hers had been lost then. What Louise said to me when she telephoned—"She is dying"—was true, was the kind of truth you perceive in a flash, she was dying, she was almost dead, the wait had not begun at that moment; at that moment it had come to an end; or rather the last wait had gone on nearly the duration of the telephone call: at the beginning she was alive and lucid, watching all of Louise's movements; then still alive, but already sightless and without a sign of acceptance when Louise said, "She is dying"; and the receiver had hardly been hung up when her pulse, the nurse said,scattered like sand. [translation modified] [*DS* 19/*AM* 38]

"More than a lifetime, more than that eternity of life . . .": this "more," this *more-than-life* [*sur-vie*], marks, at least in the passage I have just cited, a temporal extension of life, in the form of a reprieve. Before dying, in these "few minutes," she lived "more than a lifetime [*plus qu'une vie*]."

This excess, which in life triumphs over life and in time is worth more than the eternity of life, is already completely different from life or the eternity of life, but it *presents* itself, if that expression were still possible, before the *arrêt de mort*, before the death of J., "in," "life." After J.'s death, after Louise, who "must have read in my face that something was about to happen that she knew she did not have the right to see, nor anyone else in the world," has taken everyone away, the narrator remains alone with the dead woman. He is seated "on the edge of the bed." He describes her with her "stillness of a recumbent effigy and not of a living being." Mortuary sculpture, death masks and impressions, wills, embalming, and the crypt, everything that preserves [*garde*] the dead, at the same

---

perhaps: triumph over oneself is also pursuit of power (*Gewalt*). Hence, and I come back to this, the apocalyptic text of *Glas*. What I write here is related to reading, writing, teaching as apocalypse, to apocalypse as a revelation, to apocalypse in its eschatological and catastrophic sense, to the *Apokalupsis Ioannou*, the Revelation of St. John the Divine. The translators will cite *Glas*, including this passage that begins on page 196b/220b—"after developing the radiographic negative of the testamentary chrisms and bandages (why anointing and banding in the two testaments?), after attacking, analyzing, toning

time living and dead, beyond life and beyond death—this persistent motif must be followed in the "two" "*récits*" that compose *L'arrêt de mort*. "She who had been absolutely alive was already no more than a statue." Her hands still bear the contracted trace of "the immense battle that [she] had fought" [*DS* 19–20/*AM* 39–40]. Then come the call and the resurrection, the triumph of life, the moment when "this young woman [who] was dead . . . returned to life at my [call]" [*DS* 30/*AM* 60]. He calls (to) J. by her first name, but this first name is never spoken in the *récit* that he gives of its utterance. This utterance [*profération*] is forbidden to the *récit*. The name must not be spoken publicly, aloud. The initial keeps [*garde*] the secret like a grave—jealously. J.'s resurrection will be announced afterward as a piece of good "news" [*DS* 21/*AM* 43]. We shall take into account, later, the fact that the other woman, in the other *récit*, is called Nathalie, in other words, Noëlle.

I leaned over her, I called to her loudly by her first name; and immediately—I can say there wasn't a second's interval—a sort of breath came out of her compressed mouth, a sigh that little by little became a light, weak cry; almost at the same time—I'm sure of this—her arms moved, tried to rise. At that moment, her eyelids were still completely shut. But a second afterward, perhaps two, they opened abruptly and they opened to reveal something terrible that I will not talk about, the most terrible look that a living being can receive, and I think that if I had shuddered at that instant, and if I had been afraid, everything would have been lost, but my tenderness was so great that I didn't even think about the strangeness of what was happening, which certainly seemed to me altogether natural because of that infinite movement that drew me toward her, and I took her in my arms, while her arms clasped me, and not only was she completely alive from that moment on, but perfectly natural, gay and almost completely recovered. [*DS* 20/*AM* 40–41]

Between the call—the only time her name is spoken, this name that is not even disclosed—and a resurrection that is marked only by a breath,

---

their relics in a kind of developing bath, why not search there for the remains of John (*Jean*)? The Gospel and the Apocalypse, violently selected, fragmented, redistributed, with blanks, shifts of accent, lines skipped and moved out of place, as if they reached us over a broken-down teletype, a wiretap [*table d'écoute*] in an overloaded telephone exchange: 'And the light shines in the darkness, and the darkness . . . glory . . . Who is worthy to open the book and break the seals on it . . .'"—and concludes on page 198b/222b: "As his name indicates, the apocalyptic, in other words capital unveiling, in truth

there was no time ("there wasn't a second's interval"). The first "breath," the first "sigh" (we use *le dernier soupir*, "one's last breath," literally "the last sigh," to mean death), the first "cry" of the woman who has just been born, did not *follow* a call, which was nothing but a first name, spoken out loud. Resurrection, birth, or triumph of life thus will not have been the effect of a cause, but rather an absolute event, a cause even, the cause, the *causa*, *la Chose*, the *first name* itself: since now no interval or interruption separates the call from the first breath, we do not even know anymore who spoke that name for whom. She heard it before the other had finished speaking it. She is called as (is) the other, and it is like the name that is given for the first time, at birth. The time of this response (*responsa*) that weds the call, accompanies it rather than follows it, performs it as a naming rather than succeeds it, even makes it possible by giving itself unconditionally, as an unconditioned (call)—this time is contemporary with the end of *L'arrêt de mort* [147/ *DS* 80]: " . . . and to that thought I say eternally, 'Come,' and eternally it is there." The "and" ("and immediately," "and eternally") weds in a timeless time the one called and the caller, the *come* [viens] and the coming of the one who comes. In this sense, we can no longer describe the call (demand, order, desire . . .) and the response in the usual terms and according to the usual distinctions of an analysis of locutionary acts. The *come*-effect of the "first name" transcends all these categories (strictly speaking, it can thus be called a "transcendental": *qui transcendit omne genus*), and this event, at once ordinary and extraordinary, is also what *L'arrêt de mort* "recounts." But it recounts it while performing it in secret. The cryptic insistence [*instance*] of this secret is marked not only by the initial of a first name that is neither noun nor verb nor pronoun (the initial, at most, of the pronoun *Je*, J.): this insistence is constantly remarked, remarkable, noticeable, especially, as in the case of every crypt, in its relationship to the law, in an interdiction. Thus the narrator says repeatedly

---

lays bare self-hunger. In *Funeral Rites*, you recall, on the same page: 'Jean was taken away from me. . . . Jean needed a compensation. . . . I was hungry for Jean.'¹ That (*Ça*) is called a colossal compensation. The absolute phantasm as an absolute self-having [*s'avoir absolu*; cf. *savoir absolu*, "absolute knowledge"] in its most mournful glory: to engulf (one)self in order to be close-by-(one)self; to make (one)self a mouthful,ᵐ to be(come) (in a word, band (erect) [*bander*]) one's own bit [*mors*]. . . . " The apocalyptic theme of *Glas*, of course, is due not only to the fact that the Greek word (*apokalupsis*), another phenom-

that he cannot say. He is forbidden to say. So—he says. And if the *arrêt de mort* is related to judicial decision, if it says the law, it is also an *arrêt* that arrests—with a sentence, a verdict—speech and the right to speak. ("As for the rest, I don't want to say anything. . . . I have said nothing extraordinary or even surprising. What is extraordinary begins at the moment I stop [*je m'arrête*]. But I am no longer able to speak of it.") The same interdiction encrypts the resurrection at the moment when he sees the terrible *Chose*, which we know he does not see as something, something other than an act of seeing, a look, eyes, when J.'s eyelids "opened to reveal something terrible that I will not talk about, the most terrible look. . . . " Before, you remember, Louise had seen in the narrator's face "that something was about to happen that she knew she did not have the right to see, nor anyone else in the world. . . . " The *arrêt de mort* is thus the interdictory decision that arrests *L'arrêt de mort* (the "*récit*" with this title) on the verge of the event that it does not have the right to recount, but that also puts it into operation, puts it to work, makes it recount, decides, induces it to recount, starting from this interdictory suspension, makes it set out again toward the impossible *récit*, to recount that (which) it will not recount. The text comments on the title (a *parergon* or *cartouche* between the work and what is outside it, as the locus *du droit à la littérature*), a title that is thus part of it without belonging to it; but the title also states the impossibility of the text or erstwhile *récit* that it will have entitled, the impossibility of the *intitulé* [title, heading, that which is entitled]. *L'arrêt de mort*: of the *intitulé*. Or of the *en-tête*. Its condition for possibility and impossibility. An entire conjugation, in all the tenses, of law and duty [*devoir*] (I must, I had to, I should not have, I must not, I shall have to refrain from, it will turn out that I should not have),[21] all the steps [*démarches*] taken by the interdictory *pas*, in every tense [*temps*] and every mood [*mode*]. The *double bind* and the double *invagination* of this interdiction make it possible for us to read

---

enon of translation, was one recourse of the Septuagint to translate the verb *gilah*, which means "to reveal" in Hebrew, to reveal in particular the genitals, the ear, and the eyes. . . . In "Freud and the Scene of Writing"[n] I refer to Ezekiel (on this, see what Bloom says about the Chariot of YHWH and *The Triumph*) and to a certain sequence: "Then did I eat [the scroll of the law]; and it was in my mouth as honey for sweetness." A similar passage in Revelation: " . . . I took the little book . . . and ate it up; and it was in my mouth sweet as honey: and as soon as I had eaten it, my belly was bitter." Necessary

[*donnent à lire*] the unreadability of this impossible event (the after-life of resurrection), of this "news." Thus:

> . . . as she asked me how long I had been there, it seemed to me she was remembering something, or that she was close to remembering it, and that at the same time she felt an apprehension that was linked to me, or my coming too late, or the fact that I had seen and taken by surprise something I shouldn't have seen. All that came through her voice. I don't know how I answered. Right away she relaxed and became absolutely human and real again.
>
> Strange as it may seem, I don't think I gave one distinct thought, during that whole day, to the event that had allowed J. to talk to me and laugh with me again. It is simply that in those moments I loved her totally, and nothing else mattered. I only had enough self-control to go find the others and tell them J. had recovered. I don't know how they took the news [*nouvelle*]. . . . [*DS* 21/*AM* 42–43]

The narrator reports that he reported—a *nouvelle*, a *récit*, in short, a "novella"²² and a piece of good news—like an evangelist who has returned (from the dead) to report J.'s resurrection. The Christ parallel (an *arrêt* that puts someone to death, an *arrêt de mort* in accordance with the resurrection that says, "I am the truth and the life," the triumph of life, and so on) is supported by more than one witness (martyr, you might say) or piece of evidence in the narration. An effect of "superimposing" of images inscribes itself *en abyme*, beginning with the visit to the doctor, the one who first condemns J. to death. He is a believer:

> The first day, he greeted me with this statement: "I am fortunate enough to have faith, I am a believer. What about you?" On the wall of his office there was an excellent photograph of the Turin Sudario, a photograph in which he saw two images superimposed on one another: one of Christ and one of Veronica; and as a matter of fact I distinctly saw, behind the figure of Christ, the features of a woman's face—extremely beautiful, even magnificent in its strangely proud expression. One last thing

---

comparisons, effects of translation and superimprinting in *The Triumph of Life, La folie du jour,* and *L'arrêt de mort* (among others). E.g., because of the vision ("And I had a vision. . . . " "*Kai eidon.* . . . ") that gathers all these texts together on Patmos. (Hölderlin is there, with lots of people.) But also because of the imperative *Come* that forms their regular scansion. "*Pace* Not(*s*)," because of the *come*, as a superimprinting of Revelation. Tremendous problems of translation. The translators should read—and cite—all these texts in Hebrew and Greek. What happens when *eidos* is translated as "vision"? And

about this doctor: he was not without his good qualities; he was, it seems to me, a good deal more reliable in his diagnoses than most. [*DS* 9/*AM* 21–22]

What this "superimposing," multiplied *en abyme*, comes down to is not a constitution of the Gospel as a paradigm or a model for reference, as if *L'arrêt de mort* powerfully cited, or cryptically put back into operation, back to work, a great, exemplary narration. Nor is it the other way around: for one might also be tempted to read *L'arrêt de mort* as the analytic regression toward a sort of original *récit*, nuclear event-ness, an invariable sequence of which the Gospels would be only an example, a variation, a case. The relationship, it seems to me, is of a different sort: it is one of seriality without paradigm. If there is a *récit*, it is to the extent that no paradigm can determine or arrest it. Serial repetition involves paradigm-"effects" but reinserts them in the series; and this reinsertion is already, still, put into operation in *L'arrêt de mort*, which, in itself "alone" (if that's the right word), constitutes a series of *récits* (at least two), *récits* at once analogous (hence the series) and utterly different, offering no guarantee of analogy. It is by the way remarkable, since we alluded to Veronica's veil, that this episode of the Passion does not appear in any of the canonical Gospels, as Pierre Madaule points out in his *Une tache sérieuse?: récit* (Paris: Gallimard, 1973, p. 106n.). Is not Shelley's relationship in *The Triumph of Life* to those whom Harold Bloom calls Shelley's "precursors" analogous to this? Could not this "poem" be called a *nouvelle*?

The question has the following resonance: What is a *nouvelle* when it no longer relates, no longer is related as the *récit* of an event of life-after-life, nor simply produces it, but when its relationship to this "event" (*living on*) is the uncanny [*insolite*] one that we are tracking down here under the titles *L'arrêt de mort* or *The Triumph of Life*? Living-on comes about at "dawn," with the sunrise, for the one who says *I* and must not say

---

both the words *erkhou* and *hupage* by "come" and sometimes by "go"? The *Va* and *Viens* ["go" and "come"; cf. *va-et-vient*, "interrelationship"] of *Thomas l'obscur* (in two versions). Direct the entire reading of *L'arrêt de mort* toward the end, when Jesus says: "'I am Alpha and Omega, the beginning and the end, the first and the last [*prōtos kai eskhatos, ē arkhē kai to télos*].' . . . 'Yes, I come quickly [*Nai, erkhomai takhu*].' . . . And the spirit [*pneuma*] and the bride [*numphē*] say, 'Come,'" and so on. By way of the whole bibliography and sigillography of the seven seals. And of Blanchot's eschatology, in *The Last*

anything ("As for the rest, I don't want to say anything"; " . . . I, whom thoughts which must remain untold / Had kept as wakeful as . . . "). All the outpouring of light and solar glory at the beginning of *The Triumph* is here concentrated at the moment of J.'s resurrection: "J.'s waking took place at dawn, almost with the sunrise, and the dawn light charmed her." If we had the time and space here, we would have to summon up the paternal figure of the sun ("the Sun their father") that dominates the opening of *The Triumph*, until the arrival, with the moon, of "the ghost of her dead Mother," with the figure effaced, deliberately struck with insignificance, by J., the figure of her mother, the "queen mother," a mere walk-on, almost a supernumerary, a figurant, a figureless figure, the vanishing origin of every figure, the bottomless, groundless background against which J.'s life fights, and from which it is snatched away, at every moment. Since we shall never have time and space enough for this mother, here is one passage, one of her regular, stealthy passings through the text, a few lines after J.'s "waking" at "dawn":

Apparently the morphine had not affected her spirits at all: someone who is saturated with drugs can seem lucid and even profound, but not cheerful; well, she was extremely and naturally cheerful; I remember that she poked fun at her mother in the kindest manner, which was unusual. When I think of all that took place before it and after it, the memory of that gaiety should be enough to kill a man. But at the time, I simply saw that she was gay, and I was gay, too.

During that whole day she had almost no attacks, though she talked and laughed enough to bring on twenty. She ate much more than I did. . . . [*DS* 22/ *AM* 44–45]

There is a great deal to be said about this gaiety, about the quality of experience thus designated to describe what is proper to an act or instance of living on, the levity of its affirmation, of the *yes, yes, yes* to *yes* without

---

Man ("Often what he told of his story was so obviously borrowed from books that, warned immediately by a kind of suffering, one made great efforts to avoid hearing him. It was her that his desire to talk miscarried most strangely. He did not have any precise notion of what we call the seriousness of facts. The truthfulness, the exactness of what has to be said astonished him. . . . 'Now what do they mean by *event?*'—I read the question in his recoil. . . . She called him 'the professor.' . . . He wasn't addressing anyone. I don't mean he wasn't speaking to *me*, but someone other than me was listening to him. . . . Is

self-recollection, the *yes* that, saying and describing nothing, performing only this affirmation of the *yes* saying *yes* to *yes*, *must not even* [*ne doit même pas*] have, and know, itself [*s'avoir et se savoir*]. But this "need not" [*ne pas devoir*] or "must not" [*devoir ne pas*] is also an interdiction that interposes an unconscious between the event and the very experience of the event, between the living-on and the present, conscious, knowing experience of what thus comes about [*arriver*]. I—the one who says me, that is to say, me—does not know [*Je . . . ne sait pas*] what will have happened [*arriver*] to me. *J. must not know* [ne doit pas savoir] *what has happened to her*. This *ne . . . pas* is to be understood any—and every—way that you wish; it is re-cited here in every way, every mode, every mood. The narrator's fright:

> "Why," she said coldly, "are you staying *precisely* tonight?" I suppose she was beginning to know as much as I did about the events of the early morning, but at that moment I was frightened at the thought that she might discover what had happened to her; it seemed to me that would be something absolutely terrifying for anyone to learn who was naturally afraid of the night. [*DS* 24/*AM* 48]

It is thus not sure that she knows what has happened *to her*, that is, *her* coming back to life; in any event she shouldn't know it, she should not know, she must not have known, she should not have known, she would not have had to know it, found it out. . . . Here "know," *savoir*, means "discover," "learn"; these are the narrator's words. Now, what the narrator is frightened of is the possibility that J. might have "learned" or "discovered" *from him*—from his more or less irrepressible *récit*, from an account [*relation*] that he was unable to contain at the time of the event itself—the triumph of life that had happened, that had come, to her. He is frightened at the thought that he might have let something slip, might have violated the interdiction that forbids the *récit* of the event, already a past event, which has never been *present* (because she regains her breath before he

---

he still coming? Is he already going away? . . . The happiness of saying yes, of endlessly affirming. . . . He needed to be one too many [*en surnombre*]: one more, only one more. . . . The thought that is spared me at each moment: that he, the last man, is nevertheless not the last. . . . Even a God needs a witness. . . . But if I was present, he would be the most alone of all men, without even himself, without that last that he was—and thus he would be the very last."⁰ It should all have been cited, at length.) or of Nietzsche's (for example, "Oedipus. Soliloquies of the Last Philosopher. A Fragment from the

has finished speaking her first name, telling her in effect "Come," "Come again," "Come back"), because the event in itself belongs to the order of the *récit*.

This frightening thing that has come about without ever presenting itself, this event that is ineffable at the very moment it is seen, seen without there being anything to see except a look or *vision* ("her eyelids . . . opened to reveal something terrible that I will not talk about, the most terrible look . . . "), this terrible thing, the terribleness of the thing [*la chose*] is not only ineffable, unnarratable: it is interdictory, it forbids telling and even seeing (" . . . I had seen and taken by surprise something I shouldn't have seen"). But the interdiction is violated by itself ("I shouldn't have . . . "). It begins the *arrêt* of the *récit*, in other words paralyzes it but also sets it in motion with a single *pas* [pace, "not"]. The interdiction transgresses itself and produces the *pas* that crosses it: the *récit*. The *récit* that tells "what happened" without having been present, and that tells it to the very "subject" to whom it happened and who is not supposed to know—this impossible *récit* is *surpassed, overrun, "débordé,"* by its own *arrêt de mort*. What must remain beyond its reach is precisely what revives it at every moment. The forbidden thing forbids. That which forbids (that which is forbidden) happens, comes about, without attaining, without happening in or to, the *récit*. And J. must not find out from the *I* what thus happens without happening to her, the "subject" of the whole thing, of *la chose*.

Perhaps "*chose*" has always designated, in philosophy, that which does not come about [*n'arrive pas*]. Things come about, but *la Chose*, in its determination as *hupokeimenon* or *res*, is the substance to which "accidents" happen and to which predicates attach, but which cannot itself be the accident or predicate of something else. *La chose n'arrive pas à autre chose. La chose*, when defined as the *hupokeimenon*, is that to which the *sumbebekos* or accident happens, but which, being a thing, *chose*,

---

History of Posterity": "I call myself the last philosopher because I am the last human being. I myself am the only one who speaks with me, and my voice comes to me as the voice of someone who is dying. . . . "P To be cited in its entirety. But I shall reread that elsewhere. This, too, is a "fragment.") Insaturable context. And how could what I am writing here "concern" *The Triumph of Life*, which I read in a "foreign" language, and of which I lack so many contextual features? On what conditions, however . . . ? *20–27 February 1978*. Last judgment. Resurrection of the dead. Ghosts, *Doppelgänger* (Nietzsche: I

does not happen, does not come about. To this extent and in this sense at least, the history or possibility of *récit* is not essentially constitutive of *la chose*. Nor of *la chose* as *aistheton* or as *hulē*, to use the three determinations whose history—or fable—Heidegger offers us in "The Origin of the Work of Art." Here, *la Chose* is "terrible" because in its very not-happening it happens (comes about) to the "Come," in its *pas de chose* [no thing, thingly step, thingly "not"]: proceeding, progression [*procès*], as *arrêt de mort* that cannot be decided, neither life nor death, but rather LIVING ON, the very progression that belongs, without belonging, to the progression of life and death. Living on is not the opposite of living, just as it is not identical with living. The relationship is different, different from being identical, from the difference of distinctions—undecided, or, in a very rigorous sense, "vague," *vagus*, evasive, *évasé* [splayed, flared, widened out], as is said of an edge [*bord*] or its waters [*parages*]. I shall cite a passage in which "living, living on" is defined precisely as a "vague objective," at the exact moment when this comma between the two verbs is the mark of the uncertainty of a transition or apposition between them: neither conjunction, nor disjunction, nor equation, nor opposition, but merely punctuation marking a pause before the desire for an *arête*, an *arrêt*, a "firm decision," is expressed. The spacing of what could here be named *parage*.[23]

I cite this passage also because of the proximity of a *triumph*. This is one of the times that she "triumphs," absolutely, intransitively:

The pain near her heart did not go away, but the symptoms died down and she had *triumphed* once more. The treatment was discussed again: she wanted it very much, either in order to get it over with or because her energy could no longer be satisfied with a *vague* objective—*living, living on* [*vivre, survivre*]—but needed a firm decision on which she could lean heavily. (My emphasis) [*DS* 10/*AM* 23]

---

am a *Doppelgänger*, in *Ecce Homo*. The event—which "*sur-vient*" ["takes place," "occurs"; lit., "comes on"]—how will they translate this word?—consists in nothing, nothing but coming about, going on, and being gone.) Apocalypse, eschatology, the "last War," the "context" of *L'arrêt de mort*. *Come* is said, is addressed to the event that comes about. An apocalyptic superimprinting of texts: there is no paradigmatic text. Only relationships of cryptic haunting from margin to margin. No [*Pas de*] palimpsest (definitive unfinishedness). No morsel, no metonymy, no integral corpus. And thus no

Living On 157

This *vivre, survivre*, in this *parage*, delays at once life and death, on a line (the line of the least sure *sur-*) that is thus one neither of clear-cut opposition nor of stable equivalence. "Living, living on" differs and defers, like *différance*, beyond identity and difference. Its domain is indeed in a *récit* formed out of traces, writing, distance, tele-graphy. Tele-phone and tele-gram are only two modes of this telegraphy in which the trace, the grapheme in general, does not come to attach secondarily to the telic structure but rather marks it *a priori*. Differance—*arrêt de mort* or triumph of life—defers (differs like) the *récit* of (from) writing. We notice this, as it "re-marks itself," for example, in the immediate context of the passage that I just cited on the "triumph" and "living, living on." The narrator has just recounted, written, what J. had written to him ("During the beginning of my stay in Arcachon, J. wrote to me at fairly great length, and her handwriting was still firm and vigorous"). The narrator is always away, distanced (at a distance, *tele-*); he always returns from afar and finally remains at a distance. What does she write him? "She told me the doctor had just had her sign a paper in case an accident should occur. So the treatment, which consisted of a series of shots—one each day, given to her at home—was about to begin" [*DS* 9/*AM* 22]. The doctor, the one who has thus condemned her and in effect signed her death warrant by prescribing this treatment, the author of the *arrêt de mort*, asks her, the condemned woman, to release him from his responsibility as a doctor, with a signature subscribing to the *arrêt de mort*. The narrator has already signed her death warrant, subscribed to it, by telling J. that she is condemned to die, that the doctor has given her up. In the case of the paper, she must surrender, with a piece of writing signed and counter-signed, thus "giving herself death," risking death in an effort to live on. This gesture is confirmed by the demand formulated elsewhere in the text: "If you don't kill me, you'll kill me" [*DS* 15–16/*AM* 33]. Now, this treatment itself, as prescribed or or-

---

fetishism. Everything said here about double invagination can be brought to bear—a labor of translation—on what is worked out in *Glas*, for example, on the subject of fetishism, as the argument of the *gaine* ["sheath," "girdle"; cognate of *vagina*] (to be translated "vagina"? On the *gaine*, see *Glas*, p. 230b/257b; cf. also, on the subject of fetishism, "against" Hegel, Marx, and Freud, pp. 226b–27b/253b and 210a/235a. Freud: the fetish erects itself like a "monument," a "*stigma indelebile*," a "sign of triumph"). *L'arrêt de mort* and fetishism ("In her nightly terror, she wasn't superstitious at all; she faced a very great danger,

dered by the doctor, will be deferred in turn, postponed, for a reason that is still unrevealed, after a "crisis" and more than one *telephone* call. The day before the treatment "was about to begin," the paper having been signed,

> she felt a violent, stabbing pain near her heart and had such a severe attack [*crise*] of choking that she had them telephone her mother [—she does not do the telephoning herself, she *has* it done: one more supplementary relay along the way—] who then called the doctor. This doctor, like all fairly prominent specialists, was not often willing to go out of his way. But this time he came quite quickly, no doubt because of the treatment he was supposed to begin administering the next day. I don't know what he saw: he never talked to me about it. To her, he said it was nothing, and it is true that the medicine he prescribed for her was insignificant. But even so, he decided to postpone the treatment several days. [*DS* 9–10/*AM* 22]

Since it is at this point that she "triumphed once more" [*DS* 10/*AM* 23], the suspicion arises that there is perhaps a connection between the start of the treatment and the death sentence, because she triumphs when the treatment is postponed. But because she also demands death and gives it to herself, all these propositions on the triumph and the *arrêt* are reversed at every turn.

Such would be the truth beyond truth of living on [*la sur-vérité du survivre*], the hypertopia of these proceedings [*de ce procès*]. *La Chose* takes place without taking place [*a lieu sans avoir lieu*]: a *non-lieu* in the proceedings, a *non-lieu* at the "end" of the proceedings beyond even acquittal, debt, the symbolic, the judicial. (The *non-lieu* is the strange judgment in French law that is worth *more* than an acquittal: it fictively annuls the very proceedings of indictment, arraignment, investigation, detention, and trial ["*cause*"], even though, nonetheless, the investigation has indeed taken place; the archive of all this remains, and the certification of the *non-lieu*.) The unnarratable event of the coming back to life holds the *récit* breathless

---

one that was nameless and formless, altogether indeterminate, and when she was alone she faced it all alone, without recourse to any trick or fetish" [*DS* 11/*AM* 25]). Similarly, everything said here about double invagination can be brought to bear—a labor of translation—on what is said in "The Double Session" about the hymen (as syllepsis) and the pane of glass [*vitre*].⁹ A discussion, still to come, of the *vitrifying* structure of writing and desire in *L'arrêt de mort* (" . . . I saw her again, through a store window. When someone who has disappeared completely is suddenly there, in front of you, behind a pane of

for an interminable lapse of time that is not merely the time of what is narrated [*récité*]: the one who narrates [le *récitant*] (between the narrating voice and the narrative voice) is also, first, *one who lives on*. This living on [*survivance*] is also phantom *revenance* (the one who lives on is always a ghost) that is noticeable (re-markable) and is represented from the beginning, from the moment that the posthumous, testamentary, scriptural character of the *récit* comes to unfold. The narrator has spoken of the doctor's sentencing J. to death, of the way in which he himself has told her about it, of the "several sentences" that she "wrote down" and "wished to keep secret." ("I still have them. . . . No mention of me. I could see how bitter she had felt when she heard me agree to her suicide.") And here he is, sentenced himself by the same doctor, and thus living on, in the "supernumerary" "remains" of a life:

Her doctor had told me that from 1936 on he had considered her dead. Of course the same doctor, who treated me several times, once told me, too, "Since you should have been dead two years ago, everything that remains of your life is a reprieve [*est en surnombre*, is supernumerary]." He had just given me six more months to live and that was seven years ago. But he had an important reason for wishing me six feet underground. What he said was only an expression of his desire, only suggested what he wanted to happen. In J.'s case, though, I think he was telling the truth. [*DS* 5/*AM* 14–15]

This does not rule out the possibility that J.'s death sentence is *also* an expression of the narrator's desire.

The reprieve in which each moment of life is extra, super-numerary (the supernumerology—1936, two years, six months, seven years, six feet—with which everything is accounted for and all these accounts are settled), this living on, establishes this *récit*, this former *récit*-less "*récit*" (now the erasing of the designation "*récit*" is part of the *récit* of *L'arrêt de mort*), in truth beyond truth [*la sur-vérité*], the supplement of truthless truth.

---

glass, that person becomes the most powerful sort of figure [unless it upsets you]. . . . The truth is that after I had been fortunate enough to see her through a pane of glass, the only thing I wanted, during the whole time that I knew her, was to feel that 'great pleasure' again through her, and also to break the glass. . . . The strangeness lay in the fact that although the shop window experience I have talked about held true for everything, it was most true for persons and objects that particularly interested me. For instance, if I was reading a book that particularly interested me, I read it with vivid plea-

Why truth beyond truth? At the moment when the narrator has said, "I was frightened at the thought that she might discover what had happened to her; it seemed to me that would be something absolutely terrifying for anyone to learn who was naturally afraid of the night" [*DS* 24/ *AM* 48], he suspects himself of letting himself say what must not be said (that is to say, as always, the only thing to be said), the thing that would (absolutely) frighten, *la chose effrayante*. This is the beginning of what I shall call, using a figure justified elsewhere ("*Pa*ce Not(*s*)"), the stairway [*escalier*] or escalade of truth, one truth *about* another, one truth *on* (top of) another, one above or below the other, each step [*marche*] more or less true than truth. This is not a matter of impersonal or objective truth, of veracity, of telling the truth that is equivalent to the thing in question. Nor of the relationship between truth and interdiction (the truth that must not be told), a transgressive truth or a transgression of truth, truth as law or above the law.

From J. there would be a *demand for narrative*, a *demande de récit*: "Perhaps I did commit a grave error in not telling her what she was expecting me to tell her. My deviousness [*manque de franchise*] put us face-to-face like two creatures who were lying in wait for one another but who could no longer see one another" [*DS* 24/*AM* 48].

He has not concealed from her the thing that he has not told her: she knew it well enough, in a certain way, to expect him to tell her, "me to tell her." Not telling the truth, in this case, or rather being "devious," failing to be "frank," is not saying something (something that is, in a certain way, known) but simply not *saying*, not *admitting*, what is, in its content, nothing new, not admitting what is already revealed, not unveiling the revealed. One might then think that truth is here in the act of *saying*, of *reciting*, and not in the relationship of veracity between what is said or experienced and the saying of it, between the saying and the thing said,

---

sure, but my very pleasure was behind a pane of glass: I could see it, appreciate it, but not use it up. In the same way, if I met someone I liked, everything nice that happened between us was under glass and thus preserved, but also far away and in an eternal past. Yet where unimportant people and things were involved, life regained its ordinary meaning and immediacy [*actualité*], so that though I preferred to keep life at a distance . . . " [*DS* 43–44, 48/*AM* 83– 84, 91]. " . . . And perhaps I would have known something about its [*ses*] intentions that even it [*elle*] could never have known, made so cold by my distance

in this case between the narrative and what it narrates, between the *récit* and the recited (as meaning [*sens*] or as referent): all of these distinctions are called into question in this entire hypertopia. But if we were to think of truth as involving solely the act of saying, we would still be consigning truth [*confier la vérité*] to the *present* of an act (saying, narrating, reciting) or indeed of a performative (a saying or reciting that produced, in the present, the referent of the saying or *récit*, the recited referent of the *récit*, its undeferred "referred"). However, this present, too, is borne away in the stairstep (de)progression [*la démarche en escalier*] of truth (above and) beyond truth.

The truth-beyond-truth of life-after-life: the truth that J., as she lives on, is not told, is not, as in most cases, that she has been given up, that she is sentenced to die, that the illness will not spare or pardon her, that she is *going* to die or even that she *has just* [*vient de*] died, but rather that she is not dead, that she will have died and will have lived on. This is what is terrible in the thing: *la chose* as the event of living on, of life-after-life—but this event, this coming back to life, will never have been present. This is why it is truthless, more or less than true. This truth-beyond-truth provides the narrator (himself condemned, sentenced, to live on and condemned by the *double bind* of an impossible demand) with a double "excuse":

(1) "My excuse is that in that hour I exalted her far above any sort of truth and the greatest truth mattered less to me than the slightest risk of worrying her" [*DS* 24/*AM* 48–49].

If we stopped here, if that were all, we could interpret this movement in banal terms: he prefers J.'s well-being in life, her peaceful tranquility, to his own sincerity, his own relationship to truth. But this is precisely not all, and for this reason the excuse, at least the one that he has or that he gives to himself, is a double one: J. has access to, or rather does not have access to, she only approaches, *aborde*, drawing near to, a truth that is

---

that it was put under glass . . . " [*DS* 54/*AM* 101]) and in *La folie du jour* (it is glass that has almost cost him his eyesight) or in "A Primal Scene" (". . . *through the pane* . . . [*as though the pane had broken*] . . . " [in *WD* 72/ *ED* 117]). Will they translate *verre* and *vitre* with *glass*? Something else that escapes usage, using up, use-value. *Wearing away, using up, usury* of what is out of use. Surplus-value and process of fetishization. The "under-glass" quality of the text in translation, and thus of every mark. How can a translation be signed? How can a proper name be translated? Is there, from that moment

superior to his, to the truth in the name of which he forbids himself to say that which is true.

(2) "Another excuse is that little by little she seemed to approach [*se rapprocher d'*] a truth compared to which mine lost all interest" [*DS* 24/ *AM* 49].

The *parage* of truth that she only draws near to may be what she already knew yet wanted, he believes, to hear from him, but perhaps also a secret located above what he could have told her but has forbidden himself to: *la Chose effrayante*, life-after-life that has come about or come on without coming to be here and now [*sans arriver*], the approach of what has come to *pass*, is *past*, without having taken place in the present, replacing both life and death without "taking" a "place," in the time that elapses or does not elapse when a first name mobilizes and paralyzes the entire *récit*, forbids the very no/pace [*le pas*] that it sets in motion, fascinates all the writing of *L'arrêt de mort*. It can also be read as a fascinating *treatment of* truth. In the unarrestable dissemination of its titles, the *arrêt de mort* is the truth *about* truth, *on* truth, truth*less* truth *on* truth, the *récit-less récit* of truth*less* truth *on* truth.

From beginning to end. Let's start now at the end, the very end, the end of the end, the end of what I shall call for the sake of convenience and without rigor the "second part" of the "book." But this second part is "whole," perfectly autonomous. True, if we accept the entire conventional system of legalities that organizes, in literature, the framed unity of the corpus (binding, frame, unity of the title, unity of the author's name, unity of the contract, registration of copyright, etc.), *L'arrêt de mort* (in each of its versions) is *a single book*, signed by *a single author*, and made up of two narratives, two *récits*, in the first person, following in a certain order, and so forth. And everything that can call into question, in the text, this conventional system of legalities, also presents itself in its

---

on, such a thing as a proper name? And the "yes" in translation. People who get married abroad (*oui . . . oui . . .*) [in the French text: "yes, yes"]: all the guarantees in the transferring of marriage certificates. Fundamental irresponsibility for a translated text. The ideal thing is translation into a foreign writing system (Japanese, for example, for a European). But that's valid in "my" language, too. An impossible contract. Two unrelated processions. *27 February 1978.* Don't forget that N. (Nathalie) is a translator ("she translated writings from all sorts of different languages"). The narrator notes: "That was an

framework [*cadre*]. Within this framework, the strange construction of the double *récit* is held together at an invisible hinge or pivot, a double inner edge [*bord*]: the blank space between the last sentence of the first *récit* and the first of the second. There is no absolute guarantee of the unity of the two *récits*, and even less of continuity from one to the other, or even that the narrator who says *I* in each is the same. And even if, to increase the undecidedness, he starts by saying, "I will go on with this story" [*DS* 31/*AM* 61], there is no thread that continues from one story to the other, no temporal link, no character, no situation, or anything of the sort. And "this story" can refer, with its demonstrative, to a completely different story as well as to the one that has just ended with an "I stop" "at the moment" when "what is extraordinary begins" [*DS* 30/*AM* 60]. This undecidedness is never resolved. The double *récit* is constructed so as to preserve the undecidedness and to hold in suspension the demand for *récit* that, as in *La folie du jour*, demands unity from a narrator capable of remembering and of gathering (himself) together, telling "exactly" what has happened. Among other things, we can always wonder, against the law (of the registration of copyright, with all its implications, for example, of the fixed identity of the author as a "real" signatory, the bearer of a single patronymic name), whether the time of the "second" *récit* does not come, will not have come, before that of the "first." Thus the title *L'arrêt de mort* (one more supplementary meaning) can refer also to the *arrêt de mort in the récit*, almost at the "center" of it. J.'s life after the death sentence, then death, then life-after-life, then death, seem in fact to be succeeded by the long-awaited entrance of Nathalie—a first name that refers to the Nativity with the resonance of good news, tidings we have already heard. Isn't Nathalie the triumph of life?

This reading of the *arrêt de mort* at the middle of *L'arrêt de mort* is powerfully called for by the crater of the double inner edge: the "first" *récit*

---

aspect of her character that helped to mislead me about her" [*DS* 55/*AM* 104]. All these texts, it should now be clear, involve law and transgression, and the order that is *given*, and the sort of order that can be obeyed only by transgressing it beforehand. Read yesterday, among some graffiti: "do not read me." I continually ask what *must* be done or not be done (for example, in reading, writing, teaching, and so on) to find out on what is constructed the place of what takes place (for example, the university, the boundaries between departments, between one discourse and another, and so on). Today, respect-

stops at the moment the *arrêt de mort* has done its work, but this suspension also marks the moment when "what is extraordinary" in the *arrêt de mort* begins: "What is extraordinary begins at the moment I stop. But I am no longer able to speak of it." What is extraordinary begins where the "I" stops, where the narrating voice stops, at the "*arrête*" of the voice. Let us recall *The Step Not Beyond*: "'Speak on the arrête—*the line of instability—of speech.*' *As if it attended the exhaustion of dying, as if the night, having started too early, at the earliest time of day, doubted that it would ever become night."* The line of this cutting edge, this "arrist," this *arrête*, passes "between" the two *récits* of *L'arrêt de mort*. Indeed, the double *récit* revolves (in the turning of a version or a revolution) around *la raie de mort* [*raie*: line, stripe, parting, ridge], death crossed out, blocked, held in check, signed, sealed, sentenced.

The truth beyond truth of living on: the middle of the *récit*, its element, its ridge, its backbone [*arête*]. There is only one blank space in the typography of the book, between the two *récits*. Before, in the first version, there were two. By erasing, by doing away with the second blank space, in the second version—the blank space that separated the two *récits* from the sort of epilogue that was in danger of being metanarrative and pretending to gather together the two *récits*—by making this change, Blanchot has given the "middle" blank space an even more remarkable singularity. This is not the only effect of this change, but it counts.

Now, immediately after this blank space, at the bottom of one page and at the top of another, after the absolute interruption, the connectionless connection [*rapport sans rapport*], after J.'s second death, after the narrator has said, "What is extraordinary begins at the moment I stop. But I am no longer able to speak of it," on the next page, the facing page, the other shore, truth enters—thematically, and by name. As if the veil of an interdiction were finally going to be lifted—any minute now, once more.

---

ing (up to a certain point) the contract or promise that binds me to the authors of this book, I have felt it best to confine myself to the problem of the "must" ["*il faut*"] and its transgression (in the realm of reading, writing, the institution of the university, and so on—all domains that defy delimitation) from the standpoint of translation (*Über-setzung, Über-tragung*, transference, and so forth). What must *not* be said, today, if we are to follow the dominant system of norms of this domain? I do not say it; I say what must not be said: for example, that a text can stand in a relationship of transference (primarily

"I will go on with this story, but now I will take some precautions. I am not taking these precautions in order to cast a veil over the truth. The truth will be told; everything of importance that happened will be told. But not everything has yet happened [*Mais tout ne s'est pas encore passé*]" [*DS* 31/*AM* 61].

Not everything has yet happened. This is difficult to understand. When does this refer to? Whatever the answer to this question, the *récit* of *this* story, the one that begins here, will not recount a past event. It will not report, will not relate (a *rapport sans rapport*) something that would remain prior to and thus outside the writing, the *récit* or, as we can now say, the series. *L'arrêt de mort* is in series.

Not everything has yet happened. The coming of the thing, of *la chose*, its event or advent, will be also the coming of the thing to the *récit*, subsequent to the narration, at least to its *incipit*, and *la chose* will thus be a *récit*-effect. Thus the *récit* will be the cause—as well as *causa, chose* [thing, mere tool]—of what it seems to recount. The *récit* as the cause and not as the relating of an event: this is the strange truth that is announced. The *récit*'s the thing. But we must beware: this formula, "*la chose est le récit*," implies no performative presentation or production. What we have here is not that conclusion, readily drawn these days, using a logic of truth as presentation substituted for a logic of truth as representative equivalence, according to which new logic the *récit* would be the very event that it recounts, the thing presenting itself and the text presenting itself—presenting *itself*—by producing what it says. If there is performance here, it must be dissociated from the notion of presence that people always attach to the performative. What is here recited will have been that non-presentation of the event, its presence*less* presence, as it takes place place*less*ly: the *-less* (or *without*) and the *pas*, without *pas*, without the negativity of the *pas*.

I said that "truth" appeared, at least in name, in the middle, at the

---

in the psychoanalytical sense) to another text! And, since Freud reminds us that the relationship of transference is a "love" relationship, stress the point: one text loves another (for example, *The Triumph of Life loves*, transferentially, *La folie du jour*, which in turn . . .). It's enough to make a philologist laugh (or scream), and Freud himself, who, however, did speak of transference as a "new edition" (in the metaphorical sense, of course, of *Übertragung*!). On what conditions is this transferential magnetization possible between what are called textual bodies? This strange question has, perhaps, long engaged

beginning and at the end. And that I was going to begin at the end to recount it in turn. But how are we to decide, to fix [*arrêter*] the end of such a text?

I shall proceed a bit arbitrarily, as for every *arrêt*, for time is short, and I hope you will forgive me.[24] We always ask to be forgiven when we write or recite. For here I am recounting. And so I shall choose the episode of the key. There is a key in this *récit*: a "Yale" key. Like all keys, it locks and unlocks, opens and closes. This key has been stolen and concealed by N. (Nathalie). The terrifying scene that this episode will have occasioned seems to form a pendant-piece, in this second *récit*, to the scene of J.'s return to life in the first. But superimposing is something you can never be sure about, and above all we cannot strictly speaking call either of these a "scene": in neither does *la Chose* present itself, nor does anything else make itself visible—or if so, it forbids one to speak of it. This is, this will be, the moment in which *I* says "Come." This time *I* does not utter the "Come" in the conditional or virtual form or mood, or as a citation, as in the three occurrences that I have cited elsewhere ("*Pace* Not(*s*)"), and "I" is addressing himself here not to the merely grammatically feminine, the feminine gender of "thought" or "speech," *la pensée* or *la parole*, or to a neuter (beyond sexual difference), but rather, *it seems*, in the present, indeed, to a woman. True, this woman is no one ["*personne*"] ("I can say that by getting involved with Nathalie I was hardly getting involved with anyone [*personne*]: that is not meant to belittle her; on the contrary, it is the most serious thing I can say about a person [*un être*]" [*DS* 55/*AM* 103]). I must assume that you are familiar with the text. In the course of an air raid during the Second World War, in an underground shelter in the metro (already what you would call a crypt), he tells her for the first time *in French*, in his language, things that he usually tells her in a

---

(or long committed) me. Engaged me in what must not be . . . [*Dans ce qu'il ne faut pas*]. How are you going to translate that? What must not be done, in the realm of translation, transference, or the aforementioned comparative literature: for example, relating in a monstrous association the "phenomenon," "occurrence," "surrection" of "rose" in *The Triumph of Life* (so many times "arose," "rose," "I rose," "I arose") to—not the resurrection—but the "rose" of resurrection in *L'arrêt de mort*. This is what would not be serious, sober, even if effects of homonymic transference are at play already and of

fictive way or mood [*mode*], playfully, without any commitment, in her language, a *Slavic* language, for example, proposing marriage to her. As long as they spoke to each other in the language of the other [*la langue de l'autre*], it was *as if* speech were *irresponsible*. But this irresponsibility already commits the speakers and, as we shall see, the return to the mother tongue does away with commitment as well as seals it. It spells the *arrêt* of commitment.

The commitment thus *arrêté*, both in one's own language and in the language of the other, is indeed the *hymen*.

For quite some time I had been talking to her in her mother tongue, which I found all the more moving since I knew very few words of it. . . . She . . . would answer me in French, but in a different French from her own, more childish and talkative, as though her speech had become irresponsible, like mine, using an unknown language. And it is true that I too felt irresponsible in this other language [*langage*], so unfamiliar to me. . . . So I made the most friendly declarations to her in this language [*langage*], which was a habit quite alien to me. I offered to marry her at least twice, which proved how fictitious [*fictif*] my words were, since I had an aversion to marriage (and little respect for it), but in her language [*langue*] I married her, and I not only used that language lightly but, more or less inventing it, and with the ingenuity and truth of half-awareness, I expressed in it unknown feelings that shamelessly welled up in the form of that language and fooled even me, as they could have fooled her. [*DS* 61–62/*AM* 114–15]

But *tromper*, "fooling," for words that express in the language of the other a "truth of half-awareness," is also *tromper la surveillance* (as we say in "my" language, French), eluding the watchful eye of some monitor, in order to tell the truth. All the more so since the language of the other, as the language of truth, is never just the language of the other. Since it is "of the other," I invent it at every moment ("more or less inventing it"), I speak it

---

necessity within Shelley's poem, which is, moreover, full of colors and embroidered flowers. The last word that J., the woman who "lives on," has spoken, was not *la Chose* but *la Rose*, the "perfect rose," "*la rose par excellence.*" Not the "artificial roses" given to the dying Anne (*Thomas the Obscure* [78/ *ThIo* 85]), not the sand-rose, even though the woman who lives on called for it twice at the moment when her pulse "scattered like sand." Twice, at the moment of her double death, of her double *arrêt de mort*, she says, "Quick, a perfect rose." Reread *in extenso*. For example: "Another excuse is that little by

for the first time, as if at the moment of its initial establishment, of the first contract by which I adapt and adopt [*(m')approprie*] the language. At the same time, in the mythic time of this "at the same time" of the language of the other and my establishment of it, I make the contract *and* exempt myself from it. All *at once*. I am "irresponsible" and absolutely committed in the establishment of the language of the other. Is it not significant that the "at once," the "at the same time," of this *double bind*, is the occasion of the *hymen*, its chance and its law?

The words spoken in the language of the other are "true," commit the speaker, are binding, in legal proceedings, in accordance with a contract that is all the more inflexible since the words belong to the language of the other. The paradox of the heteronomous dissymmetry that is due to the apparently formal element in the language before any consideration of content: the obligation is binding to whatever extent the words of the obligation are "fictitious," "fictive." There is commitment only in the language of the other, which I speak, of necessity, irresponsibly and fictively, in expropriation, but the language of the other is more contractual, contracts more, is closer to the conventional, fictive origin, to the extent that I invent it and thus adopt, appropriate it, mythically, in the present act of each spoken word. The language of the other lets the spoken word have the word, and commits us to keep our word. In this sense, there is "language of the other" whenever there is a speech-event. This is what I mean by "trace."

I must now propose a long reading. We have here the passage from the language of the other to *my* language, the mother tongue, the theme of which should also be related to the figure of the mother as *figurant*, walk-on, extra, super, in this *récit* and in certain others. Here, a sudden intrusion, the event that comes to pass in the metro when I say to the other, in my language this time, what was reserved for the other language, truth as

---

little she seemed to approach a truth compared to which mine lost all interest. Toward eleven o'clock or midnight she began to have troubled dreams. Yet she was still awake, because I spoke to her and she answered me. She saw what she called 'a perfect rose' [*une rose par excellence*] move in the room. During the day I had ordered some flowers for her that were very red but already going to seed, and I'm not sure she liked them very much. She looked at them from time to time in a rather cold way. They had been put in the hall for the night, almost in front of her door, which remained open for some time. Then

Living On   169

fiction that commits and provokes—*la Chose*, the theft of the little "Yale" key. This comes immediately after the passage that I just cited.

> They did not fool her at all; I am sure of that. And perhaps my frivolity, though it made her a little frivolous too, aroused disagreeable thoughts more than anything else, not to speak of one other thought about which I cannot say anything. Even now, when so many things have become clear, it is difficult for me to imagine what the word marriage could have awoken [*faire naitre*] in her. She had once been married, but that business had left her only the memory of the unpleasant details of the divorce. So that marriage was not very important to her either. And yet why was it that the only time, or one of the only times, she answered me in her own language, was after I had proposed marriage to her: the word was a strange one, completely unknown to me, which she never wanted to translate for me, and when I said to her: "All right, then I'm going to translate it," she was seized by real panic at the thought that I might hit on it exactly, so that I had to keep both my translation and my presentiment to myself. [*DS* 62–63/*AM* 115–16]

The interdiction remains [*demeure*]: there is "one other thought about which I cannot say anything," and the only "answer," "*réponse*," that she gives to his proposal of marriage is neither *yes* nor *no* but an untranslatable word: not only in a foreign language but also "strange" and unknown to him. The risk of his perhaps being able to translate it nevertheless, makes its untranslatability more an interdiction than an impossibility. If he translated it, there would be an answer, the "response" of a *sponsa* (fiancée, a promise made), and this possibility is maddening for her. It is this understanding of a *yes* (which must be untranslatable and uncitable, must remain outside the language, strange and foreign), this understanding between them, which, along with "madness" and "insane words," will make her flee, will interrupt the hymen even as it consummates it in the confusion of their tongues.

---

she saw something move across the room, at a certain height, as it seemed to me, and she called it 'a perfect rose.' I thought this dream image came to her from the flowers, which were perhaps disturbing her. So I closed the door. At that moment she really dozed off, into an almost calm sleep, and I was watching her live and sleep when all of a sudden she said with great anguish 'Quick, a perfect rose,' all the while continuing to sleep but now with a slight rattle. The nurse came and whispered to me that the night before that word had been the last she had pronounced: when she had seemed to be sunk in com-

It is possible that the idea of being married to me seemed like a very bad thing to her, a sort of sacrilege, or quite the opposite, a real happiness, or finally, a meaningless joke. Even now, I am almost incapable of choosing among these interpretations. Enough of this. As I said, I was deluding myself much more than I was her with these words, which spoke within me in the language of someone else [*la langue d'une autre*]. I said too much about it to her not to feel what I was saying; inwardly I committed myself to honoring these strange words; the more extreme they were, I mean alien [*étrangers*] to what might have been expected of me, the more true they seemed to me because they were novel, because they had no precedent; the more I wanted, since they could not be believed, to make them believable, even to myself, especially to myself, putting all my effort into going farther and farther and building, on what might have been a rather narrow foundation, a pyramid so dizzying that its ever growing height dumbfounded even me. Still, I can put this down in writing: it was true; there cannot be any illusions when such great excesses are involved. My mistake in this situation, the temptations of which I see most clearly, was much more the result of the distance I imagined I was maintaining from her by these completely imaginary [*fictifs*] ways of drawing close to her. Actually, all that, which began with words I did not know and led me to see her much more often, to call her again and again, to want to convince her, to force her to see something other than a language in my language [*autre chose qu'un langage dans mon langage*], also urged me to look for her at an infinite distance, and contributed so naturally to her air of absence and strangeness that I thought it was sufficiently explained by this, and that as I was more and more attracted by it, I was less and less aware of its abnormal nature and its terrible source.

No doubt I went extremely far, the day we took shelter in the metro. It seems to me that I was driven by something wild, a truth so violent that I suddenly broke down all the frail supports of that language [*langue*] and began speaking French, using insane words that I had never dreamt of using before and that fell on her with all the power of their madness. Hardly had they touched her when I was physically aware that something was being shattered. Just at that moment, she was swept away from me, borne off by the crowd [*ravie par la foule*], and as it

---

plete unconsciousness, she had abruptly awakened from her stupor to point to the oxygen balloon and murmur, 'A perfect rose,' and had immediately sunk [*et aussitôt avait sombré*] again. / This *récit* chilled me" [*DS* 24–25/*AM* 49–50]. *18 March 1978*. "*et aussitôt*": to translate this, like everything said above about the "*et*/and," the translators will have to consult (or refer the reader to) the Greek "at the same time," *hama*, and *en tō ephexēs* ("immediately") as they are treated in "*Ousia* and *Grammē*" [in *Margins of Philosophy*]. What is a *refer-*

Living On 171

hurled me far away, the unchained spirit of that crowd struck me, battered me, as if my crime had turned into a mob [*foule*] and was determined to separate us forever. [*DS* 63–64/*AM* 116–19]

Shall we leave this text on its own power?

We should neither comment, nor underscore a single word, nor extract anything, nor draw a lesson from it. One should not, one should refrain from—such would be the law of the text that gives itself, gives itself up, to be read [*qui se donne à lire*]. Yet it also calls for a violence that matches it in intensity, a violence different in intention, perhaps, but one that exerts itself against the first law only in order to attempt a commitment, an involvement, with that law. To move, yieldingly, toward it, to draw close to it fictively. The violent truth of "reading."

This is what is happening right here. With great violence, I draw three motifs from the citation.

(1) The fiction of the foreign language is intended to keep a distance, indeed infinite distance, within all the rapprochement, proximation, propriation, appropriation. *Pas d'Ent-fernung*: de-distance. The *pas* is less susceptible of definition by words like "fiction," "language," "language of the other," than it is itself capable of remarking on them, drawing our attention to them [*il . . . les donne . . . à remarquer*].

(2) Where does this "truth" come from, the "truth so violent" of *I*'s repatriation in his own language? From the fact that the reappropriation does not take place and that he discovers the language of the other in his "own" language, French, in the utterly new words that he speaks in it. Between the two experiences or the two events or the two languages, the relationship is once more one of double invagination. Just as in the previous experience, when he was speaking Nathalie's language, but this time within his language, his "mother" tongue, he initiates, discovers, *establishes*,

---

ence, a reference to a thing, to a text, to one text, to the other? What is this word "reference"? And the reference of a certain "perfect rose"? The absolute crypt, unreadability itself. And yet the "references" call for an "infinite finite analysis," an infinite-finite reada-translatability. Do not go on about the symbolism of the flower (I have done so elsewhere, at length, precisely about the rose). "Symbol" of life (the rosiness of cheeks, imitated by makeup in *L'arrêt de mort*), "symbol" of death (funeral flower) or of love, the rose is also the

creates; he speaks in words that are "novel," that have "no precedent." If he begins "speaking French," he does so "using insane words that I had never dreamt of using before." Hence their *madness*, madness for both him and her. We can also say that these "French" words are *untranslatable* for him, absolutely familiar and absolutely foreign. He speaks his mother tongue *as* the language of the other and deprives himself of all reappropriation, all specularization in it. The effect of commitment, of breaking and entering, of heteronomous expropriation, gives truth this over-violence: within my "mother" tongue I have broken all the safety-devices ("I suddenly broke down all the frail supports of that language"), everything that authorizes awareness or consciousness and the illusion [*leurre*] of appropriation with respect to language. Will it be said that by letting the trace of the other involve or commit me in this linguistic expropriation I am breaking with what is maternal in the mother tongue? Or on the contrary with the paternal law that kept me at a distance from what was maternal?[25] Perhaps only with these figures of the law, with these extras, walk-ons, these figurants of an unfigurable law.

(3) The hymen *s'arrête*: it comes about *and* is immediately forbidden. It is the *double-bind*[26] structure of this event: its "madness." The interruption of the hymen—which is nothing other than its coming to be, its event—does not arise from any decision. No one has the initiative. As soon as the words have "touched" her, she is "swept away from me, borne off by the crowd": she does not leave, nor do I, and this "sweeping away" consigns what it carries off, to *dispersion* (the event, the *coup*—blow, stroke, "suddenly"—the pulse once more "scatters like sand") and to *anonymity*. All the same, the crowd (dispersion and anonymity) brings in no verdict of acquittal. The crime has taken place (and every hymen intervenes, like a crime, "between perpetration and the memory of it" as in Mallarmé's *Mimique*[27]), and its dissemination dissolves or absolves

---

paradigm of that which never has to account for itself ("die Rose ist ohne warum," "the rose has no why or wherefore"), the enigmatically arbitrary that signifies the non-significance of the arbitrary, of the thing with no why or wherefore, without origin and without end. (Cf. "The *Sans* of the Pure Cut" and all of the reading, in a seminar at Yale on *La chose*, of Heidegger's text on "Die Rose ist ohne warum." To be continued elsewhere, as is what concerns Ponge's rose and Celan's.) If the rose is not the thing, a thing, and not *la Chose*

it in the crowd only by multiplying it incalculably ("as if my crime had turned into a mob and was determined to separate us forever"). And my crime is that I loved her, proposed marriage to her, this *alliance*—but in a language [*langue*] that I have never been able to reappropriate or even understand, whether it be her (Slavic) language, a foreign language, or insane words (themselves foreign) in "my" language. My crime is that I proposed marriage to her in language [*langage*] that could commit me only if it was the other's, thus only if I did not understand it as mine and if it thus did not commit me, if even as it bound me, was binding upon me, it set me free. But this is always the case, always "normal": a language [*langue*] can never be appropriated; it is mine only as the language of the other, and vice versa. The essential irresponsibility of the promise or the response: this is the crime of the hymen. The violence of a truth stronger than truth. The crime of the hymen takes place without taking place and repeats itself endlessly, by the throng [*en foule*], like sand, like the *arrêt de mort*: interminable proceedings.

What happens then? There's no justifying this trip, nor this series of leaps and omissions (and I am referring to writing as well as to reading). He has lost her and is looking for her. First, although "at her house [*chez elle*], no one had answered the telephone," he goes there, thinking "that she was not answering it" on purpose. But even at the door there is no answer: it is "deaf." Yet "every time I had gone, she had been there" in that room [*DS* 64/*AM* 119–20]. The last words of *L'arrêt de mort*: "and to that thought [*et à elle*] I say eternally, 'Come,' and eternally she/it is there [*elle est là*]" [*DS* 80/*AM* 147]. In this room he cannot even "make out the trail [*trace*] she had left in passing through" or wait for her, having thus "replaced her." Replaced *her*: the woman named Nathalie, the first name that celebrates the birth of Christ, as we have noted, but also the first name of the woman who gave birth, in the *récit*, to Christiana, whom

---

either. Understand the perfect *rose* not as thing but as word, breath, a word breathing its last: adjective, noun (common or proper), immediately nominalizable predicate (*rose, la rose, le rose, Rose* ["pink" (adj.), "rose" (n.), "pink" (n.), "Rose"]). The first word of the first scene of the first act of a play (Genet's *Paravents* [*Screens*], for example; see *Glas*), it retains, out of context, the reserve of all those powers (*Rose!*) of a name beyond names, the reserve that it still retains when it becomes the last word (*par excellence*) of the last act: of the

at this moment "I cursed... for being [away] in the country, where she could not stop her mother from getting lost." Feeling "lost" himself rather than uneasy for Nathalie's sake, he is like "a wanderer in search of nothing." Has she drowned herself? No, suicide horrifies her. Then comes the moment when he stops [arrête] wandering. He reaches [arrête] a sort of decision, coolly arrived at, that one is tempted to compare to the moment in the "first" récit when he (the same one, another) returns, then calls her back to life, then "gives" her death: "reason returned to me, at least a fairly cool and lucid feeling that said to me: the time has come, now you have to do what has to be done." His resolution reached [arrêt d'une résolution] is purely formal in nature. In any case, we are told nothing of its content: what you have to do is do what has to be done. *Il faut "il faut"*: he gives himself this pure order or prescription at the same time that he receives it. He will return home, but home is not home, for two reasons. First, he lives in hotels, has no place of his own. Second, because there are two places, two hotel rooms: one, in an almost empty hotel with no owner present (it's wartime, and he's been called up), a room in which "I had nothing... but some books" and where "I almost never went," and went "at night [only if] it was really necessary"; the other, in the hotel on the rue S., where "I had asked N. never to go." She called him there one morning and "what I said," his "response," makes him hate the place. As he goes back there on this particular evening, he notes that "the strange thing" is that he does not think at all that she might be waiting there. He doesn't feel like sleeping in either place, so he tries to get a room in "a rather shady hotel," but since that hotel is full, he returns to the one on the rue d'O., the one where he "almost never [*presque pas*]" stays. His room there is like a crypt: with the elevator out of order, it is reached by way of a stairwell [*escalier*] with "a cold smell of earth and stone." The cryptic topology of this dark room, this obscure chamber, has the resonance of a certain triumph of life. It is

---

dead woman and of death, of *la Chose par excellence*. Rose: rose: "rose": I, a rose, rose. Its own subject and predicate, a tautology into which the other, however, has intruded, a flower of rhetoric without properties, with no proper meaning, a reiterated self-citation. "A rose is a rose is a rose is a rose": in *The Infinite Conversation*, Blanchot says that this line of Gertrude Stein's disturbs us because it is "the site of a perverse contradiction" (see the passage that follows, p. 343/[*EI*] 503). When speaking of the "narrative voice," he mentioned a *for intérieur* [usually "conscience," "inner tribunal," "heart of hearts"] without intimacy, an enclave larger than its inhabitant but which this inhabitant nevertheless carries within him; he haunts rather than inhabits it. The relationships of inclusion or inherence that link the part to the whole cannot be fixed, defined, *arrêter*, in terms of boundaries. The part includes the whole, and life triumphs over life. "Everything about that room, plunged in the most profound darkness, was familiar to me; I had penetrated it, I carried it in me, I gave it life, a life that is not life, but that is stronger than life and that no force in the world could ever overcome" [*DS* 65–67/*AM* 120–24]. This *camera obscura* is a secret; no one goes there, and he keeps the key in his wallet. Hence the transgression that follows, the theft of a key and a letter (important for the address it bore), a crypt broken into, desecrated—and a representationless scene of *la Chose*: this scene is what I was coming to.

. . . the elevator was not working and in the stairwell, from the fourth floor on up, a sort of strange musty smell came down to me, a cold smell of earth and stone that I was perfectly familiar with because in the room it was my very life. I always carried the key with me, and as a precaution I carried it in a wallet. Imagine that stairwell plunged in darkness, where I was groping my way up. Two paces from the door I had a shock [*je fus frappé par un coup*]: the key was no longer there. My fear had always been that I would lose that key. Often, during the day, I would search my wallet for it; it was a little key, a Yale key, I knew every detail of it. This loss brought back all my anxiety in an instant, and it had been augmented by such a powerful certainty of unhappiness that I had that unhappiness in my mouth and the taste of it has remained there ever since. I was not thinking anymore. I was behind that door. This might seem ridiculous, but I think I begged it, entreated it, I think I cursed it, but when it did not respond, I did something that can only be explained by my lack of self-control: I struck it violently with my fist, and it opened immediately.

---

a "wily perversity" [*IC* 385/*EI* 564]. Here the translators might amass references:[r] to Rilke, of whom Blanchot is a prodigious reader—to all his "rose"'s and all his "roses" (a formidable *anthology*, from which, because space is limited and for the sake of translation, I shall extract here only this line, from "Les roses," a poem written by Rilke *in French*: "Rose, toi, ô chose par excellence complète. . . . " Read and translate in full.); to Kierkegaard, of whom Blanchot is a prodigious reader ("The seal is yours, but I keep it. But in a seal, as you

I will say very little about what happened then: what happened had already happened long ago, or for a long time had been so imminent that not to have revealed it, when I felt it every night of my life, is a sign of my secret understanding with this premonition. I did not have to take another step to know that there was someone in that room. That if I went forward, all of a sudden someone would be there in front of me, pressing up against me, absolutely near me, of a proximity that people are not aware of: I knew that too. Everything about that room, plunged in the most profound darkness, was familiar to me; I had penetrated it, I carried it in me, I gave it life, a life that is not life, but that is stronger than life and that no force in the world could ever overcome. That room does not breathe; there is neither shadow nor memory in it, neither dream nor depth; I listen to it and no one speaks; I look at it and no one lives in it. And yet, the most intense life is there, a life that I touch and that touches me, absolutely similar to others, that clasps my body with its body, marks my mouth with its mouth, whose eyes open, whose eyes are the most alive, the most profound eyes in the world, and whose eyes see me. May the person who does not understand that come and die. Because that life transforms the life that shrinks away from it into a falsehood.

I went in; I closed the door. I sat down on the bed. Blackest space extended before me. I was not in this blackness, but at the edge of it, and I confess that it is terrifying. It is terrifying because there is something in it that scorns man and that man cannot endure without losing himself. But he must lose himself; and whoever resists will founder, and whoever goes forward will become this very blackness, this cold and dead and scornful thing in the very heart of which lives the infinite. This blackness stayed next to me, probably because of my fear: this fear was not the fear people know about, it did not break me, it did not pay any attention to me, but wandered around the room the way human things do. A great deal of patience is required if thought, when it has been driven down into the depths of the horrible, is to rise little by little and recognize us and look at us. But I still dreaded that look. A look is very different from what one might think, it has neither light nor expression nor force nor movement, it is silent, but from the heart of the strangeness its silence crosses worlds and the person who hears that silence

---

know, the letters are reversed, from this it follows that the 'yours,' by which you validate the certainty of possession, appears as a 'mine' from my side. Herewith have I sealed this parcel, and I would ask you to do likewise with the enclosed rose before it is put away in the temple archive";[8] the reversal "yours"/"mine" takes place, of course, only in Danish)—to so many others. *L'arrêt de mort* as another *Roman de la rose* (we know that this text, too, presents considerable problems of the unity or duplicity of the "I," the narrator or

Living On 177

is changed. All of a sudden the certainty that someone was there who had come to find me became so intense that I drew back from her, knocked violently into the bed, and immediately saw her distinctly, three or four paces from me, that dead and empty flame in her eyes. I had to stare at her, with all my strength, and she stared at me, but in a strange way, as if I had been in back of myself, and infinitely far back. Perhaps that went on for a very long time, even though my impression is that she had hardly found me before I lost her. At any rate, I remained in that place for a very long time without moving. I was no longer at all afraid for myself, but for her I was extremely afraid, of alarming her, of transforming her, through fear, into a wild thing that would break in my hands. I think I was aware of that fear, and yet it also seems to me that everything was so entirely calm that I could have sworn there was nothing in front of me. It was probably because of that calm that I moved forward a little, I moved forward in the slowest possible way, I brushed against the fireplace, I stopped again; I recognized in myself such great patience, such great respect for that solitary night that I made almost no movement; only my hand went forward a little, but with great caution, so as not to frighten. I wanted most of all to go toward the armchair, I saw that armchair in my mind, it was there, I was touching it. In the end I got to my knees so that I would not be too large, and my hand slowly crossed through the dark, brushed against the wooden back of the chair, brushed against some cloth: there had never been a more patient hand, nor one more calm, nor more friendly; that is why it did not tremble when another hand, a cold hand, slowly formed beside it, and that hand, so still and so cold, allowed mine to rest on it without trembling. I did not move, I was still on my knees, all this was taking place at an infinite distance, my own hand on this cold body seemed so far away from me, I saw myself so widely separated from it, and pushed back by it into something desperate that was life, that all my hope seemed to me infinitely far away, in that cold world where my hand rested on this body and loved it and where this body, in its night of stone, welcomed, recognized and loved that hand.

Perhaps this lasted several minutes, perhaps an hour. I put my arms around her; I was completely motionless and she was completely motionless. But a mo-

---

the author). And to place here this rose on the most abyss-like of crypts, these "discovered fragments" by Bataille, on Laure (just published by Jérôme Peignot, Laure's nephew): "Walking through the streets, I discover a truth that will not leave me in peace: that sort of painful contraction of my whole life that for me is related to Laure's death [in October 1938, dates found at the beginning of *L'arrêt de mort*] and to the sparse autumn sadness, is also for me the only way to 'crucify' myself. . . . [*11 October*.] As Laure was dying, I found

ment came when I saw that she was still mortally cold, and I drew closer and said to her: "Come." I got up and took her by the hand; she got up too and I saw how tall she was. She walked with me, and all her movements had the same docility as mine. I made her lie down; I lay down next to her. I took her head between my hands and said to her, as gently as I could, "Look at me." Her head actually did rise between my hands and immediately I saw her again three or four paces from me, that dead and empty flame in her eyes. With all my strength, I stared at her, and she too seemed to stare at me, but infinitely far behind me. Then something awoke in me, I leaned over her and said, "Now don't be afraid, I'm going to blow on your face." But as I came near her she moved very quickly and drew away (or pushed me back). [*DS* 66–70/*AM* 122–29]

(Citing or not citing is always equally unjustifiable, in the eyes of the law that concerns me here. What must we do to allow a text to live? Are we to take it—and how—or merely to "brush against" it? Say to it, "Come"? Isn't that what one always does "at home," i.e., in accordance with the violent law of one's own *economy*, here of mine? But we have just seen how the at-home of a room, what properly belongs to an economy, someone's own economy, is anonymously dedicated, divides itself and submits to the other who was waiting there for him already, without waiting for him, and how he said "I remained [*je restai*]," then "I stopped [*je m'arrêtai*] again." The rest has just been read [*vient d'être lu*].)

The "Come" that has just rung out will be cited, after a time in which we are told of "the obstacle that must be overcome" and of what is said to have "triumphed over an immense defeat, and is even now triumphing over it, and at each instant, and always, so that time no longer exists for it" [*DS* 72/*AM* 133]. In the interval between the first occurrence, event, coming of the "Come" in the *récit* and the first citation of it, an interval that I'll leave for you to read, that I'll let you read (it's like letting someone, or something, live), he sees her "in the morning," like J., in the

---

in the then ruined garden, among the dead leaves and wilted plants, one of the prettiest flowers I've ever seen: a rose, 'autumn-colored,' barely opened. Distracted as I was, still I picked it and took it to Laure. Laure was then lost in herself, lost in an undefinable delirium. But when I gave her the rose, she emerged from her strange state, smiled at me, and spoke one of her last intelligible sentences: 'It's gorgeous,' she said to me. Then she brought the flower to her lips and kissed it with a mad passion as if she wished to hold on to ev-

room and "quite gay" [*DS* 70 "quite cheerful"/*AM* 130]. This is a time of coldness beyond cold. A semblance of "natural life" [*DS* 72 "natural manner"/*AM* 132] has returned. "Naturally, what I had to do was live with her, in her apartment: I had to take my revenge on that door" [*DS* 72/ *AM* 133–34]. And here is the citation of the one single "Come," "one single word" in its serial repetition:

> ... I felt determined to transform the most simple details of life into so many insignificant words, that my voice, which was becoming the only space where I allowed her to live, forced her to emerge from her silence too, and gave her a sort of physical certainty, a physical solidity, which she would not have had otherwise. All this may seem childish. It does not matter. This childishness was powerful enough to prolong an illusion that had already been lost, and to force something to be there that was no longer there. It seems to me that in all this incessant talking there was the gravity of one single word, the echo of that "Come" that I had said to her; and she had come, and she would never be able to go away again. [*DS* 73/*AM* 134–35]

"Come": a single word, unique, and yet, in and of itself, entwined, interlaced, in a series. Truth beyond truth inscribes its own effacement there, in the middle of and on the invaginated boundaries of the *récit*, of these crypts, death- or bridal chambers that bring about [*donnant lieu à*] this double *récit*, this *arrêt de mort* that is finally only its own homonym. After the theft of the key—the event of a hymen that brings at once alliance and separation, when "as I came near her she ... drew away" ("joined: separated"—*Awaiting Oblivion*[28]), in the crypt—another *arrêt de mort* punctuates the *récit*. Each time beyond decision, in a serial repetition that does not change the uniqueness of the event. Hence the extraordinary lightness, slightness, the indifferent distractedness, the strange or insignificant coldness that is allied, in narrative affect, with a bottomless sorrow

---

erything that was slipping away from her. But it lasted only an instant: she threw down the rose the way children throw down their toys and became once more alien to everything that came near, breathing convulsively. *12 October.* ... Laure's dying was almost finished when she raised with a weary movement one of the roses that had just been spread before her, and she cried out almost in a voice absent and infinitely pained: 'The rose!' (I believe those were her last words.) ... At that same moment I was recalling what I had felt

and mourning without measure. At the very moment when unhappiness is "immense," one must not "have faith," he says, "in dramatic decisions. There was no drama anywhere. In me it had in one second become weaker, slightly distracted, less real.... I knew that if I did not immediately again become a man carried away by an unbridled feeling I was in danger of losing both a life and the other side of a life" [*DS* 74/*AM* 136–37]. Thus we come to the other *arrêt de mort*, and the other theft: in the wallet, she had found not a letter but a card, and an address, the address of a sculptor who would make a cast of her head and her hands—enough to turn her into an effigy.

Before reading this passage, let us recall the "first" *récit*, the "stillness of a recumbent effigy" [*DS* 19/*AM* 39], the narrator's request for permission to "have [J.] embalmed" [*DS* 21/*AM* 43]. Earlier he "had sent a very beautiful cast of J.'s hands to ... a professional palm reader and astrologer" [*DS* 10/*AM* 23]. To embalm, to make a death mask or cast, is indeed to set about the *arrêt de mort* in its double triumph, and indeed the chambers of this desire are in a sort of *funeral home*.[29] This comes about (again) in series in the two *récits*. There is an *arrêt* between the two deaths, and thus hypertopia: between the two deaths in each *récit*, and between the two *arrêts de mort* from one *récit* to the other. Two *récits* in one, one *récit* in two, synonymous, homonymous, anonymous. *He* (the narrator, whose identity is doubly problematic: he has no name [*pas de nom*], and there is no guarantee that he does not have two, from one half-*récit*—or half-mourning—to the other) loves them. He loves them ... dead. He loves (*by*) seeing them. He loves (*by*) seeing them dead. But when he sees them they die—when he sees them, and when they see him with that terrible look of theirs, see him as their death—with these looks, they die, are dead. Die, are dead, when he loves them—die, are dead, of this love. Moreover, he can love, desire, only behind a pane of glass, he says elsewhere. One

---

that very morning: 'Take a flower and look at it until you and the flower are in harmony....' That was a *vision*, an *inner vision* maintained by a silently felt necessity."ᵗ *20–27 March 1978.* Resurrections. Easter week. The translators should refer to the end of my apocalypse (*Glas*), entirely concerned with the paschal conjunction. The Christ-like figure again, of the "who?," of the X. of *L'arrêt de mort*, over whom "it's about time we raised a cross," says the doctor

imagines a glass coffin: this is one thematic of this *récit*—and of others—that I reserve here. But each woman is also the double, death mask, cast, ghost, body at once living and dead, of the other. Separated by a pane of glass uncrossable from one story to the other. Separated: joined. There are two of them, absolutely different, absolutely other, infinitely separated by the *arrêt de mort* between two heterogeneous *récits*. They are each bound to "me" (to "me," to the one who says *I* in each instance and who is not necessarily the same, who is perhaps not the same precisely because he, the same in name or first name, is linked, bound, in accordance with a double hymen and twice says *yes*, twice *Come*) in accordance with a double vow. By the same double token [*coup*], himself by the same token double, *I* becomes two, absolutely foreign to himself, divided, partitioned in his crypt: he belongs to two different *récits*, two different vows; he has another, a woman, dictate to him what he says and tell him what has to be done—another, a woman, who inspires. Everything is decided, we have seen, in the moment of an insufflation in which we no longer know who has the absolute initiative. Even the mouth of one of those women, "open to the noise of agony [*agonie*], did not seem to belong to her; it seemed to be the mouth of someone I didn't know, someone irredeemably condemned, or even dead" [*DS* 28/*AM* 56]. Interruption, this connectionless connection [*rapport sans rapport*] of the *arrêt*, passes not only between J. and N. but also, with the same interminable stroke [*trait*], inside me, the ego, the henceforth insideless insides of the *récitant*. But if the two women are different, utterly other "in relation to" [*par rapport à*] each other, each one *is* the other. Each one signifies and preserves [*garde*] the other. Each one *remains*—the other. For and by the other. Each signs the other's *arrêt de mort*. One dies *while* the other lives, lives on, comes—again. *While: as: when: in order that: because: as soon as:* this is the timeless time of the "and," of the "and immediately" that recurs, that comes back, so often

---

who condemns him. The translators will have to refer here to what is said about chiasmus, about χ (*chi*) and the *ichthus* in "+ R (Into the Bargain)" [in *The Truth in Painting*] (in reference to Adami) and in Hillis Miller's article "Ariadne's Thread" (*Critical Inquiry*, 3:1 [1976]: 75). There is another X., in *L'arrêt de mort*, the creator of that "process that is strange when it is carried out on living people, sometimes dangerous, surprising, a process

in the *récit* to describe the *simul* without causality, without absolute synchrony, without order. For the narrator: the death of one is what keeps the other under guard—preserves the other, preserves [him] from the other. Thus in the time of the "and" they must—*il faut*—they must both die so that, each time, the other will live. One dies *and* the other lives: an *immediately* that weds symbiosis to synthanatosis in a triumph without identity, without identicalness. In a double signature, he himself signs *their arrêt de mort*, at their request, their demand, he says, in order to preserve them, keep them, embalm them, encrypt them . . . *and* his *arrêt de mort*, with and in the same hand. What binds him to each of the two dead women (alliance, ring, vow, hymen, double affirmation, yes, yes, come, come: come back, come again—"come," again), each of these two revenants, living on as ghostly fiancées—this bond is double not because it commits him twice, attaches him to two women, to two identities: this hymen is a *double bind each time*, because each of these bonds that bind is, in itself, double. Each time is several times at the same time: several dates in one. But the event does not, for all that, lose its uniqueness of each time. I/It signifies, desires, *arrête* life death, the life the death of the other so that the other lives *and* dies, the other of the other—who is without being the same. For there is an other of the other, and it is not the same: this is what the order of the symbol seeks desperately to deny. The double bond to each woman *signifies* to each woman the *arrêt de mort* (death *and* life-after-life / life-after-death) so that the other's *arrêt de mort* will be possible (so that she will live on and cease to live). "L'arrêt de mort," the *arrêt de mort*, thus designates the title of the book and the "totality" or set of a *récit* that is never gathered together to form one *récit* and that thus questions even the unity of its "title," as well as the unity of the narrator. *L'arrêt de mort / Death Sentence* would thus follow this *double bind* whose terrifying *figura*, figure, face, traverses the *récit* that is forbidden, inter-dicted in the

---

that . . . Abruptly . . . " [*DS* 75/*AM* 138]. X. is the name of the sculptor, the one who, *par excellence*, fixes life death [*arrête la vie la mort*]. *Arrêt* without *Aufhebung*: of translation. Economy. Temptation, but it's impossible, to recount the history of this text (countless episodes: for example, the Yale Seminar in 1976, Venice, the lecture in Belgium—the feminist "leader,"[u] a prodigious reader of Blanchot, who realizes, after the fact, that it was hard for her

quasi-middle of it, over above beyond its double inner border, over above beyond the untranslatability that holds one *récit* apart [*écart*] from the other. From/of one *récit* to the other, from/of one woman to the other, language [*langue*] is every (bit) other.

But there are enough signs that make it possible to read [*donnant à lire*] one *récit* in the other, and the double overrun of these two inner borders, so that *double invagination* is here no longer simply a formal structure. It is related in an essential way to the *double bind* that ties the "narrator" to each of these two women—related in an essential way to the triumph of life or to the *arrêt de mort* interrupted in the "middle," the "middle" "of it," at the *very place* where the *relationship* of the "book" *to itself*, in its fragile binding, is formed, the *relationship* of the *I to himself*, his alliance with himself, his ring, his anniversary, the alliance that joins him to himself. This *very* place, the *very same* place, being the place, the locus, of interruption, is also the place where double invagination gathers together what it interrupts in the strange *sameness* of this place. The *arrêt de mort* calls forth what it forbids: the death of the other whom it is supposed to preserve. One *récit* (one woman) makes the other die and live in a movement that is unarrestable and unnarratable. By the same (double) token, activity comes down to [*revient à*] passivity, making a person die *comes down* to letting a person die, making a person live *comes down* to letting a person live. But in going from *making* to *letting*, we are no longer passing from one opposite to the other, not passing into passivity. The passivity of "letting" is different from the passivity of couples and pairs, e.g., the pair active/passive.

Each lives off and dies *of* the other, preserves the other, preserves and loses the other's narrator. The "and" is to be understood each time as a conjunction that does not join logically, for example, in contradiction, nor according to chronology, succession or absolute simultaneity, nor accord-

---

to bear that a "man" should have dared the "mad hypothesis" of the *hymen* between the two women; she used the most academic criteriology against me, demanded "proof," and so on—reading "Morella," the thought of that Miss Blind bent over the corrections of *The Triumph*, hesitations about the title—I had first thought of "Living On—in Translation" and "Translations"—my calculations about the English—how will they render the *il faut* or perhaps

ing to some fundamental ontology. This *and* must be understood, if possible, as it appears in the story, where it seems to be unreadable in terms of any of the *conjunctions* that I have just mentioned. And the conjugality of the *double bind* between the two women and the narrator (if there is only one narrator), joins or weds this *and* to itself *as* an *arrêt de mort*. One example, although we could give a long series of them: "I called to her loudly by her first name; and immediately—I can say there wasn't a second's interval—a sort of breath came out of her compressed mouth . . . " [*DS* 20/*AM* 40]; " . . . and to her [*et à elle*] I say eternally, 'Come,' and eternally she is there" [*DS* 80/*AM* 147]. This "and"-, "and immediately"-writing, as it annihilates time in the ring of eternal return, yokes affirmation to itself in its *récit*, in the being-at-the-same-time of the other beyond time, in the accompaniment of that which is not accompanied—this "and"-writing returns, recurs, rather regularly when the narrative voice is (lets itself be) heard in Blanchot's texts—in all the other texts signed by him. It is like a silent gliding, the elusiveness of a cause that does not accompany its effect, of a before *and* an after that are indistinct in a movement's soft, light no/pace [*pas*]. And that, nonstop, stops and stops nothing; without a rest, arrests and arrests nothing; *sans arrêt*, *arrête* and *arrête* nothing.

Each woman lives off *and* dies of the other, *and* the same for the other, each woman preserving the other's narrator, *and* they lose him immediately. What do they preserve him from? From loneliness *with* the other, from the single vow with the other. But in both cases—double vow, single, unique vow—they sign the narrator's *arrêt de mort*: he can live in accordance neither with the single nor with the double alliance.[30] I am, he is, moreover, one who is "living on" in the two *récits*, each time promised (given up, condemned) by a doctor to imminent death, like another anonymous Christ (X., *chi*, chiasma, raising "a cross over him"). I have already cited the "first" *récit*; this is from the "second": "he [an

---

the *faut-il* that is the imprint of prescription in "Living On"?—the Paris Seminar in 1974 or 1975 on "Die Aufgabe des Übersetzers," what my friend Koitchi Toyosaki said to me yesterday, the article in *The Work of Fire* entitled "Translated From . . . "[v] [it begins thus: "In *For Whom the Bell Tolls*, Robert Jordan, discovering the importance of the instant he is in the process of living, repeats to himself the word 'now' in many languages: now, *maintenant*,

editor] thought I was nearing my end, he telephoned the doctor, who also gave me up for lost [*m'enterrait*] every few weeks, and got this opinion from him: 'X.? My dear sir, it's about time we raised a cross over him.' A few days later, the doctor told me this as though it were an excellent joke" [*DS* 47/*AM* 89]. Later, in the course of a story about blood that should be analyzed: "The doctor put me in his clinic; he thought I was dying" [*DS* 47/*AM* 90]. A couple of pages later: "The night before, I had been on the point of dying" [*DS* 49/*AM* 93].

The two women, like the doctor, sign his death warrant, and he signs theirs, but always in a countersignature, because the death that is "given" is always requested, demanded, by the one who receives it *and immediately* gives it to himself or herself, in order to sign it, with/from/in the hand of the other.

And thus we see: there would be . . . another hymen.

Among these three survivors, as they live on, there can be an *arrêt* only of death. No/pace of [*pas d'*] infidelity, more than one fidelity, no more of just one fidelity. *Three, to lose: lost.* He, the sole narrator, in his improbable and divisible identity, can live neither the single nor the double alliance, and he preserves himself, makes/lets one woman preserve him from the other, using one terror to avoid the other, and the double *récit*, as we have perhaps seen adequately, ensures the possibility of the impossible *arrêt de mort*. Nothing seems capable of surpassing this terrifying, triumphant affirmation—unless it comes to hold in store/check something even worse [*garder du pire*]. Unless there is something even worse—and thus more desirable, more madly terrifying—for the narrator: *the hymen between the two women*. What if the structure of the *récit*, the interruption between the two stories, guaranteed at first the non-meeting of J. and N.? And what if it were this—that the two women love each other and approach one another [*se rapprochent*], before him and without him—what if

---

ahora, now, *heute*. But he is a little disappointed . . . " (*WF* 176/*PF* 173)], the five pages in *Friendship* entitled "Translating" [last words: " . . . with the conviction that, in the end, translating is madness" (61/*A* 73)], and so on), but I count the words and I give up. Economy. Political. If there is something that arrests translation, this limit is not due to some essential indissociability of meaning and language, of signified and signifier, as they say. It is a matter of

it were this hymen that the *arrêt de mort* was both to forbid, as absolute terror, and thus, since every *arrêt de mort* calls forth what it suppresses, to make/let it live, be readable, die [*donner à vivre, à lire, à mourir*] in the unconscious, imperceptible structure of this *récit*? I am speaking here of the fascination of one woman by the other, across the uncrossable glass partition that separates the two stories. They do not know each other, have never met; they inhabit two utterly foreign worlds. They telephone each other ("Come") across the infinite distance of a no-connection [*d'un sans rapport*]. The narrator is between them, saying *I*, with an *I* identical and other, from one *récit* to the other. In him, before him, without him, they are the same, the same one, "two images superimposed on one another" [*DS* 9/*AM* 21], a "photographic" superimposing; they are utterly different, completely other, and they love, unite, and call to each other: *Come*.

Of course, nothing on the manifestly readable surface of the *récit*s makes it possible to sustain such a mad hypothesis. How could the character from one *récit* desire, marry, fascinate the character from another *récit*? And if we wished to consider *L'arrêt de mort* a single *récit*, joined to itself by the supposed identity of the character who says *I*, how could we fail to see that J. and N., in the story, have no connection, no relationship with each other, do not meet, just as the two series of events in which they are involved never intersect? Of course. No normal category of readability, then, could give credence to the mad hypothesis according to which the double invagination that attracts us in this *récit* could make it possible to read [*donner à lire*] the unreadable hymen between the two women: one *with(out)* the other. I am speaking here neither of an intention nor of a construction on the part of the "author"—which does not mean that the interruption between author and narrator, or indeed between the two women, is simple: it is as ambiguous as the interruption

---

economy (economy, of course, remains to be thought) and retains an essential relationship with time, space, counting words, signs, marks. The unity of the word is not to be fetishized or substantialized. For example, with more words or parts of words the translator will triumph more easily over *arrêt* in the expression *arrêt de mort*. Not without something left over, remain(s), of course, but more or less easily, strictly, closely, tightly. Beware of the "new mode of

of every *arrêt de mort*. As ambiguous, moreover, as differantial de-distance (*Entfernung*): from one *récit* to the other, they—the two women, the two voiceless voices, tele-phone one another: *come*. And the relationship, the connection, between the two *récits* would be tele-graphic in nature [*de téléscription*]. Furthermore, I am speaking here neither of an intention nor of a construction on the part of the "narrator"—which does not mean that the interruption between narrating voice and narrative voice, the two voices, the two women, one *without* the other, is simple: it remains as improbable as the interruption of every *arrêt de mort*. And yet something like X-ray analysis or "blood" [*sang*] analysis can make readable [*donner à lire*] that which is unreadable in this narrative body. A moment ago I drew (on) the "blood" that circulates in one of the two stories, the "mysterious" blood, "so unstable that it was astonishing to analyze"[*DS* 47/*AM* 90], the "madness of blood" in which the narrator seeks "hope of escaping the inevitable" [*DS* 61/*AM* 113] .

This readability of unreadability is as improbable as an *arrêt de mort*. No law of *normal* reading can guarantee it in its *legitimacy*. By normal reading I mean every reading that *ensures knowledge* transmittable *in its own language*, in a language unchanging (identical to itself), in a school or academy, knowledge constructed and ensured in institutional constructions, in accordance with *laws* made so as to resist (precisely because they are weaker) the ambiguous threats with which the *arrêt de mort* troubles so many conceptual oppositions, boundaries, borders. The *arrêt de mort* brings about the *arrêt* of the law. The double invagination of this narrative body in deconstruction overruns and exceeds not merely the oppositions of values that make the rules and form the law in all the schools of reading, ancient and modern, before and after Freud; it overruns a delimitation of the fantasy, a delimitation in the name of which some would here abandon, for example, the

---

expression" of the "totally new language" and the like. Economy: stricture and not *coupure*, rupture. It is always an *external* constraint that arrests a text in general, i.e., *anything*, for example, life death. What is arrested here: the authenticity (*Eigentlichkeit*) of a being-for-death. Think exteriority from the angle of this economy of the *arrêt*. *Arrêt*: the greatest "bound" energy, "banded (erect)," *bandée*, tightly gathered around its own limit, retained, inhibited

mad hypothesis to "my" fantasy-projection, to that of the one who says "I" here, the narrator, the narrators, or me, who am telling you all this whole fable. This unreadability will have taken place, *as* unreadable, will have become readable [*se sera donne à lire*] right here, as unreadable, from the very bottom of the crypt in which it remains. It will have taken place where it remains: that's the proof. From here on it's up to you to think what will have taken place, to work out both the conditions for its possibility and its consequences. As for me, I must break off here, interrupt all this, close the parenthesis, and let the movement continue without me, take off again, or stop, arrest itself, after I simply note this: in everything that happens, it's as if the narrator desired (in other words forbade)—from the moment he comes to say *I* onward—one thing: that the two women should love one another, should meet, should be united in accordance with the hymen. *Not [pas] without him/it, and immediately without him/it.* That they, these two other women, others of the other, should not merely resemble each other but should be the same in the impossible *parti(cipa)tion*: this is what he desires, what he would die of, what he desires like the death that he would "give" himself. This is absolute terror: the bottomless boundless abyss of that which is single, *unique*—the other death, laughable, the most simply insignificant death, the most fatal. And immediately *la Chose* is its double. It remains [*reste*] its double. But now we shall be able to make out the *arrestance* of this *reste*.

At about ten o'clock Nathalie said to me:
"I telephoned X.; I asked him to make a cast of my head and my hands."
Right away I was seized by a feeling of terror. "What gave you the idea of doing that?" "The card." She showed me a sculptor's card that was usually with the key in my wallet. [*DS* 75/*AM* 137]

(*Hemmung, Haltung*) *and immediately* disseminated. Sand. Empty, unloaded itself, spontaneously. In the trance of the trans-. On the word *transe*, the translators should cite *Glas*, at great length (e.g., pp. 22–23b/30b). Trans/partition. *Trépas* [death: *trans* + *passus*]. *Trespassing.*ʷ To be related, without translation, to all the *trans*-'s that are at work here. I hope that they will not believe that, escorted by this mob, this procession of doubles, ghosts, *transes, folies du*

Should we say that he gave her the idea of or the desire for the death mask, as he had wished to embalm the other woman, in order to preserve both of them, to keep them alive-and-dead, living on? Yes *and* no. Yes, because it is indeed thanks to him, next to him, *on him*, that she *finds* this "idea," this direction, this destination, this address, this "card." No, because she *finds* them only by stealing them from him, from a place where he was hiding them, in a crypt, a crypt next to his body, clinging to his skin, the wallet, an object that is detachable from him, neither clothing nor itself a body proper, a safe [*coffre*] containing other detachable objects, a card, keys, and the like. These detached objects are of a particular nature: they operate, orient, open, close; they make something readable or keep it secret. They, like the wallet that contains them, are not objects or simply things. "It seems to me you don't always behave very sensibly with that wallet," he tells her [*DS* 75/*AM* 137].

At this point the exchange of a *yes* takes a particular form and responds to specific demands ("'Say yes,' and I took her by the hand . . . ," then "I nodded yes [*je fis signe que oui*]. I was still holding her hand . . . " [*DS* 76/*AM* 139]) in the course of a scene that I cannot cite here. Then—as "yes" responds to nothing, nothing but the other "yes," itself—then the "terrible thing," the "victory over life," the "will to triumph" [*l'"intention triomphale"*], "glory," the "madness of victory" will all be evoked, named; then, too, will come the cry of "yes, yes, yes!"

She looked so human, she was still so close to me, waiting for a sort of absolution for that terrible thing that was certainly not her fault.
   "It was probably necessary," I murmured.
   She snatched at these words.
   "It was necessary, wasn't it?"
   It really seemed that my acquiescence reverberated in her, that it had been in some way expected, with an immense expectancy, by an invisible responsibil-

---

jour, manic jubilations and triumphs, I have produced here an underground or shady translation of *The Triumph of Life*, and for example, of "The crowd gave way, & I arose aghast / Or seemed to rise, so mighty was the trance, / And saw like clouds upon the thunder blast / The million with fierce song and maniac dance / Raging around; such seemed the jubilee. . . . " I have amassed references (to "things" and "texts," they would say) but in truth what

ity to which she lent only her voice, and that now a supreme power, sure of itself, and happy—not because of my consent, of course, which was quite useless to it, but because of its victory over life and also because of my loyal understanding, my unlimited abandon—took possession of this young person and gave her an acuity and a masterfulness that dictated my thoughts to me as well as my few words.

"Now," she said in a rather hoarse voice, "isn't it true that you've known about it all along?"

"Yes," I said, "I knew about it."

"And do you know when it happened?"

"I think I have some idea."

But my tone of voice, which must have been rather yielding and submissive, did not seem to satisfy her will to triumph.

"Well, maybe you don't know everything yet," she cried with a touch of defiance. And, really, within her jubilant exaltation there was a lucidity, a burning in the depths of her eyes, a glory that reached me through my distress, and touched me, too, with the same magnificent pride, the same madness of victory.

"Well, what?" I said, getting up too.

"Yes," she cried, "yes, yes!"

"That this took place a week ago?"

She took the words from my lips with frightening eagerness.

"And then?" she cried.

"And that today you went to X.'s to get . . . that thing?"

"And then!"

"And now that thing is over there, you have uncovered it, you have looked at it, and you have looked into the face of something that will be alive for all eternity, for your eternity and for mine! Yes, I know it, I've known it all along."

I cannot exactly say whether these words, or others like them, ever reached her ears, nor what mood led me to allow her to hear them: it was a minor matter, just as it was not important to know if things had really happened that way. But I must say that for me it seems that it did happen that way, setting aside the question of dates, since everything could have happened at a much earlier time. But the truth is not

---

I have just written is without reference. Above all, not to myself or to texts that I have signed in another language. Precisely *because of* this jubilant multiplicity of self-references. "In order to come into being as text, the referential function had to be radically suspended" (Paul de Man, "The Purloined Ribbon," in *Glyph 1*. Cite in full.). Transreference. How can one sign in translation, in another language? Living on—in/after whose name, in/after the

contained in these facts. I can imagine suppressing these particular ones. But if they did not happen, others happen in their place, and answering the summons of the all-powerful affirmation that is united with me, they take on the same meaning and the story is the same. It could be that N., in talking to me about the "plan," wanted only to tear apart with a vigilant [*jalouse*] hand the pretenses we were living under. It may be that she was tired of seeing me persevere with a kind of faith in my role as man of the "world," and that she used this story to recall me abruptly to my true condition and point out to me where my place was. It may also be that she herself was obeying a mysterious command, which came from me, and which is the voice that is always being reborn in me, and it is vigilant too, the voice of a feeling that cannot disappear. Who can say: this happened because certain events allowed it to happen? This occurred because, at a certain moment, the facts became misleading and because of their strange juxtaposition entitled the truth to take possession of them? As for me, I have not been the unfortunate messenger of a thought stronger than I, nor her/its plaything, nor her/its victim, because that *thought*, if she/it has conquered me, has only conquered through me, and in the end has always been equal to me. I have loved her/it and I have loved only her/it, and everything that happened I wanted to happen, and having had regard only for her/it, wherever she/it was or wherever I might have been, in absence, in unhappiness, in the inevitability of dead things, in the necessity of living things, in the fatigue of work, in the faces born of my curiosity, in my false words, in my deceitful vows, in silence and in the night, I gave her/it all my strength and she/it gave me all her/its strength, so that this strength is too great, it is incapable of being ruined by anything, and condemns us, perhaps, to immeasurable unhappiness, but if that is so, I take this unhappiness on myself and I am immeasurably glad of it and to that thought, to her I say eternally, "Come," and eternally she/it is there. [*DS* 78–80/*AM* 142–47]

---

name of what? How will they translate that? Of course, I have not kept my promise. This telegraphic band produces an untranslatable supplement, whether I wish it or not. Never tell what you're doing, and, pretending to tell, do something else that immediately crypts, adds, entrenches itself. To speak of writing, of triumph, as *living on*, is to enunciate or denounce the manic fantasy. Not without reiterating it, and that goes without saying.

Note: A lecture delivered in 1979 at Saint Louis College in Brussels and at the Studium Generale of the University of Freiburg-im-Brisgau. A first version of this lecture was published in a special issue of the journal *Nouva Corrente* (84, 1981), prepared and prefaced by Stefano Agosti. [The translation by Tom Conley first appeared in *SubStance*, Vol. 10, No. 2, Issue 31 (1981): 5–22.—Ed.]

Title to Be Specified

Translated by Tom Conley

The T-i-t-l-e-e-r

Were I to venture stopping here, to pronounce this, the t-i-t-l-e-e-r, had I audacity enough to be satisfied with it, or be convinced to leave you with what I have just uttered, no doubt you still could not tell how to take it.

In more than one way the titleer can be taken, meant or even understood.

For as long as there is attention drawn to what we calmly call a "context," or for as long as a *consistent* discourse will not have encircled an event of language of this sort in its path, what I have just risked, or even suspended, in pronouncing *the titleer* would probably allow your reception or your understanding to remain open, and open to question.

What happens to you (in hearing *the titleer*) certainly is neither for nought nor void, nor even totally indeterminate. You hear something quite well (the *titleer*), you begin to press toward several possible meanings of words, or of pieces of words, or of syntactical groupings that are sifted in shadow; you make them cross their paths or cross each other as if they were virtual sentences (*the title . . . here*, in three words, for example, or of a common noun placed and suspended like a title, if at least—another conceptual possibility is opened—you knew the Old French word (the *titrier* spelled t.i.t.r.i.e.r. [or the *titleer* spelled t.i.t.l.e.e.r.]).[1]

But your moment of discomfit, these doubts drifting about the waves or the semantic froth in the air, you don't dominate them. They leave you awash on the border of a shore where you want to arrive safe and sound or even, I would say, arrive *yourself*. Awash because this suspension does not allow floating on the high sea, but in view of certain borders in whose harbor we wait—time suspended as our vessels are brought to a standing or a stopover—to depart or arrive. In any case the desire, if it chills the hearing of these words that form perhaps neither a sentence nor a discourse—*le titrier*, the titleer—this desire draws, or at least calls you to this bank [*rive*] where meaning can finally be stopped, fixed, anchored—with the most precise mooring of a legitimacy. From these waters [*parages*], you want to see the shore, you wish to discern the lines of the border.

And for that reason you would like to know what I mean when I pronounce the t i t l e e r.

Now I'm off to tell you all about it.

That—"I'm off to tell you all about it"—is what is called a promise, a commitment, a plighted word. Now were I not faithful to this plighted word, did I not keep it (what is always possible in the case, for example, where I might place my promise between quotation marks and bind myself to an endless commentary of statement, "I'm off to tell you all about it"), the discursive event of the promise would remain suspended on the border of a certain border, half empty—but emptied of what? not of meaning [*non pas de sens*] but of something else that is neither reference nor even truth. It will assume a position, like a ruse of a dummy or a simulacrum, inside a scene that, to be riddled with fiction, will be none the less effective.

In announcing "Title (to be specified)" for this lecture, I have made a promise. But what kind of promise? Right off [*D'abord*] we might think that the locution, "Title (to be specified)," has come in a provisional fashion to take the place of the title. Like a blank check, it indicated the empty spot of a title to be filled in which, as such, there would be found the *true* title. Therefore I have promised to give a true title to my lecture this evening, and I promise to conform and adhere to it. But naturally this limit, this delay, this differance of title[2] was possible only in the space of convention, thanks to the agreement or to the contract that was passed among you and foremost, among the appointed and legitimate authorities of the premise. According to very complex resources—too varied and rich here however to be placed on exhibit—of an implicit contract, these appointed authorities have trusted me, have accredited me with a faith in the plighted word. But what therefore had I promised? Nothing more than coming, and to come and speak, here, before you, but without specifying what, without committing myself to anything other than coming and coming to speak. All the same about anything on condition that at the given moment I furnish the true title to my speech (what was quoted until now being only a false, temporary title placing in check the title to come) and that somehow I have my remarks conform to this title—or this title to my remarks—so that between the entitled (another name for the title) and the remarks thus entitled, between the entitled entitling and the entitled entitled there is surely the most adequate agreement.

But a prudent analysis of the politico-juridical context of this event would make all this business rather evident: if the legitimate authorities of these premises signed a blank check honoring me with an invitation to speak about anything under a title remaining still "to be specified," it is only in authorizing the titles they recognize in me that merits such confidence. A whole legitimizing process is implied in this contract, and it forms infinitely complex networks of sub-contracts, implicit evaluations, codes of admissibility, more or less virtual legal protocols, in brief, of the establishment of a set of titles—this time not in the meaning of what entitles or names a work, a discourse, a corpus, but of what appoints, what legitimizes a function or gives status—a law (for example, a right to speak in given conditions, etc.). But the two meanings of the word *title* in one law appeal to both, to a jurisdicity that I would rightfully like to interrogate.

In analyzing the protocol of this bizarre situation in which we find ourselves, at the border of a speech that has begun without having begun, that, still without a specific title, is going to speak about who knows what, in my opinion it seems hardly contestable that in according me some kind of carte blanche they have rightfully or wrongfully judged—the difference matters little—or they have *had* to judge that I have already pledged enough to merit the apparent confidence that they have conferred upon me without the cost of too much risk, and that therefore I had title enough to ask that they allow me not to specify the title in advance. These titles, I mean those that rightfully or wrongfully are recognized as mine, do not pass only because of copyright or collegial legitimacy, for the analogies that could be made of it would be a fine linkage for all kinds of juridical, juridico-political, philosophico-juridical problems, and the like. But they are of little interest to me this evening. All the same, this evening, like every evening, I feel somewhat obscurely that, if the titles in question—in this instance I mean mine—inspire a confidence propped up on all sorts of norms and guarantees, on a whole social contract; nonetheless mixed in this is a vague disquiet, a suspicion, an apprehension before an always possible, indeed imminent catastrophe: in the audience there is someone who, sitting in the back, under very polished amenities [*abords*] and despite the display of evident civility, does not always respect the fundamental contracts. And what would happen if he were not to come tonight? And, in coming, if he were not to speak? Or if in speaking, he spoke about anything? Or if in speaking of this or that or one thing or another, he were not to give a title to his speech, if he were to leave the title blank ("to be specified") or if he were to invent a title bearing rapport neither with what he says nor with what we have the right to expect from him in these premises—that is to say, truly nowhere? And were this intolerable situation to last one or two hours without anyone daring to interrupt him?

So I warn you that this is about to happen.

I declare that I have the intention neither of replacing my "title (to be specified)" by any other nor of having it specified in any way. And we are going to remain on the border; we are not going to leave these waters [*ces parages*].

The title is here. (*Le titre y est.*)

By that I mean, now I'm off to tell you all about it, as I promised a moment ago.

Let's say that I mean the following in the form of a thesis: a title always has the structure of a name, inducing effects of the proper name and under this title it remains in quite a unique fashion, foreign to language as discourse, in the very way it introduces an anormal referential function and a violence, an illegality that founds the law and the right of its procedure.

All of a sudden we begin to see an unfurling of theses that I am not going to have to prove. In place of demonstration, in its stead, I shall put forward an account of sorts, a story, a *récit*. The premises of a demonstration will perhaps be marked and therefore the passage of the story will be more economical.

Suppose that *The Titleer* is a title, the title of a book, of a painting, or of a lecture. *Somewhere* it must be *legible*. *Legible* somewhere, implying right off a script, a trait, a mark. And there is no title without legibility of a trace. To defend this affirmation, I am not only referring to some primitive or etymological meaning in recalling that *titulus* will have signified from the very beginning an inscription, a little trait or a little sign, in brief an elliptical, economical, visible, short but legible mark incising a surface, a support, a panel, or a board. Without need for this philological guarantee of the word *title*, of the title "title," I have to sustain that an analysis of the *functioning* of every title is possible and demonstrates that there cannot be a purely phonic title without possibility of its being recorded [*archivation*] and without a code of legibility. Legibility, I specified, of the title having to be *somewhere*: by that I imply no theory of the title can be rid of a topology. No title without spacing, of course, and also without the rigorous determination of a topological code defining *borderlines* [*arrêtant des lignes de bordures*]. A title takes place only on the border of a work: were it to let itself be incorporated in the corpus it entitles, were it only to be a part, like one of its internal elements or one of its pieces, it would no longer play the role of having title-value. Were it completely outside, detached and separated from the body by a distance greater than that which the law, right, and code ordain, there would be no more title. Such words—for example, *the titleer*—would play the role of a title, for example, to my speech, but only if placed a bit ahead and on the border of my text, in accord with a whole topological prescription. This prescription must model itself on a conventional code. But the same words, pronounced *inside* of my text and my discourse or even encountered *elsewhere*—in a dictionary or in another text—will no longer have title-value but only a rapport in some homonymic way with *the titleer* as title.

I feel that you are already protesting. I have just said that a title had to be legible; now for a while, even here, nothing is either visible or legible, but only audible, and there remains however the overriding question of the title of my remarks. Justly: there will be a title only when the possibility of a reading will be set and when the false title you have read or heard as having being read, archived, filed, recorded, and programmed, at the spot where this false title will finally be replaced by a true, authentic, and fitting title. Suppose that the *titleer* is this title: the word can claim to be that only when its legibility will have suspended its equivocation in the eye of the law [*la loi*]—for it is of law [*du droit*] that I have come to speak with you this evening—and where we will have had to decide if it might be spelled (of *orthography*, of law and writing, of justice and the law [*droit*] in relation to writing [*graphie*] have I come to exchange with you this evening) the *title* (. . .) *here* (*le titre y est*), a phrase of two (four) words or the *titleer* (*le titrier*) in just one word (or two). In the two cases of a complete sentence or a name, what assumes title-value will function like a name or even a proper name, and this will be the case even if the referential structure of this proper name is completely singular and paradoxical, as I will try to show in a while. Had I opted for the sentence—*the title (is) here (le titre y est)*—as title, this sentence would somehow become the name or proper name of a text I am supposed to sign; it would refer to this text across all sorts of other possible references and other semantic values it ostensibly shares with the same sentence—the title (is) here—that would be found elsewhere in another context. Naturally one of the complications here that happens to put the law to the test in playing and betting on it—for it is a game in which neither winner nor loser can ever be specified—is due to the fact that the word "title" is part of the title and that, in this phonetic writing across the audible element, the noun *titleer* happens at once to double, assemble together, and send away the univocality of the sentence. All the more since, now that the time has come for me to specify it—at least if only that were possible—the noun *titleer* would signify at least two things. In Old French a *titleer* (*titrier*) was a monk responsible for the archive of the titles of a monastery. He was an archivist, the archivist par excellence, for if every archivist must prevail over the order of titles—how can there be an archive without a title [*pas d'archives sans titre*]—what is to be said of a guardian of titles? But in a more recent and pejorative, devaluating meaning, what is of most interest to me, here, is that a titleer refers to a falsifier of titles, a forger of bogus titles, a fabricator of counterfeit titles, as we would almost say of counterfeiters in thinking of what is called *entitling* or *titrage* of money in a rather narrow sense.

I. "The Counterfeit"

Having decided to proceed in a more reflective than definitive manner, by way of exemplum, *récits* or samples of *récits* rather than by concepts, I thought first off that we might speak of the title of one of Baudelaire's brief *récits*. Despite its brevity, it defies every kind of résumé. It seems to be about two friends (of whom one is the narrator) who, in leaving a tobacco shop, meet a beggar. The narrator's friend gives him a false coin and brags about it to his friend who, lost in the spirals of reflection, finally explains why he cannot forgive him. The *récit* is entitled "La fausse monnaie" ("The Counterfeit"). For essential reasons that are bound to the referential structure of the title suspended the way it is, we cannot define, determine, or specify the indivisible trait binding this title to what it is supposed to relate to. On cursory reading it designates the false coin, in effect, at stake in the narrated account, not just of the real false coin or of the false coin in general, but even more generally, of this false coin as recited or narrated content that apparently forms the principal or major object of the fiction. But the title can be implied otherwise: this *récit* that is the discourse of the narrator, its narration as well as the *récit* signed Baudelaire are fictions or simulacra—more or less figuratively we might say—of the false coin. In order to limit myself to this first fold—there would be many more and more complex at that, but for lack of time I shall stick to this one—the title "The Counterfeit" ("La fausse monnaie") has at least two implications, two references: let's say roughly the story recounted by the text, the story of the counterfeit coin, *and* the fictional structure of the narrative text. It is divided and suspended, but in each case it designates the false currency, something like a forgery issued by a falsifier, by a titleer of sorts.

But that is not all—and yet, however, with the apparent complexity of the text that I am describing in this fashion, you must realize that I am restricting myself to a very summary analysis of the borders of this text. As soon as claiming to entitle the content of the story or even the referent of the content—the truly false coin—the title also entitles the textual fiction, its value at least for being equivocal. We cannot tell what it entitles; it is askew, cockeyed, and risks becoming the title itself, at least insofar as it is a title or an entitling border, of the false coin. It is a risk—but not for sure. And hardly for sure it remains undecided, imprecise, unspecified, always to be specified. Somewhat as if the title "The Counterfeit" uttered or let itself be uttered in the name of its personification: in refusing to let you know if I am the title of the story told (the story of the false coin) or of the narrative fiction (*récit as* false coin), I am entitling nothing precise; thus I am "The Counterfeit"; I am the title; I entitle only myself. I am no more than my own event, the performance of my title; yes, I am, myself, the title, "The Counterfeit." But this personification, this self-presentation in the first person is properly a specification that he does not give.[3] For, in order that the currency can be false money, it is essential to the structure of its guise as counterfeit not to be presented as is, but as coin *passing for* real money. The false money announced or denounced for what it personifies at the same time has nothing to do with what it is. In order to entitle or function as a title, the title cannot be presented in a present discourse; it cannot say, "There you see what I am and what I mean." For that, essential are its emplacement, its *topos* being suspended on the border, and its heterogeneity with respect to a discourse, its value as inscriptive trait structurally undecidable or, if you like, always *to be specified*. As a title, "The Counterfeit," a disturbing homonym of every other identical locution, of every other counterfeit, must be read without showing or disclosing itself as "The Counterfeit." The titleer, whom we will ascertain to be the faithful archivist of a religious institution or a falsifier bent on circulating his contraband within it, is always at work. In the same way "title (to be specified)" or "the titleer" utters, without uttering: I am—I entitle myself—true false title.

II. Le pré

But I stated that I found this example unconvincing for this evening's performance.

Concerned too about not putting on exhibit certain titles of mine that circulate more and more with a stamp resembling that of a false coin, I had still contemplated analyzing closely (*de près*) the title of this immense poem by Ponge called *Le pré*. I would have recalled the forces and practical violences of a proper noun suspended above a text treating in every one of its conditions the thing called the field as well as the *word pré*, the word *pré* as noun, with its nominal reference, and even still the fragment of the word *pré* as the present prefix in the word "present" and in so many others, the word *prêt* (ready) as an adjective (*le prêt* [loan] as noun is not treated thematically although in my opinion it has an organizing role around which all of *Le pré* [The Field] is indebted, and *La fabrique du pré* retains a more visible trace of it), the word *près* [near] as an adverbial or prepositional locution with all these signifying values, all these more or less thematic references identical not only in the unity of a *récit*, a myth, a fable, or a drama that we cannot describe here, but also in a brief, economical elliptical title: *Le pré*.

In terms of grammar, we can say that this title has a nominal form, but we can show that every title, even when it does not have the grammatical form of a noun (besides, which is extremely rare), produces a nominal effect, nominalizing—I would even say, an effect of the proper name. In the title of a title, *Le pré* condenses the whole network of motifs and tangled titles (the thing, "*pré*," the word "*pré*"), the words as a noun [*pré* (field), *prêt* (loan)], as prefixes and pieces of words (*pré-*), as adjective (*prêt*), as adverb (*près*). Poem of language that it is, *Le pré* praises all these referential trajectories, multiplying and crossing them, *en abyme* or buried under the border of a line that, in the text, separates the text itself, an internal and external border, in separating it from the body of the signature Francis Ponge, whose initials repeat those of *Fenouil* (Fennel) and *Prêle* (Horsetail) inside the poem, on the other side of the bar:

Save the initials, to be sure,
Since they are also those
Of *Fenouil* and of *Prêle*

Who tomorrow will grow above.

Francis Ponge

> But in speaking elliptically the law of the text, *Le pré*, the title "*Le pré*" names the text, calls and designates it, discloses it, and says (*sagt, zeigt*) it as just where everything in the writing of language grows, eats, presents, and is presented as *phusis*, then keeps in the grave. *Le pré* names, prenames, invites, calls (*heisst*), watches over, summons all the *pré*'s or *prê*'s of the text, but before the whole text as *pré*. And the *pré* as absolute pretext. In doing this the title not only induces you to read all the *fields, proximations,* or *loans* in sight displayed [*les* prés *ou* près *ou* prêts *posés, parés, et présents*] in the poem, all the accents that make it sing its song or the spellings that normalize it. It also gives you an order, it enjoins you—if at least you know how to read it; it makes the law, it bespeaks you without speaking, it gives you something to read: *je suis le pré*, I am the field, I present myself like the field and, if you want to know what field means, what *pré* means, what it is that *pré* says, you *must* read me right off (*d'abord*), you *must* begin by reading me, you *must* read and understand me precisely first (*préalablement*).
>
> Thus here the title is ready (*prêt*) to fabricate the law since the enigmatic reserve in the ellipse where it is kept—near the border, on the border, neither in nor out of the poem, suspended in its proper name.
>
> But you remarked it: it only makes the law right from a violence before the law. In violating the normality of discourse, in throwing into disorder the habitual functioning of reference, in abusing contextual indetermination to accumulate equivocation, in placing about the name the abandonment [*le désert*] of the sentence, in accumulating in the oracular power of the proper name the entire resource of mute sentences, it founds its own state, its own legitimacy, the imperium of law legitimized over violence—but a violence right away that is the economy of the language of writing. It is this madness of the title that concerns me tonight, this stroke of force laying down the law in the course of a rape, and of an incessant violation, a rape perpetuated across the law.
>
> Across the law? What does that mean? If I translate "across the law" by "rape of the law" we have yet to know whether rape *of* the law signifies the law violated or the law violating. The madness of the title is perhaps that no choice exists between these two possibilities. Because there is no

choice signifies perhaps not that we are limited to one of these possibilities, but that the two are as necessary as incompatible, obligating according to the inflexible stricture [*loi*] of a double law and a *double bind*.⁴

III. The Madness of the Title

In forgoing both "La fausse monnaie" and *Le pré*, I have chosen recourse to another exemplary title for this evening's performance. It is about the title of a "*récit*" by Maurice Blanchot. For this title of "*récit*" forms one of the most problematic stakes of the text. If I have finally chosen this example it is because the "story," told according to one of the most unwarranted narrative structures, is a showdown with the law. The narrator—at least he who says *I*, who never happens to form a *récit* and therefore to become a narrator any more than he who happens to say "I," at the outer limit, to account for his identity or identify himself in the way that the lawmen ask of him—the presumed [*prétendu*] narrator, then, rather than the so-called [*soi-disant*] narrator, has accounts to settle with the law, at the request and provocation of the law at least according to two figures or two forms: one of a sort of feminine allegory that he calls the Law and another of doctors who could be called forensic pathologists and who, in the name of society, summon him to tell a true *récit* of the accident that befell him or of the aggression victimizing him. Because of this instance of the law I choose this example.

In effect, the very schematic and preliminary analysis I am venturing before you this evening sticks to the border of a work—which I only project—on law [*droit*] and literature that I would like to entitle "Du droit à la littérature."⁵ At issue would be, for example, the history and structure of juridico-literary relations. Here I will define neither the premises nor even the most general perspectives of such a problematic. I would not have the time to do so. I shall have to be happy with this: what I am sketching here in the title of the title would perhaps claim place inside the more systematic analysis of a sequence or of a grand historical configuration of juridico-literary procedures: what institutes a new relation in Western Europe among, let us say, first off, literary production; then, positive law [*le droit positif*]; and finally, the critical institutions of evaluation: of the traditional guard, of archivation, entitling and titled legitimization, of the institution of competencies, all of which the *Universitas* is the form and premise par excellence. The model of the *Universitas* in which we work in the West—more or less well for some time now—has been set in place, with of course important but secondary variants in respect to a grand principal structure, at a moment when—and in relation with—the inscription in positive law of the fundamental decrees that order the propriety of works, copyright, reproduction, translation. This event, of which neither the structure nor content can I describe here, has had an essential, internal, and decisive relation with what others would call the inside most intrinsic to the production of literary and artistic forms in general.

So the instance of the title (whether of the title of the work, the corpus, the legitimizing title in general, of the title authorizing the author's authority, guaranteeing the evaluation, evaluating criticism, etc.) situates the spot or one of the essential borderlines and therefore the line of rapport, the most apparent *Bezug* let us say, between writing and law [*loi*], between so-called literary writing and law [*droit*]. About this general perspective in which I am involved elsewhere, here I will say nothing more (we could, if you wish, come back to this during the discussion). I simply wanted to open the discussion in order, precisely, to justify it right away and to legitimize the choice of my example in order, then, to account for what entitles me to speak to you about *La folie du jour* [*The Madness of the Day*] by Maurice Blanchot.

Following normal appearances, *La folie du jour* is normalized by literary and editorial law, as the title of a work, of a book of small format published, as the date of its copyright by deposit of duty copy indicates, in 1973. On its cover, under the name of the author and above the name of the editorial enterprise conventions prescribe us to recognize the title *La folie du jour* (Montpellier: Fata Morgana).

Title to be specified. It must be specified and made precise, but how? A title is always an economy awaiting *its* determination, its specificity, its *Bestimmtheit*, what it determines and what determines it. Determining and determined, determination always *returns* to it. It returns in the direction whence it is responsible *de jure* and in the direction that has always promised return from elsewhere, and according to a very unique mode of return.

Of the immense reading that the unending book promotes, and whose very structure defies every border and frame, I shall retain here only a few traits worthy of showing how and in what way, in playing on its law [*jouant sa loi*], *La folie du jour* is a madness of the title. To use the expression "stake one's law" (*jouer sa loi*) is the very equivocation of import to me. To stake the law is to twist or transgress the law, but it also can mean to repeat or mime one's law, and at the same time. In both cases it is to summon the law as such. So it is that the law of the border is itself borderless: tantamount to saying that it never summons [*comparaît*] itself as such.

What therefore are the irregularities [*dérèglements*], and what are the laws of these irregularities that, in the case of *La folie du jour*, emplace the title as the law while forbidding it to function normally, to be determined in precise specification, to be identified and to summon [*rassembler*] in being summoned?

I restrict myself to the typical traits of this turnaround that goes out of control [*dérèglement*]. Such maddening twists spin around this: *the sense of the title is a certain manner of not having any and its event is one of not taking place*. No more meaning and/is no more place, therefore.[6]

No more meaning (*pas de sens*). I recognize in *La folie du jour* its title-value, its title titled for reason of its *place* and of the juridical conventions that its *topos* obeys. No criterion of internal reading (either linguistic or semantic) allows me to discuss or contest the title of its title. Met elsewhere, the same words, "la folie du jour"—which moreover do not form, strictly speaking, a statement—will not have title-value, whether separated or detached from the book, the corpus or from the context born in mind or, on the contrary, that simply they are found written *inside*. Thus in the text bearing this title, "La folie du jour," the expression "la folie du jour" is to be read at least once. And evidently it (*elle*) does not have the function of a title: "But often I lay dying without saying anything. In the end, I grew convinced that I saw the madness of the day face-to-face. That was the truth: the light was going mad, the brightness had lost all reason [*bon sens*] . . . " (*FJ* 22 [*MD* 11]). Despite their apparent identity, these two occurrences of the expression "la folie du jour" have absolutely heterogeneous functions. It is not because one of them is taken in a phrastic remark ("I grew convinced that I saw the madness of the day face-to-face") that the title seems to have been drawn off a fragment. Were the whole sentence retained as a title as it can happen to be in certain cases, the entire sentence would have a sort of nominal role as title and value heterogeneous to that of the "same" sentence inside the book. Here, then, topology poses the law. It cannot be said that the two locutions are simply homonyms. To a certain point they are synonyms although their mode, function, and *value* are not reducible one to the other. In the title the locution allows a supplementary meaning to be grafted to it, which reads thus: this is a title, I am the title. Then the signatory or, if you prefer, the locutor is not the same. *In* the book, "La folie du jour" is signed—so to speak—by the narrator, or at least by whoever says "I" from the very first word onward and, besides, by the person who does not happen, that is the whole story, to become a narrator, to form a *récit*, and even, at the limit of stating *I*, to be identified under his "I."[7] On the other hand, the responsibility for the title is not incumbent upon the supposed narrator—required elsewhere by lawmakers inside the "*récit*." The title, we must, rightfully, suppose that the author, Maurice Blanchot, is responsible for it before the law—publisher, copyright, etc. But if the law obliges one to suppose the real and identifiable author, the title is nonetheless a fiction (Blanchot does not sign this title as he signs a check or a testimony before the examining magistrate). Presumably by a real author, the title still is part of a so-called literary fiction; but it does not play a role [*partie*] in the same fashion as what is found inside the same fiction, in, for instance, the other occurrence of "la folie du jour." There is a fiction nominating and guaranteeing the unity of the fictional corpus in which it has no role. It must be found on the outer border of what it entitles.

Separated from the border, the two occurrences must nevertheless belong to the same set, to what one calls the same context, here in the form of a corpus or a work: this book. And according to a certain rapport of ordered proximity. This relation is not citational. In the duplicity of this occurrence it is impossible to say which is the original and which repeats the other. This iteration without origin grows hollow or unfolds its abyss according to the measure of this pace-of-(non-)meaning (*ce pas-de-sens*) that oversteps polysemy toward a borderless dissemination, toward the borderless border of the disseminal text. In order to see, let us try counting the possible meanings of the expression *la folie du jour*; let us try counting with them, recounting them, taking account of them, accounting for them.

(1) If we pay heed to the idiomatic syntagm "du jour," which in

French signifies "today," "here and now" (as in the locution "the order of the day," "the man of the hour" to mark the marking or remarkable thing of the present hour). *La folie du jour* is what makes an event today, that of the hour, today and of no other, and even that of the day today as the place and date of the event, and in a way, its signature. And in the text thus entitled there is enough to support this meaning. At stake is the event or advent of madness, of going mad at such an instant. Where do we situate the event? Did it ever really take place? Whatever the enigma, the event is named several times, and even in a certain place, as the order of the day. We simply cannot tell whether it took place, what taking place means, or even if what had taken place was no more than a vision. You can read (*FJ* 18–20)⁸ the passage beginning with "Dehors, j'eus une courte vision," which is closed by "Tout cela était réel, notez-le." In the center the one who tries to say "I" explains, "This brief scene excited me to the point of delirium. I was undoubtedly not able to explain it to myself fully and yet I was sure of it, that I had seized the moment when the day, having stumbled against a true event, would begin hurrying to its end. Here it comes, I said to myself, the end is coming, something is happening, the end is beginning."

(2) A second meaning comes forth immediately to parasitize the preceding. The event of the day (madness) is not only what happens *this day*, even today; it is the order *of* the day itself ("I had seized the moment when the day, having stumbled against a true event, would begin hurrying to its end. Here it comes, I said to myself . . . "). An event of the day, therefore, as present time and the possibility of the event, of the present, of the moment. A presence of the present, happening from the possibility of something happening, to appear and to take place. An event of the eventuality and possibility of the *récit*, day to day.

(3) It passes, is passed, and passes by the day as *day*,⁹ if you will, in the day as in *daylight*,¹⁰ the ether of evidence, the milieu of visibility. It is justly the most evident meaning of a text that recounts or fails to recount the impossible endeavor to make a "*récit*," of the *récit* of a traumatic event that almost costs the *sight*—therefore the day—of the one who is supposed to say "I," the person whom I do not call the narrator: for following this event when he risked his sight—or the day, he is found enshrouded; in a hospital or police institution in which the official representatives of the

society and figures of the law are exacting from him a *récit* of the events, in their alleging that, given his title (as a writer) and therefore his competence, he must be able to furnish an ordered *récit* of himself. He tells the *récit* without telling it; presently we shall return to it. The madness of the day is also in French the madness of *daylight*[11] from which he was almost deprived and which therefore strikes him more than ever ("I nearly lost my sight, because someone crushed glass in my eyes" [*FJ* 21/*MD* 11]).

(4) This fourth meaning is still divided, all of which is going to give to "day" a fourth, fifth, sixth, indeed a seventh meaning.

We shall up"date" a week of meanings. The day as "sight" or as "vision" (vision as a visual perception *or* a quasi-hallucinating apparition) is what we see, surely. The day is what we see right off. But it is also light itself, designating both the visual faculty (as they say to designate the eye, the organ of sight) and the visibility or possibility of sight. Now the possibility of seeing, daylight as element of visibi*lity* and milieu of the visible, that day is not visible, no more than the sun of Plato. In this sense, it is night, blindness—what happens to the day or makes happen to the day. And in this text there is a history of the day, an *internal* history—of interiorization, indeed of internment, of the revolution of the day that hastens toward its end as soon as it appears. This turning, this career, this course is also a story of creation—when there was light—and resurrection. There is a madness inherent to the day like its story, its becoming-night, its passage into its contrary. Light is mad because it is black; it loses its meaning and all "common sense." And this madness will have been truth. He who almost "lost his sight" thus enters into the "shocking cruelty of the day"; he can "not look, but . . . not help looking," and he notes it directly:

Once the glass had been removed, they slipped a thin film under my eyelids and over my eyelids they laid walls of cotton wool. I was not supposed to talk because talking pulled at the anchors of the bandage. "You were asleep," the doctor told me later. I was asleep! I had to hold my own against the light of seven days—a fine conflagration! Yes, seven days at once, the seven deadly lights, become the spark of a single moment, were calling me to account. Who would have imagined that? At times I said to myself: "This is death. In spite of everything, it's really worth it, it's impressive." But often I lay dying without saying anything. In the end, I grew convinced that I saw the madness of the day face-to-face. That was the truth: the light was going mad, the brightness had lost all reason [*bon sens*]; it assailed me irrationally, without control, without purpose. That discovery bit straight through my life. [*FJ* 21–23/*MD* 11–12]

(5) Another meaning, but now I no longer can count them, a summary being impossible. In the paragraph I have just read, you remarked that "accounts" were demanded.

If it accepts polysemy, the law, the law of reason or the reason as law demands, requires that we even distinguish among our senses. Aristotle explains it quite well. Law demands that we at least be able to enumerate the identities of meanings and articulate them among each other in a calculable narration, in an account, in a *récit* (*erzählen*) or accounting (*zählen*). But here the account proves to be impossible. Either singular or plural, it is the day that demands an account: "Yes, seven days at once, the seven deadly lights, become the spark of a single moment, were calling me to account."

Therefore the day is also the law—which demands an account, as representatives of the law are going to demand a *récit* of the person who says *I*, to recount and account for what happened to him. On the other hand, the law does not only appear in guise of its representatives; it appears in person as a feminine figure in a duel of love and death with the one who somehow manages to say *I*. Identification, then, between the law and the day, the days (there are seven, in seven meanings, as in the *récit* of Genesis, but also deadly like the sins). Thus an identification is remarked among the day of the madness of the day and the law, the madness of law who is also madness of law [*droit*] and reason. It is especially remarkable in a long sequence (*FJ* 23–29/*MD* 12–14) that interprets the force of law, authority (it is also the authority of the author, his competence, his entitling legitimacy) as a possibility of seeing, surveilling, having under its eyes: synoptic tables, panoramas, panopticons using the entire day. So in this sequence the word "day" becomes richer still and, if we may remark, it twists maddeningly once again in overstepping another supplementary (non)meaning [*à faire un pas de sens supplémentaire*].

(6) For essential reasons we cannot account for the economy of the idiom, of the economy of the economy, of the *idion* of the *oikos*, of the law of *oikos*. Now in the French idiom, "jour" compounds with two locutions having to do with *birth*, if not with resurrection: "to see the day" (*voir le jour*), to be born, and "give the day" (*donner le jour*), to bear or engender. As it is a legitimate sense, if you look over the semantic register of birth with all the other meanings of "day," you can go on forever. So the author-

ity of the representatives of the law that are posed here as forensic pathologists is held to have everything under their eye, but it is he, the patient, who tries to say "I," and it is he, in saying "I," who gives them the day; put otherwise, it is he who engenders them: he gives birth to the law that surveils and persecutes him in exacting of the "instructed" person that he is (the word returns periodically to recall what his title and competence are) a true *récit*.

I was an educated man! But perhaps not all the time. Talented? Where were these talents that were made to speak like gowned judges sitting on benches, ready [*prêts*] to condemn me day and night?

I like the doctors quite well, and I did not feel belittled by their doubts. The annoying thing was that their authority loomed larger by the hour. . . . Throwing open my rooms, they would say, "Everything here belongs to us." . . . They would challenge my story: "Talk," and my story would put itself at their service. In haste, I would rid myself of myself. I distributed my blood, my innermost being among them, lent [*prêtais*] them the universe, gave them the day [*leur donnais le jour*]. . . . I reduced myself to them. The whole of me passed in full view before them, and when at last nothing was present but my perfect nothingness and there was nothing more to see, they ceased to see me too. Very irritated, they stood up and cried out, "All right, where are you? Where are you hiding? Hiding is forbidden, it is an offense," etc. [*FJ* 27–29/*MD* 14]

Therefore it is he who gives the right of day to the persecuting law, and even later, the Law herself will say, "'Oh, I see the day, oh God,' etc." [*FJ* 34/*MD* 17]. He is *before* the law that he *pro*duces and *pro*creates.

We are reading for the moment, I recall, only the title and, even, a sole word of the title, "day." Were we to consider the diverse syntactical possibilities of the expression "the madness of the day" (*folie du jour*), polysemy would be driven mad over and over again. The text plays on the double genitive. The word "jour" happens to determine the madness that happens one day, or that happens in daylight, but it is also the madness belonging to the day, to the maddening daylight losing "all common sense." Thus there is freed a step over supplementary (non)meaning belonging at once to the series, to the law of the series of others and crossing its border in a heterogeneous space.

(7) And "la folie du *jour*" can also be understood as the madness of "jour," of the word or the sense of "jour," the madness that has justly to

do with this dispersion without source or unity, without common reason, without proportion, without *logos*, without common sense, without the sense or direction of meaning or of the word "day," or of the noun "day." That is a word, a name without sense, without law, out(side of) law; and this outlaw makes the law. That is the madness: that *logos* is mad, that the discourse of reason is unable to assure itself of its meaning, of the *single* meaning of the day and, if not of univocality, at least of totalization of the remembering order, even of remembrance of the history of the polysemy of the day, of a day. From then on the madness of the day is also the madness of the word, of the noun "day," a madness of this titular element insofar as a simulacrum of unity, a simulacrum of the law, a simulacrum of the trial that at once has the appeal of authority, gives daylight to law while playing the law, maddening and twisting the judgment and the *critical decision*. We can no longer account for the economy of the linguistic, verbal, and even nominal instance that produces the effect of the title. Madness not only inhabits the meaning of "day," but the word "day" as a nominative of the title, that is to say as a proper noun between quotation marks. There is madness: a proper name between quotation marks; and if the word "day" is not between quotation marks on the cover of the book, the text will have imposed the public reading of these quotation marks. The question remains: what does the law make of a citation without quotation marks?

A step over the border of meaning [*pas de sens*], I was saying, in the title, and as I was adding: in a certain way the title will not have taken place. For a title to take place, a border must at least separate it from what it entitles, and the line of this limit must be lawfully indivisible from a line. Now all the writing of *La folie du jour* is made to stake this law. According to juridical conventions, what appears to be the first line of the *récit*, its upper border if you will, is found to bear only the double (neither the original nor the citation) of the "same" false *incipit* that, inside, if it can be said, of the "*récit*," responds to the request of the forensic pathologists. Here is the "beginning" of the book. You see the necessity for the display:

I am not learned; I am not ignorant. I have known joys. That is saying too little: I am alive, and this life gives me the greatest pleasure. And what about death? When I die (perhaps any minute now), I will feel immense pleasure. [*FJ* 9/*MD* 5]

Now on the next to last page of the book, we are born to read that this first line, this first page was only the *récit* begun at the injunction or request of the representatives of the law, all leading you to defy any mark of the true beginning of the book that rolls itself into *a part greater than the whole*. Here are the three last paragraphs of the book, the last, at least in copyright, but still those preceding the first:

I had been asked: Tell us "*just* exactly" what happened. A *récit*? I began: I am not learned; I am not ignorant. I have known joys. That is saying too little. I told them the whole story and they listened, it seems to me with interest, at least in the beginning. But the end was a surprise to all of us. "That was the beginning," they said. "Now get down to the facts." How so? The *récit* was over!

This paragraph, which is only a part of the general *récit*, envelops here the whole *récit* as one of its folded parts, and it collapses the upper border, the incipit of the book, upon itself. There is a first invagination incorporating the border and internalizing the outer front of the first sentence, the one looking toward the title as an internal surface. The external surface has become the internal surface. But that is not all. The same invagination is going to internalize the other border, this time the lower border, that of the last word. I take up my reading where I had left it off.

How so? The *récit* was over!
  I had to acknowledge that I was not capable of forming a *récit* out of these events. I had lost the sense of the story: that happens in a good many illnesses. But this explanation only made them more insistent. Then I noticed for the first time that there were two of them and that this distortion of the traditional method, even though it was explained by the fact that one of them was an eye doctor, the other a specialist in mental illness, constantly gave our conversation the character of an authoritarian interrogation, overseen and controlled by a strict set of rules. Of course neither of them was the chief of police. But because there were two of them, there were three, and this third remained firmly convinced, I am sure, that a writer, a man who speaks and who reasons with distinction, is always capable of recounting the facts that he remembers.
  A *récit*? No. No *récit*, never again [*pas de récit, plus jamais*]. [*FJ* 36–38/*MD* 18]

This "last" sentence, this apparently final line figures right at the lower border of the body. Though it speaks of the resolution no longer to write *récits*, it remains a part of the internal surface, so to speak, of its border, of a *récit* finished no more than a *récit* that did not take place, whose demand was made but which the ostensible narrator could not perform in a competent way, yet which he told at once in an incompetent and more than competent fashion, in a successful non-performance. Now in restricting ourselves to the structure of the last trait of the line, of this still divisible border, the "A *récit?*" (including its question mark) is still the double (neither original nor citation) of "A *récit?*" that opened, two paragraphs above, what I then called the invagination of the upper border: "A *récit?* I began: I am not learned; I am not ignorant. . . . " Folding over the lower border above within the lower invaginated border, the last sentence, what in copyright and in all critical competence is called the last sentence, produces another invagination crossing the first according to the figure of a chiasm. This doubly chiasmatic invagination of the borders does not allow us to discern in the reading the indivisible limit of a beginning from an end. It carries away the condition for every dictatorial emergence of a title, the title implying these critical effects of the border, the possibility of discerning indivisible borders. All the more since the titling locution, "La folie du jour," is the undiscerned double of its occurrence inside the corpus. There you see why in all rigor the title exercises its authority only in order not to take place, to remain interminably "to be specified,"[12] interminably undecidable, reserved, in reserve in the ellipsis of a nominal formula that economizes the whole.

The economy of the undecidable is not to the contrary incompatible with dissemination. Perhaps I have not underlined it enough (for want of time), but all that I have remarked of the title could have been assembled together under the title of economy and even of political economy. The title draws its title-value from its power to produce value and surplus-value through the economic operation, the operation of economy—or thrift and potentiation of surplus. And this is not tautological; it is rather a tautological ruse and the law of this *oikos*, of this *oikonomia*, and I believe as I have at least suggested, it is far from being simple and direct; it is not ruled by a sole orthogonal line. When surplus-value expands as far as the abyss, the law [*droit*], economy, and politics that the title of the title calls forth have to be reconsidered.

I never demand of philology, and even less of what others call etymology, the guarantee of a concept. On the contrary, and Heidegger recalls it here and there, from what is given to think one can look both to history of the language and to the sciences that, in order to deal with it, must suppose it. There we must demand of the sciences of languages the right of their titles. Perhaps, and from what we have just glimpsed in the madness of day, or of the title, or the noun, we can accede better to such etymological hypotheses about the word, about the noun "title." Through the Latin *titulus,* some refer to a radical contained in the Greek *tiō* (I esteem, I evaluate, honor, valorize), whence *timē,* evaluation, value, price to pay, juridical estimation, for example, of a penalty or a debt. And with the properly *axiomatic* register of economo-politico-juridical evaluation, some take it back to the Sanskrit root *ci* where entire folds of meaning are assembled together in the idea of *re-assembling,* justly of reunion, colligation in the mind, on the inside: whence the meanings of to remark, to research, to recognize, to pursue, to venerate, to honor, etc. This motif about the assembling evaluation, the axio-economy that goes to its limit, to the *bewahren* of *Wahrheit,* to this truth of which Heidegger says, in a sense that is neither void, contradictory, nor dialectical, that it is nontruth. *Die Wahrheit ist Un-wahrheit* (in "The Origin of the Work of Art"). In the *economic* violence of its ellipse, the title is the truth without truth of what it re-assembles. There is no title to resemble or reassemble, and what we have just proven is that a reassembling never takes place.

  One more step and I leave you. *La folie du jour* has a history. I do not know if it can be accounted for. Before appearing in the form of what rightfully is called a book, *La folie du jour* was published in a review, nearly (*près*) a quarter of a century before. But was this the same *La folie du jour*?

  No semblance of transformation in the body of the text from one version to another, from the review to the book.

  And yet, the title was otherwise, and because of the history of the title I have spoken of the two versions. At least. What was the first title? In all rigor it remains difficult to say. The so-called first version appeared in the review *Empédocle* in May 1949. This review, which published only several numbers, bore on its table of contents, on its cover—and I would like to have drawn your attention to all these frames and all these juridico-political dimensions of *protokollon* (of the first page)—announcing its authors and titles, this: Maurice Blanchot, *A récit?* On the table of contents, the title was therefore "*A récit?*" with this question mark that makes of the title a doublet of this double occurrence that we took up a while ago. The fold taken, I leave you now to complicate for yourselves the very chiasmatic invagination of the borders in the account of its history, in the story of its inscriptions and erasures keeping the memory of the inscriptions and former titles, the instance of the copyright happening to make an archive of the whole textual body in the national or world library. Were I to be authorized to abuse your patience further, I would turn again another page to show you that on the inside of the same review, so to speak, the table of contents is reproduced entirely, and this time, the title *A récit* no longer bears a question mark, no more than in the third occurrence of the same title, above the first line of the so-called *récit* accounted for before us. In effect there can be read: *A récit* by Maurice Blanchot.

Of all these subversions playing about the law, can we esteem that they mock the law, that they transgress or reveal its precarious historicity? Not at all, or all these sophistications would not be possible; they would have no force without the instance of the law they seem to defy; they would have no reason for it without drawing Reason from it, without provoking it—to produce it in twisting it, this very reason whose madness they demonstrate rather than opposing to it, from the outside, another madness. Precisely this madness of the law, this *hubris* of the title, this denatured extravagance of the entitling authority is called forth here and is recounted under this mad title: la folie du jour.

A lecture, you will ask, or a reading? Never again. In sum I have been invited, let us not say summoned, but honored by an invitation. In the title of a lecturer invited to present a discourse provided with a specific title. And to bind my discourse to my title, that is to say to fill in contract or promise the title in blank for which I have been accredited: *title (to be specified)*. Is it the same, now? Will I have been specific? Under what title have I spoken to you? And by what entitlement? It is a bit late for me to ask such questions, but perhaps you will continue to ask them yourselves.

All the more since the title is here, you will give it to me, it was never lacking.

Note: Paper presented in July 1979 on the occasion of an international colloquium on *Genre* that was organized at Strasbourg by J.-J. Chartin, Ph. Lacoue-Labarthe, J.-L. Nancy, and S. Weber, under the auspices of the University of Strasbourg and Johns Hopkins University (Baltimore). The first version of this text was published in a bilingual edition by the journal *Glyph* 7 (1980) and in its English translation by the journal *Critical Inquiry* (Fall 1980), then in a volume edited by W. J. T. Mitchell (*On Narrative* [Chicago/London: University of Chicago Press, 1981]). I want to thank the author of the English translation, Avital Ronell. [Ronell's translation (absent some omitted paragraphs) was then published "with some editorial modifications made in light of the revised version published in 1986 in *Parages*" in *Acts of Literature*, ed. Derek Attridge (New York: Routledge, 1992). This version has been revised to follow the text published in the revised edition of *Parages* published in 2003.—Ed.]

The Law of Genre

Translated by Avital Ronell

Genres are not to be mixed.
I will not mix genres.
I repeat: genres are not to be mixed. I will not mix them.
Now suppose I let these utterances [*énoncés*] resonate all by themselves.
Suppose: I abandon them to their fate, I set free their random virtualities and turn them over to your audience, to your auditory grasp, to whatever mobility they retain and you bestow upon them to engender effects of all kinds without my having to stand behind them.
I merely said, and then repeated: genres are not to be mixed; I will not mix them.
As long as I release these utterances (which others might call speech acts) in a form yet scarcely determined, given the open context out of which I have just let them be grasped from "my" language—as long as I do this, you may find it difficult to choose among several interpretative options. They are legion, as I could demonstrate. They form an open and essentially unpredictable series. But you may be tempted by *at least* two types of audience, two modes of interpretation, or, if you prefer to give these words more of a chance, then you may be tempted by two different genres of hypothesis. Which ones?
On the one hand, it could be a matter of a fragmentary discourse whose propositions would be of the descriptive, constative, and neutral genre. In such a case, I would have named the operation that consists of

"genres are not to be mixed." I would have designated this operation in a neutral fashion without evaluating it, without recommending or advising against it, certainly without binding anyone to it. Without claiming to lay down the law or to make this an act of law, I merely would have summoned up, in a fragmentary utterance, the sense of a practice, an act or event, as you wish: which is what sometimes happens when we revert to "genres are not to be mixed." With reference to the same case, and to a hypothesis of the same type, same mode, same genre—or same order: when I said, "I will not mix genres," you may have discerned a foreshadowing description—I am not saying a prescription—the descriptive designation telling in advance what will transpire, predicting it in the constative mode or genre, that is, it will happen thus, I will not mix genres. The future tense describes, then, what will surely take place, as you yourselves can judge; but for my part it does not constitute a commitment. I am not making you a promise here, nor am I issuing myself an order or invoking the authority of some law to which I am resolved to submit myself. In this case, the future tense does not set the time of a performative *speech act*[1] of a promising or ordering type.

But another hypothesis, another type of audience, and another interpretation would have been no less legitimate. "Genres are not to be mixed" could strike you as a sharp order. You might have heard it resound the elliptical but all the more authoritarian summons to a law of a "do" or "do not" that, as everyone knows, occupies the concept or constitutes the value of *genre*. As soon as the word "genre" is sounded, as soon as it is heard, as soon as one attempts to conceive it, a limit is drawn. And when a limit is established, norms and interdictions are not far behind: "Do," "Do not" says "genre," the word "genre," the figure, the voice, or the law of genre. And this can be said of genre in all genres, be it a question of a generic or a general determination of what one calls "nature" or *phusis* (for example, a biological *genre* in the sense of *gender/genus* or the human *genre*, a genre of all that is in general), or be it a question of a typology designated as nonnatural and depending on laws or orders that were once held to be opposed to *phusis* according to those values associated with *tekhnē, thesis, nomos* (for example, an artistic, poetic, or literary genre). But the whole enigma of genre springs perhaps most closely from within this parti(cipa)tion between the two genres of genre that, neither separable nor inseparable, form an odd couple of one without the other in which each evenly serves the other a citation to appear in the figure of the other, simultaneously and indiscernibly saying "I" and "we," me the genre, we genres, without it being possible to think that the "I" is a species of the genre "we." For who would have us believe that we, we two, for example, would form a genre or belong to one? Thus, as soon as genre announces itself, one must respect a norm, one must not cross a line of demarcation, one must not risk impurity, anomaly, or monstrosity. And so it goes in all cases, whether or not this law of genre be interpreted as a determination or perhaps even as a destination of *phusis*, and regardless of the weight or range imputed to *phusis*. If a genre is what it is, or if it is supposed to be what it is destined to be by virtue of its *telos*, then "genres are not to be mixed"; one *should not* mix genres, one *owes it to oneself not* to get mixed up in mixing genres. Or, more rigorously: genres should not intermix. And if it should happen that they do intermix, by accident or through transgression, by mistake or through a lapse, then this should confirm, since, after all, we are speaking of "mixing," the essential purity of their identity. This purity belongs to the typical axiom: it is a law of the law of genre, whether or not the law is, as one feels justified in saying, "natural." This normative position and this evaluation are inscribed and prescribed even at the threshold of the "thing itself," if something of the genre "genre" can be so named. And so it follows that you might have taken the second sentence in the first person, "I will not mix genres," as a vow of obedience, as a docile response to the injunction coming from the law of genre. In place of a constative description, you would then hear a promise, an oath; you would grasp the following respectful commitment: I promise you that I will not mix genres, and, through this act of pledging utter faithfulness to my commitment, I will be faithful to the law of genre, since, by its very nature, the law invites and commits me in advance not to mix genres. By publishing my response to the imperious call of the law, I would correspondingly commit myself to be responsible.

Unless, of course, I were actually implicated in a wager, a challenge, an impossible bet—in short, a situation that would exceed the matter of merely engaging a commitment from me. And suppose for a moment that it were impossible not to mix genres. What if there were, lodged within the heart of the law itself, a law of impurity or a principle of contamination? And suppose the condition for the possibility of the law were the *a priori* of a counter-law, an axiom of impossibility that would confound its sense, order, and reason?

I have just proposed an alternative between two interpretations. I did not do so, as you can imagine, in order to check myself [*m'y arrêter*]. The line or trait that seemed to separate the two bodies of interpretation is affected *straightaway* by an essential disruption that, for the time being, I shall let you name or qualify in any way you care to: as internal division of the trait, impurity, corruption, contamination, decomposition, perversion, deformation, even cancerization, generous proliferation, or degenerescence. All these disruptive "anomalies" are engendered—and this is their common law, the lot or site they share [*partagent*]—by repetition. One might even say by *citation* or re-citation [*ré-cit*], provided that the restricted use of these two words is not a call to strict generic order. A citation in the strict sense implies all sorts of contextual conventions, precautions, and protocols in the mode of reiteration, of coded signs, such as quotation marks or other typographical devices used for writing a citation. The same holds no doubt for the *récit* as a form, mode, or genre of discourse, even—and I shall return to this—as a literary type. And yet the law that protects the usage, in *stricto sensu*, of the words *citation* and *récit* is threatened intimately and in advance by a counter-law that constitutes this very law, renders it possible, conditions it, and thereby renders it impossible—for reasons of edges in the waters [*parages*] on which we shall run aground in just a moment—to edge through, to edge away from, or to hedge around the counter-law itself. The law and the counter-law serve each other citations summoning each other to appear, and each recites the other in this proceeding [*procès*]. There would be no cause for concern if one were rigorously assured of being able to distinguish with rigor between a citation and a non-citation, a *récit* and a non-*récit*, or a repetition within the form of one or the other.

I shall not undertake to demonstrate, assuming it is still possible, why you were unable to decide whether the sentences with which I opened this presentation and marked this context were or were not repetitions of a citational type; or whether they were or were not of the performative type; or certainly whether they were, both of them, together—and each time together—the one or the other. For perhaps someone has noticed that, from one repetition to the next, a change had insinuated itself into the relationship between the two initial utterances. The punctuation had been slightly modified, as had the content of the second independent clause. Theoretically, this barely noticeable shift could have created a mutual independency between the interpretative alternatives that might have tempted you to opt for one or the other, or for one and the other of these two sentences. A particularly rich combinatory of possibilities would thus ensue, which, in order not to exceed my time limit and out of respect for the law of genre and of the audience, I shall abstain from recounting. I am simply going to assume a certain relationship between what has just now happened and the origin of literature, as well as its aborigine or its abortion, to cite one of our hosts, Philippe Lacoue-Labarthe.

Provisionally claiming for myself the authority of such an assumption, I shall let our field of vision contract as I limit myself to a sort of species of the genre "genre." I shall focus on this genre of genre that is generally supposed, and always a bit too rashly, not to be part of nature, of *phusis*, but rather of *tekhnē*, of the arts, still more narrowly of poetry, and most particularly of literature. But at the same time, I take the liberty to think that, while limiting myself thus, I exclude nothing, at least in principle and de jure—the relationships here no longer being those of extension, from exemplary individual to species, from species to genre as genus or from the genre of genre to genre in general; rather, as we shall see, these relationships are a whole order apart. What is at stake, in effect, is exemplarity and its whole *enigma*—in other words, as the word *enigma* indicates, the *récit*—which works through the logic of the example.

Before going about putting a certain example to the test, I shall attempt to formulate, in a manner as elliptical, economical, and formal as possible, what I shall call the law of the law of genre. It is precisely a principle of contamination, a law of impurity, an economy of the *parasite*. In the code of set theory, if I may use it at least figuratively, I would speak of a sort of *participation without belonging*—a taking part in without being part of, without having membership in a set. With the inevitable dividing of the trait that marks membership, the boundary of the set comes to form, by invagination, an internal pocket larger than the whole; and the outcome of this division and of this abounding remains as singular as it is limitless.

To demonstrate this, I shall hold to the leanest generalities. But I should like to justify this initial indigence or asceticism as well as possible. For example, I shall not enter into the passionate debate that poetics has brought forth on the theory and the history of genre-theory, on the critical history of the concept of genre from Plato to the present. My stance is motivated by these considerations: in the first place, we now have at our disposal some remarkable and, of late, handsomely enriched works dealing either with primary texts or critical analyses. I am thinking especially of the journal *Poètique*, of its issue entitled "Genres" (32), and of Genette's opening essay, "Genres, 'Types,' Modes." From yet another point of view, *The Literary Absolute* has already created quite a stir in this context, and everything that I shall risk here should perhaps resolve itself in a modest annotation on the margins of this magistral work that I assume you have read. I could further justify my abstention or my abstinence here simply by acknowledging the terminological luxury or rapture as well as the taxonomic exuberance that debates of this kind, in a manner by no means fortuitous, have sparked: I feel completely powerless to contain this fertile proliferation—and not only because of time constraints. I shall put forth, instead, *two* principal *motives*, hoping thereby to justify my keeping to scant preliminary generalities at the edge of this problematic.

To what do these two motives essentially relate? In its most recent phase—and this much is certainly clear in Genette's propositions—the most advanced critical axis has led to a rereading of the entire history of genre-theory. This rereading has been inspired by the perception—and it must be said, despite the initial denial [*dénégation*], by the correction—of two types of misconstruing or confusion. On the one hand, and this will be the first motive or ground for my abstention, Plato and Aristotle have been subjected to considerable deformation, as Genette reminds us, insofar as they have been viewed in terms alien to their thinking, and even in terms that they themselves would have rejected; but this deformation has usually taken on the form of *naturalization*. Following a classical precedent, one has deemed natural structures or typical forms whose history is hardly natural but, rather, quite to the contrary, complex and heterogeneous. These forms have been treated as *natural*—and let us bear in mind the entire semantic scale of this difficult word whose span is so far-ranging and open-ended that it extends as far as the expression "natural language," by which term everyone agrees tacitly to oppose natural language only to a formal or artificial language without thereby implying that this natural language is a simple physical or biological production. Genette insists at length on this naturalization of genres: "The whole history of the theory of genres is imprinted with these fascinating outlines that *inform and deform the* often irregular *reality* of the literary field—patterns whose designers claim to have discovered a natural 'system' precisely where they are constructing a factitious symmetry with the help of a copious supply of fake windows" (italics added).[2]

In its most efficacious and legitimate aspect, this critical reading of the history (and) of genre-theory is based on an opposition between nature and history and, more generally—as the allusion to an artificial construct indicates ("where they are constructing a factitious symmetry")—on an opposition between nature and what can be called the series of all its others. Such an opposition seems to go without saying; placed within this critical perspective, it is never questioned. Even if it has been tucked away discreetly in some passage that has escaped my attention, this barely visible suspicion clearly had no effect on the general organization of the problematic. This does not diminish the relevance or fecundity of a reading such as Genette's. But a place remains open for some preliminary questions concerning his presuppositions, for some questions concerning the boundaries where it begins to take hold or take place. The form of these boundaries will contain me and rein me in. These general propositions whose number is always open and indeterminable for whatever critical interpretation will not be dealt with here. What however seems to me to require more urgent attention is the relationship of nature to history, of nature to its others, *precisely when genre is on the line.*

Let us consider the most general concept of genre, from the minimal trait or predicate delineating it permanently through the modulations of its types and the regimens of its history: it rends and defends itself by mustering all its energy against a simple opposition that arises from nature and from history, as from nature and the vast lineage of its others (*tekhnē, nomos, thesis,* then *spirit, society, freedom, history,* etc.). Between *phusis* and its others, *genos* certainly locates one of the privileged scenes of the process and, no doubt, sheds the greatest obscurity on it. One need not mobilize etymology to this end and could just as well equate *genos* with birth, and

birth in turn with the generous force of engenderment or generation—
phusis, in fact—as with race,[3] familial membership, classificatory genealogy or class, age class (generation), or social class; it comes as no surprise
that, in nature and art, genre, a concept that is essentially classificatory
and genealogico-taxonomic, itself engenders so many classificatory ver-
tigines when it goes about classifying itself and situating the classificatory
principle or instrument[4] within a set. As with the class itself, the principle
of genre is unclassifiable; it tolls the knell of the knell (*glas*), in other words,
of *classicum*, of what permits one to call out (*calare*) orders and to order
the manifold within a nomenclature. *Genos* thus indicates the place, the
now or never of the most necessary meditation on the "fold," which is no
more historical than natural in the classical sense of these two words, and
which turns *phuein* over to itself across others that perhaps no longer relate
to it according to that epoch-making logic that was decisory, critical, op-
positional, even dialectical but rather according to the trait of an entirely
different contract. *De jure*, this meditation acts as an absolute prerequisite
without which any historical perspectivizing will always be difficult to
legitimate. For example, the Romantic era—this powerful figure indicted
by Genette (since it attempted to reinterpret the system of modes as a system of genres)—is no longer a simple era and can no longer be inscribed
as a moment or a stage placeable within the trajectory of a "history" whose
concept we could be certain of. Romanticism, if something of the sort
can be thus identified, is also the general repetition of all the folds that in
themselves gather, couple, divide *phusis* as well as *genos* through the genre,
and through all the genres of genre, through the mixing of genre that is
"more than a genre," through the excess of genre in relation to itself, as to
its abounding movement and its general assemblage that coincides, too,
with its dissolution.[5] Such a "moment" is no longer a simple moment *in*
the history and theory of literary genres. To treat it thus would in effect
implicate one as tributary—whence the strange logic—of something that
has in itself constituted a certain Romantic motif, namely, the teleological
ordering of history. Romanticism *simultaneously* obeys naturalizing and
historicizing logic, and it can be shown easily enough that we have not yet
been delivered from the Romantic heritage—even though we might wish
it so and assuming that such a deliverance would be of compelling interest
to us—as long as we persist in drawing attention to historical concerns

and the truth of historical production in order to militate against abuses or confusions of naturalization. The debate, it could be argued, remains itself a part or effect of Romanticism.

A second motive detains me at the threshold or on the edge of a possible problematic of genre (as) history and theory of history and of genre-theory—another genre, in fact. For the moment, I find it impossible to decide—impossible for reasons that I do not take to be accidental, and this, precisely, is what matters to me—I find it impossible to decide whether the possibly exemplary text that I intend to put to the test does or does not lend itself to the distinction drawn between *mode* and *genre*. Now, as you may recall, Genette demonstrates the stringent necessity of this distinction; and he rests his case on the "confusion between modes and genres" (417 [*The Architext* 61/*Introduction à l'architexte* 66]). This implies a serious charge against Romanticism, even though "the romantic reinterpretation of the system of modes as a system of genres is neither de facto nor de jure the epilogue to this long history" (415 [58/63]). This confusion, according to Genette, has aided and abetted the naturalization of genres by projecting onto them the "privilege of naturalness that inheres *legitimately* in the three modes . . . " (421 [70/74]). Suddenly, this naturalization "sets up these archigenres as ideal or natural types, which they are not and cannot be: no archigenre could totally escape historicity *while at the same time retaining a generic definition*. There are modes (for example: the *récit*); there are genres (for example: the novel); the relationship between genres and modes is complex and doubtless not, as Aristotle suggests, one of simple inclusion" [421 (71/75–76)].[6]

If I am inclined to poise myself on this side of Genette's argument, it is not only because of his ready acceptance of the distinction between nature and history but also because of its implications with regard to mode and to the distinction between mode and genre. Genette's definition of mode contains this singular and interesting characteristic: it remains, in contradistinction to genre, purely formal. Reference to a content has no pertinence. This is not the case with genre. The generic criterion and the modal criterion, Genette says, are "absolutely heterogeneous": "each genre was defined essentially by a specification of content that was in no way prescribed by the definition of its mode" (417 [61/66]). I do not believe that this recourse to the opposition of form and content, this distinction between mode and genre, need be contested, and my purpose is not to challenge isolated aspects of Genette's argument. One might just question the presuppositions for the legitimacy of such an argument. One might also question the extent to which his argument can help us read a given text when it behaves in a given way with regard to mode and genre, especially when the text does not seem to be written sensibly within their limits but rather about the very subject of those limits and with the aim of disrupting their order. The limits, for instance, of that mode that would be, according to Genette, the *récit* ("There are modes [for example: the *récit*]"). Of the (possibly) exemplary text that I shall address shortly, I shall not hasten to add that it is a "*récit*," and you will soon understand why. In this text, the "*récit*" is not only a mode, and a mode put into practice or put to the test because it is deemed impossible; it is also the name of a theme. It is the nonthematizable thematic content of something of a textual form that assumes a point of view with respect to the genre, even though it perhaps does not come under the heading of any genre—and perhaps no longer even under the heading of literature, if it indeed wears itself out around genreless modalizations, and would confirm one of Genette's propositions: "Genres are properly literary [or aesthetic] categories, whereas modes are categories that belong to linguistics or (more exactly) to an anthropology of verbal expression" (418 [64/68–69]).[7] In a very singular manner, the *récit* that I will discuss presently makes the *récit* and the impossibility of the *récit* its theme, its impossible theme or content at once inaccessible, indeterminable, interminable, and inexhaustible; and it makes the word "*récit*" its titleless title, the mentionless mention of its genre. This text, as I shall try to demonstrate, seems to be made, among other things, to *make light* of all the tranquil categories of genre-theory and -history in order to upset their taxonomic certainties, the distribution of their classes, and the presumed stability of their classical nomenclatures. It is a text destined, at the same time, to summon up these classes by conducting their proceeding, by proceeding from the proceeding to the law of genre. For if the juridical code has frequently thrust itself upon me in order to hear this case, it has done so to call as witness a (possibly) exemplary text and because I am convinced fundamental rights are bound up in all of this: the law itself is at stake.

These are the two principal reasons why I shall keep to the liminal edge of (the) history (and) of genre-theory. Here now, very quickly, is the law of abounding, of *excess*, the law of participation without membership, which I mentioned earlier. It will seem meager to you, and even of staggering abstractness. It does not particularly concern either genres, or types, or modes, or any form in the strict sense of its concept. I therefore do not know under what title the field or object submitted to this law should be placed. It is perhaps the limitless field of general textuality. I can take each word of the series (genre, type, mode, form) and decide that it will hold for all the others (all genres of genres, types, modes, forms; all types of types, genres, modes, forms; all modes of modes, genres, types, forms; all forms of forms, etc.). The trait common to these classes of classes is precisely the identifiable recurrence of a common trait by which one recognizes, or should recognize, a membership in a class. There should be a trait upon which one could rely in order to decide that a given textual event, a given "work," corresponds to a given class (genre, type, mode, form, etc.). And there should be a code enabling one to decide questions of class-membership on the basis of this trait. For example, a very humble axiom, but, by the same token, hardly contestable—if a genre exists (let us say the novel, since no one seems to contest its generic quality), then a code should provide an identifiable trait and one that is identical to itself, authorizing us to adjudicate [*arrêter*] whether a given text belongs to this genre or perhaps to that genre. Likewise, outside of literature or art, if one is bent on classifying, one should consult a set of identifiable and codifiable traits to determine whether this or that, such a thing or such an event belongs to this set or that class. This may seem trivial. Such a distinctive trait *qua* mark is however always *a priori remarkable*. It is always possible that a set—I have compelling reasons for calling this a text, whether it be written or oral—re-marks on this distinctive trait within itself. This can occur in texts that do not, at a given moment, assert themselves to be literary or poetic. A defense speech or newspaper editorial can indicate by means of a mark, even if it is not explicitly designated as such, "Voilà! I belong, as anyone may remark, to the type of text called a defense speech or an article of the genre newspaper-editorial." The possibility is always there. This does not constitute a text *ipso facto* as "literature," even though such a possibility, always left open and therefore eternally remarkable, situates perhaps in every text the possibility of its becoming literature. But this does not interest me at the moment. What interests me is that this re-mark—ever possible for every text, for every corpus of traces—is absolutely necessary for and constitutive of what we call art, poetry, or literature. It underwrites the eruption of *tekhnē*, which is never long in coming. I submit this axiomatic question for your consideration: Can one identify a work of art, of whatever sort, but especially a work of discursive art, if it does not bear the mark of a genre, if it does not signal or mention it or make it remarkable in any way? Let me clarify two points on this subject. First, it is possible to have several genres, an intermixing of genres or a total genre, the genre "genre" or the poetic or literary genre as genre of genres. Second, this re-mark can take on a great number of forms and can itself pertain to highly diverse types. It need not be a designation or "mention" of the type found beneath the title of certain books (novel, *récit*, drama). The remark of belonging need not pass through the consciousness of the author or the reader, although it often does so. It can also refute this consciousness or render the explicit "mention" mendacious, false, inadequate, or ironic according to all sorts of over-determined figures. Finally, this remarking-trait need be neither a theme nor a thematic component of the work—although of course this instance of belonging to one or several genres, not to mention all the traits that mark this belonging, often has been treated as theme, even before the advent of what we call "modernism." If I am not mistaken in saying that such a trait is remarkable in every aesthetic, poetic, or literary corpus, then consider this paradox, consider the irony (which is irreducible to a consciousness or an attitude): this supplementary and distinctive trait, a mark of belonging or inclusion, does not properly pertain to any genre or class. The re-mark of belonging does not belong. It belongs without belonging, and the "without" (or the suffix "-less") that relates belonging to non-belonging appears only in the timeless time of the blink of an eye. The eyelid closes, but barely, an instant among instants, and what it closes is verily the eye, the view, the light of day. But without the respite or interval of a blink, nothing would come to light. To formulate it in the scantiest manner—the simplest but most apodictic—I submit for your consideration the following hypothesis: a text could not *belong* to any genre. Every text *participates* in one or several genres, there is no [*pas de*] genreless text; there is always a genre and genres, yet such participation never amounts to belonging. And not because of an abundant overflowing or a free, anarchic, and unclassifiable productivity, but because of the *trait* of participation itself, because of the effect of the code and of the generic mark. In marking itself with, a text demarcates itself from, genre. If remarks of belonging belong without belonging, participate without belonging, then *genre-designations cannot be simply part of the corpus*. Let us take the designation "novel" as an example. This should be marked in one way or another, even if it does not appear in the explicit form of a subtitled designation, and even if it proves deceptive or ironic. This designation is not novelistic; it does not, in whole or in part, take part in the corpus whose denomination it nonetheless imparts. Nor is it simply extraneous to the corpus. But this singular *topos* places within and without the work, along its boundary, an inclusion and exclusion with regard to genre in general, as to an identifiable class in general. It gathers together the corpus and, at the same time, in the same blinking of an eye, keeps it from closing, from identifying itself with itself. This axiom of non-closure or non-fulfillment enfolds within itself the condition for the possibility and the impossibility of taxonomy. This inclusion and this exclusion do not remain exterior to one another; they do not exclude each other. But neither are they immanent or identical to each other. They are neither one nor two. They form what I shall call the *genre-clause*, a clause stating at once the juridical utterance, the precedent-making designation and the law-text, but also the closure, the closing that excludes itself from what it includes (one could also speak, without winking, of a floodgate [*écluse*] of genre). The clause or floodgate of genre declasses what it allows to be classed. It tolls the knell [*glas*] of genealogy or of genericity, which it however also brings forth to the light of day. Putting to death the very thing that it engenders, it cuts a strange figure; a formless form, it remains nearly invisible, it neither sees the day nor brings itself to light. Without it, neither genre nor literature comes to light, but as soon as there is this blinking of an eye, this clause or floodgate of genre, at the very moment that a genre or a literature is broached, at that very moment, degenerescence will have begun, the end is beginning.

The end is beginning; this is a citation. Maybe a citation. I might have taken it from the text that seems to me to bring itself forth as an example, as an example of this unfigurable figure of clusion.

What I shall try to convey to you now will not be called by its generic or modal name. I shall not say this drama, this epic, this novel, this novella, or this *récit*—certainly not this *récit*. All of these generic or modal names would be equally valid or equally invalid for something that is not even quite a book, but was published in 1973 in the editorial form of a small volume of thirty-two pages. It bears the title *La folie du jour*. The author's name: Maurice Blanchot. In order to speak about it, I shall call this thing "La folie du jour," its given name that it bears legally and that gives us the right, as of its publication date, to identify and classify it in our copyright records at the Bibliothèque Nationale. One could fashion a non-finite number of readings from *La folie du jour*. I have attempted a few myself, and shall do so again elsewhere, from another point of view. The *topos* of view, sight, blindness, *point of view* is, moreover, inscribed and traversed in *La folie du jour* according to a sort of permanent revolution that engenders and virtually brings to the light of day points of view, twists, versions, and reversions of which the sum remains necessarily uncountable and the account, impossible. The deductions, rationalizations, and warnings that I must inevitably propose will arise, then, from an act of unjustifiable violence. A brutal and mercilessly depleting selectivity will obtrude upon me, upon us, in the name of a law that *La folie du jour* has, in its turn, already reviewed, and with the foresight that a certain kind of police brutality is perhaps an inevitable accomplice to our concern for professional competence.

What will I ask of *La folie du jour*? To answer, to testify, to say what it has to say with respect to the law of mode or the law of genre and, more precisely, with respect to the law of the *récit*, which, as we have just been reminded, is a mode and not a genre.

On the cover, below the title, we find no mention of genre. In this most peculiar place that belongs neither to the title nor to the subtitle, nor even simply to the corpus of the work, the author did not affix, although he has often done so elsewhere, the designation "*récit*" or "novel," maybe (but only maybe) by erroneously subsuming both of them, Genette would say, under the unique category of the genre. About this designation that figures elsewhere and that appears to be absent here, I shall say only two things:

(1) On the one hand it commits one to nothing. Neither reader nor critic nor author is bound to believe that the text preceded by this designation conforms readily to the strict, normal, normed, or normative definition of the genre, to the law of the genre or of the mode. Confusion, irony, the shift in conventions toward a new definition (in what name should it be prohibited?), the search for a supplementary effect, any of these things could prompt one to entitle as *novel* or *récit* what in truth or according to yesterday's truth would be neither one nor the other. All the more so if the words *récit, novel, ciné-roman, complete dramatic works*, or, for all I know, *literature* are no longer in the place that conventionally mentions genre but, as has happened and will happen again (shortly), they are found to be holding the position and function of the title itself, of the work's given name.

(2) Blanchot has often had occasion to modify the genre-designation from one version of his work to the next or from one edition to the next. Since I am unable to cover [*aborder*] the entire spectrum of this problem, I shall simply cite the example of the designation "*récit*" effaced between one version and the next of *L'arrêt de mort* at the same time as a certain epilogue is removed from the end of a double *récit*, which, in a manner of speaking, constitutes this book. This effacement of "*récit*," leaving a trace that, inscribed and filed away, remains as an effect of supplementary relief that is not easily accounted for in all of its facets. I cannot arrest the course of my lecture here, no more than I can pause to consider the very scrupulous and minutely differentiated distribution of the designations "*récit*" and "novel" from one narrative work to the next, no more than I can question whether Blanchot distinguished the genre and mode designations, no more than I can discuss Blanchot's entire discourse on the difference between the narrating voice and the narrative voice that is, to be sure, something other than a mode. I would point out only one thing: at the very moment the first version of *L'arrêt de mort* appears, bearing mention as it does of "*récit*," the first version of *La folie du jour* is published with another title about which I shall momentarily speak.

La folie du jour, then, makes no mention of genre or mode. But the word "*récit*" appears at least four times in the last two pages in order to name the theme of *La folie du jour*, its sense or its story, its content or part of its content—in any case, its decisive proceedings and stakes. It is a *récit* without a theme and without a cause entering from the outside; yet it is without interiority. It is the *récit* of an impossible *récit* whose "production" occasions what happens or, rather, what remains, but which does not relate it, nor relate to it as to an outside reference, even if everything remains foreign to it and out of bounds. It is even less feasible for me to relate to you the story of *La folie du jour*, which is staked precisely on the possibility and the impossibility of relating a story. Nonetheless, in order to create the greatest possible clarity, in the name of daylight itself, that is to say (as will become clear), in the name of the law, I shall take the calculated risk of flattening out the unfolding or coiling up of this text, its permanent revolution whose rounds are made to recoil from any kind of flattening. And this is why the one who says "I," and the one after all who "speaks" to us, who "recites" for us, this one who says "I" tells his inquisitors that he cannot manage to constitute himself as narrator (in the sense of the term that is not necessarily literary) and tells them that he cannot manage to identify with himself sufficiently or to remember himself well enough to gather the story and *récit* that are demanded of him—which the representatives of society and the law require of him. The one who says "I" (who does not manage to say "I") seems to relate what has happened to him or, rather, what has nearly happened to him after presenting himself in a mode that defies all norms of self-presentation: he nearly lost his sight following a traumatic event—probably an assault. I say "probably" because *La folie du jour* wholly upsets, in a discreet but terribly efficient manner, all the certainties upon which so much of discourse is constructed: the value of an event, first of all, of reality, of fiction, of appearance, and so on, all this being carried away by the disseminal and mad polysemy of "day," of the word "day," which, once again, I cannot dwell upon here. Having nearly lost his sight, having been taken in by a kind of medico-social institution, he now resides under the watchful eye of doctors, handed over to the authority of these specialists who are representatives of the law as well, forensic doctors who demand that he testify—and in his own interest, or so it seems at first—about what happened to him so that remedial justice may be dispensed. His faithful *récit* of events should render justice unto the law. The law demands a *récit*.

Pronounced five times[8] in the last three paragraphs of *La folie du jour*, the word "*récit*" does not seem to designate a literary genre but rather a certain type or mode of discourse. That is, in effect, the appearance of it. Everything seems to happen as if the *récit*—the question of or rather the demand for the *récit*, the response, and the nonresponse to the demand—found itself staged and figured as one of the themes, objects, stakes in a more bountiful text, *La folie du jour*, whose genre would be of another order and would in any case overstep the boundaries of the *récit* with all its generality and all its genericity. The *récit* itself would of course not cover this generic generality of the literary corpus named *La folie du jour*. Now we might already feel inclined to consider this appearance suspect, and we might be jolted from our certainties by an allusion that "I" will make: the one who says "I," who is not by force of necessity a narrator, nor necessarily always the same, notes that the representatives of the law, those who demand of him a *récit* in the name of the law, consider and treat him, in his personal and civil identity, not only as an "educated" [e.g., *MD* 13/*FJ* 27] man—and an educated man, they often tell him, ought to be able to speak and recount; as a competent subject, he ought to be able to know how to piece together a story by saying "I" and "just exactly" how things happened to him—they regard him not only as an "educated" man, but also as a writer. He is writer and reader, a creature [*animal*] of "libraries," *the* reader of this *récit*. This is not sufficient cause, but it is, in any case, a first clue and one whose impact incites us to think that the required *récit* does not simply remain in a relationship that is extraneous to literature or even to a literary genre. Lest we not be content with this suspicion, let us weigh the possibility of the inclusion of a modal structure within a vaster, more general corpus, whether literary or not and whether or not related to the genre. Such an inclusion raises questions concerning edge, borderline, boundary, and abounding that do not arise without a fold.

What sort of a fold? According to which fold and which figure of enfoldment?

Here are the three final paragraphs; they are of unequal length, with the last of these comprising approximately one line:

I had been asked: Tell us "*just* exactly" what happened. A *récit*? I began: I am not learned; I am not ignorant. I have known joys. That is saying too little. I told them the whole story and they listened, it seems to me with interest, at least in the beginning. But the end was a surprise to all of us. "That was the beginning," they said. "Now get down to the facts." How so? The *récit* was over!

I had to acknowledge that I was not capable of forming a *récit* out of these events. I had lost the sense of the story [*histoire*]: that happens in a good many illnesses. But this explanation only made them more insistent. Then I noticed for the first time that there were two of them and that this distortion of the traditional method, even though it was explained by the fact that one of them was an eye doctor, the other a specialist in mental illness, constantly gave our conversation the character of an authoritarian interrogation, overseen and controlled by a strict set of rules. Of course neither of them was the chief of police. But because there were two of them, there were three, and this third remained firmly convinced, I am sure, that a writer, a man who speaks and who reasons with distinction, is always capable of recounting the facts that he remembers.

A *récit*? No. No *récit* [*pas de récit*], never again. [*MD* 18/ *FJ* 36–38]

In the first of the three paragraphs that I have just cited, he claims that something is to begin after the word "*récit*" punctuated by a question mark ("A *récit*?"—herein implied: they want a *récit*, is it then a *récit* that they want? "I began . . . "). This something is nothing other than the first line on the first page of *La folie du jour*. These are the same words, in the same order, but this is not a citation in the strict sense for, stripped of quotation marks, these words commence or recommence a quasi-*récit* that will engender anew the entire sequence comprising this new point of departure. In this way, the first words ("I am not learned; I am not ignorant . . . ") that come after the word "*récit*" and its question mark, that broach [*entame*] the beginning of the *récit* extorted by the law's representatives—these first words mark a collapse that is unthinkable, unrepresentable, unsituable within a linear order of succession, within a spatial or temporal sequentiality, within an objectifiable topology or chronology. One sees, without seeing, one reads the crumbling of an upper boundary or of the initial edge in *La folie du jour*, uncoiled according to the "normal" order, the one regulated by common law, editorial convention, positive law, the regime of competency in our logo-alphabetical culture, etc. Suddenly, this upper or initial boundary, which is commonly called the first line of a book, is forming a pocket inside the corpus. It is taking the form of an *invagination* through which the trait of the first line, the *borderline*,[9] as it were, splits while remaining the same and traverses yet also bounds the corpus. The "*récit*" that he claims is beginning at the end, and by legal requisition, is none other than the one that has begun from the beginning of *La folie du jour* and in which, therefore, he gets around to saying that he/it begins, etc. And it is without beginning or end, without content and without edge. There is only content without edge—without boundary or frame—and there is only edge without content. The inclusion (or occlusion, inocclusive invagination) is interminable: it is an analysis of the *récit* that can only turn in circles in an unarrestable, inenarrable, and insatiably recurring manner—but one terrible for those who, in the name of the law, require that order reign in the *récit*, for those who want to know, with all the required competence, "just exactly" how this happens. For if "I" or "he" continued to tell what he has told, he would end up endlessly returning to this point and beginning again to begin, that is to say, to begin again with an end that precedes the beginning. And from the viewpoint of objective space and time, the point at which he stops is absolutely unascertainable ("I told them the whole story . . . "), for there is no "whole" story except for the one that interrupts itself in this way.

A lower edge of invagination will, if one can say so, respond to this "first" invagination of the upper edge by intersecting it. The "final line" resumes the question posed *before* the "I began" ("A *récit*?") and bespeaks a resolution or promises it, tells of the commitment made no longer to give a *récit*. As if he had already given one! And yet, yes (yes and no), a *récit* has taken place. Hence the last word: "A *récit*? No, no *récit*, never again." It has been impossible to decide whether the recounted event and the event of the *récit* itself ever took place. Impossible to decide whether there was a *récit*, for the one who barely manages to say "I" and to constitute himself as narrator recounts that he has not been able to recount—but what, just exactly? Well, everything, including the demand for a *récit*, and so on. And if an assured and guaranteed decision is impossible, this is because there is nothing more to be done than to commit oneself, to perform, to wager, to allow chance its chance—to make a decision that is essentially edgeless, without safeguard, bordering perhaps only on madness [*sans garde-fou*]. Yet another impossible decision follows, one that involves the promise "No, no *récit*, never again": Is this promise a part of or apart from the *récit*? Legally speaking, it is party to *La folie du jour*, but not necessarily to the *récit* or to the simulacrum of the *récit*. Its trait splits again into an internal and external edge. It repeats—without citing—the question apparently posed above (A *récit?*) of which it can be said that, in this permanent revolution of order, it follows, doubles, or reiterates it in advance. Thus another lip or invaginating loop takes shape here. This time the lower edge creates a pocket in order to come back into the corpus and to rise again on this side of the upper or initial line's line of invagination. This would form *a double chiasmatic invagination of edges*:

> A. "I am not learned; I am not ignorant . . . "
> B. "A *récit?* I began:
> A'. "I am not learned; I am not ignorant . . . "
> B'. "A *récit?* No, no *récit*, never again."

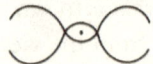

The *I* of "I began" seems to bear all the responsibility of the *récit*, at least of the *récit* that could be said to be *included* and that nevertheless also becomes larger than what apparently comprises it. *I* figures the beginning, the very act of beginning, recalling at the same time that it is found *en arkhē*, in the beginning, the first word of the book: "I am not learned; I am not ignorant." S/he and me and *I* are asked at once to begin and to repeat, to relate the facts. And to take up in sum one's responsibilities. But in order to relate the facts, there begins a relation that relates another account in which the *I* is included. On the other hand [*d'autre part*], here figured as a point, an eye, a point of view in the diagram I have just sketched, *I* seems not to be a part of the lineage of the two *récits* forever enveloped and overlapped. The inaugural decision to respond to the demand and to "begin" the *récit* is not part of the *récit*, no more than is, at the end of the book, the "No, no [*pas de*] *récit*, never again," an inverse resolution that seems to cite nothing either. "I began" and "No, no *récit*, never again" could then resemble some of the *récit*'s *quasi-transcendental* commitments, moreover according to different, but equally external, modes to the very content of the narration. The first describes or notes, in the past, a sort of performative: I begin, I began. The other enunciates, in a more manifestly performative mode, in the present, a decision engaging the future. The decision to begin and then to interrupt forever the relating, to take some responsibility or other confronted with the demand of/for the *récit*, that is what would come to rip the fabric of a narrative text while it tends to envelop itself indefinitely within itself. I had to begin and end, even if I begin with the end, if "the end is beginning."

Would it be so simple? and so reassuring, after all, as the purity of a transcendental or a performative can always be? The two resolutions appear to be inaugural, to be sure, and the final one even has the form of an inaugural decision come to interrupt spontaneously every possible sequence. But these two resolutions immediately become once again *moments of passage*, within the general *récit* titled *La folie du jour*. If, after "I began: I am not learned; I am not ignorant . . . ," the simulacrum of repetition continued on according to its own logic and the internal necessity of its movement, turning infinitely on itself, the "I began" and the "No, no *récit*, never again" would without fail find themselves inscribed therein, linked together, caught up again in the general web, in the citation and the narration, in the madness of a fiction that no decidability could surely interrupt. "I began" and the "No, no *récit*, never again" are part of the sequel [*suite*], the *consequence* of the text that *I* begin(s) to cite. They are, if one can say this, *implicitly cited*, re-implicated in this singular continuum. No tearing [*Pas de déchirure*], never again between A, B, A', B', not even within B and B', between the question and the response.[10]

It is thus impossible to decide whether an event, *récit*, *récit* of event, or event of *récit* took place. Impossible to settle upon [*arrêter*] the simple borderlines of this corpus, of this ellipse unremittingly repealing itself within its own expansion. When we fall back on the poetic consequences enfolded within this dilemma, we find that it becomes difficult indeed to speak here with conviction about a *récit* as a determined mode included within a more general corpus or one simply related, in its determination, to other modes or, quite simply, to something other than itself. All is *récit* and nothing is; the exit out of the *récit* remains *within* the *récit* in a *non-inclusive* mode, and this structure is itself related so remotely to a dialectical structure that it even inscribes dialectics in the *récit*'s ellipse. All is *récit*, nothing is: and we shall not know whether the relationship between these two propositions—the strange conjunction of the *récit* and the *récit*-less—belongs to the order of the *récit* itself. What indeed happens when the edge pronounces a sentence?

Faced with this type of difficulty—the consequences or implications of which cannot be deployed here—one might be tempted to take recourse in the law or the rights that govern published texts. One might be tempted to argue as follows: all these insoluble problems of delimitation are raised "on the inside" of a book classified as a work of literature or literary fiction. Pursuant to these juridical norms, this book has a beginning and an end that leave no opening for indecision. This book has a determinable beginning and end, a title, an author, a publisher, its distinctive denomination is *La folie du jour*. At this place, where I am pointing, on this page, right here, you can see its first word; here, its final period, perfectly situable in objective space. And all the sophisticated transgressions, all the infinitesimal subversions that may captivate you are not possible except within this enclosure for which these transgressions and subversions moreover maintain an essential need in order to take place. Furthermore, on the inside of this normed space, the word "*récit*" does not name a literary operation or genre, but a current mode of discourse, and it does so regardless of the formidable problems of structure, edge, set theory, the part and whole, etc., that it raises in this "literary" corpus.

That is all well and good. But in its very relevance, this objection cannot be sustained—for example, it cannot save the modal determination of the *récit*—except by referring to extra-literary and even extra-linguistic juridical norms. The objection makes an appeal to the law and calls to mind the fact that the subversion of "La folie du jour" needs the law in order to take place. Whereby the objection reproduces and accomplishes its staging within *La folie du jour*: the *récit*, mandated and prescribed by law but also, as we shall see, commanding, requiring, and producing law in turn. In short, the whole critical scene of competence in which we are engaged is *party* to and *part* of *La folie du jour*, in whole and in part, the whole is a part.

The whole does nothing but begin. I could have begun with what resembles the absolute beginning, with the juridico-historical order of this publication. What has been lightly termed the first version of *La folie du jour* was not a book. Published in the journal *Empédocle* (No. 2, May 1949), it bore another title—indeed, several other titles. On the journal's cover, here it is, one reads:

Maurice Blanchot
Un récit? [A *Récit?*]

Later, the question mark disappears twice. First, when the title is reproduced within the journal in the table of contents:

Maurice Blanchot
Un récit

then below the first line:

Un récit
par
Maurice Blanchot

Could you tell whether these titles, written earlier and filed away in the archives, make up a single title, titles of the same text, titles of the *récit* (which of course figures as an impracticable mode in the book), or the title of a genre? Even if the latter were to cause some confusion, it would be of the sort that releases questions already implemented and enacted by *La folie du jour*. This enactment enables in turn the denaturalization and deconstitution of the oppositions nature/history and mode/genre.

What could the words "A *récit*" refer to in their manifold occurrences and diverse punctuations? And precisely how does reference function here? In one case, the question mark can *also* serve as a supplementary remark indicating the necessity of all these questions as the insolvent character of indecision: Is this a *récit*? Is it a *récit* that I entitle? asks the title in entitling. But also, announcing outside the inside of the story: Is it a *récit* that they want? What entitles them? Is it a *récit* as discursive mode or as literary operation, or perhaps even as literary genre or literary fiction *on the theme* of mode and genre? Likewise, the title could excerpt, as does a metonymy, a fragment of the *récit* without a *récit* (to wit, the words "a *récit*" with and without a question mark), but such an iterative excerpting is not citational. For the title, guaranteed and protected by law but also making law, retains a referential structure that differs radically from the one underlying other occurrences of the "same" words in the text. Whatever the issue—title, reference, or mode and genre—the case before us always involves the law and, in particular, the relations formed around and to law. All the questions that we have just addressed can be traced to an enormous matrix that generates the non-thematizable thematic power of a simulated *récit*: it is this inexhaustible writing that recounts without telling and that speaks without recounting.

Récit of a *récit*-less *récit*, a *récit* without edge or boundary, *récit* all of whose visible space is but some border of itself snatched from itself, without "self," consisting of the framing edge without content, without modal or generic boundaries—such is the law of this textual event, of this text that also speaks the law, its own and that of the other as reader of this text that, speaking the law, also imposes itself as a law text, as the text of the law. What, then, is the law of the genre of this singular text? It is law, it is the figure of the law that will also be the invisible center, the themeless theme of *La folie du jour* or, as I am now entitled to say, of "A *récit*?"

This law, however, as law of genre, is not exclusively binding on the genre *qua* category of art and literature. But, paradoxically, and just as impossibly, the law of genre also has a controlling influence and is binding on that which draws the genre into engendering, generations, genealogy, and degenerescence. You have already witnessed its approach often enough, with all the figures of this degenerescent self-re-engendering of a *récit*, with this figure of the law that, like the day that it is, challenges the opposition between the law of nature and the law of symbolic history. The remarks that have just been made on the double chiasmatic invagination of edges should suffice to exclude any notion linking all these complications to pure form or one suggesting that they could be formalized outside the content. The question of the literary genre is not a formal one: it covers the motif of the law in general, of generation in the natural and symbolic senses, of birth in the natural and symbolic senses, of the generation difference, sexual difference between the feminine and masculine genre/gender, of the hymen between the two, of a relationless relation between the two, of an identity and difference between the feminine and the masculine. The word *hymen* tells us several things. It not only points toward a paradoxical logic that is inscribed without however being formalized under this name; let us not forget everything that Philippe Lacoue-Labarthe and Jean-Luc Nancy tell us in *The Literary Absolute* about the relationship between genre (*Gattung*) and marriage, as well as about the intricate bonds of serial connections begotten by *gattieren* ("to mix," "to classify"), *gatten* ("to couple"), *Gatte/Gattin* ("husband/wife"), and so forth.[11]

Once articulated within the precinct of Blanchot's entire discourse on the neuter, the most elliptical question would inevitably have to assume this form: What about a neutral genre/gender? Or one whose neutrality would not be *negative* (not . . . not; neither . . . nor), nor dialectical, but affirmative, and *doubly affirmative* (yes, yes; or . . . or)?

Here again, due to time limitations but also to more essential reasons concerning the structure of the text, I shall have to excerpt some abstract fragments. This will not occur without a supplement of violence and pain.

As first word and surely most impossible word of *La folie du jour*, "I" presents itself as *self (moi), me, a man*. Grammatical law leaves no doubt about this subject. The first sentence, phrased in French in the masculine ("Je ne suis ni savant ni ignorant" and not "Je ne suis ni savante ni ignorante"), says, with regard to knowledge, nothing but a double negation (*not . . . not; neither . . . nor*). Thus, no glint of *self-presentation*. But the double negation gives passage to a double affirmation (yes, yes) that enters into alignment or alliance with itself. Forging an alliance or marriage-bond ("hymen") with itself, this boundless double affirmation utters a measureless, excessive, immense *yes*: both to life and to death.

I am not learned; I am not ignorant. I have known joys. That is saying too little: I am alive, and this life gives me the greatest pleasure. And what about death? When I die (perhaps any minute now), I will feel immense pleasure. I am not talking about the foretaste of death, which is stale and often disagreeable. Suffering dulls the senses. But this is the remarkable truth, and I am sure of it: I experience boundless pleasure in living, and I shall take boundless satisfaction in dying. [*MD* 5/ *FJ* 9]

Now, seven paragraphs further along, the chance and probability of such an affirmation (one that is double and therefore boundless, limitless) is granted to woman. It returns to woman. Rather, not to woman or even to the feminine, to the female genre/gender, or to the generality of the feminine genre but—and this is why I spoke of chance and probability— "almost always" to women. It is "almost always" women who say *yes, yes*. To life to death. This "almost always" avoids treating the feminine as a general and generic force; it makes an opening for the event, the performance, the uncertain contingencies [*aléa*], the encounter. And it is indeed from the contingent experience of the encounter that "I" will speak here. In the passage that I am about to cite, the expression "men" occurs twice. The second occurrence names the sexual genre, the sexual difference (*aner, vir*—but sexual difference does not occur between a species and a genre); in the first occurrence, "men" comes into play in an indecisive manner in order to name either the genre of human beings (the *genre humain*, named "species" in the text) or sexual difference.

Men want to escape from death, bizarre *species* that they are. And some of them cry out "Die, die" because they want to escape from life. "What a life! I'll kill myself, I'll give in." This is lamentable and strange; it is a mistake.

Yet I have met *beings* who have never said to life, "Quiet!", who have never said to death, "Go away!" Almost always women, beautiful creatures. Men are assaulted by terror.... (My emphasis.) [*MD* 7/ *FJ* 12–13]

What has thus far transpired in these seven paragraphs? Almost always women, beautiful creatures, relates "I." As it happens, encounter, chance, affirmation of chance do not always manage to happen. There is no natural or symbolic law, universal law, or law of a genre/gender here. Only almost always, "almost always women" (comma of apposition), "beautiful creatures." Through its highly calculated logic, the comma of apposition leaves open the possibility of thinking that these women are not beautiful and then, on the other hand, as it happens, capable of saying *yes, yes* to life to death, of not saying *quiet, go away* to life to death. The comma of apposition lets us think that they are beautiful, women and beauties, these creatures, insofar as they affirm both life and death. Beauty, the feminine beauty of these "beings," would be bound up with this double affirmation.

Now I myself, who "am not learned ... not ignorant," "I experience boundless pleasure in living, and I shall take boundless satisfaction in dying." In this random claim that links affirmation almost always to women, beautiful ones, it is then more than probable that, as long as I say *yes, yes*, I am a woman and beautiful. I am a woman, and beautiful. Grammatical sex (or anatomical as well, in any case, sex submitted to the law of objectivity): the masculine gender [*genre*] is thus affected by the affirmation through a random drift that could always render it other. A sort of secret coupling would take place here, forming an odd marriage ("hymen"), an odd couple, for none of this can be regulated by objective, natural, or civil law. The "almost always" is a mark of this secret and odd hymen, of this coupling that is also perhaps a mixing of genders/genres. The genders/genres pass into each other. And we will not be barred from thinking that this mixing of genres, viewed in light of the madness of sexual difference, may bear some relation to the mixing of literary genres.

"I," then, can keep alive the chance of being a female or of changing sex. Transsexuality permits me, in a more than metaphorical and transferential way, to engender. "I" can give birth, and many other signs that I cannot mention here bear this out, among other things the fact that on several occasions I "bring something forth to the light of day." In the rhetoric of *La folie du jour*, the idiomatic expression "to bring forth to the light of day" (*donner le jour*) is one of the players in an exceedingly powerful polysemic and disseminal game that I shall not attempt to reproduce here. I only retain its standard and dominant meaning that the spirit of linguistics gives it: *donner le jour* is to give birth—a verb whose subject is almost always maternal, that is to say, generally female. At the center, closely hugging an invisible center, a primal scene could have alerted us, if we had had the time, to the *point of view* of *La folie du jour* and to "A Primal Scene."[12] This is also called a "brief scene" [*MD* 10/*FJ* 18].

"I" can bring forth to light, can give birth. To what? Well, precisely to law or more exactly, to begin with, to the representatives of law, to those who wield authority—and let us also understand by this the authority of the author, the rights of authorship—simply by virtue of possessing an overseer's right, the right to see, the right to have everything in sight. This panoptic and this synopsis demand nothing else, but nothing less. Now herein lies the essential paradox: from where and from whom do they derive this power, this right-to-sight that permits them to have "me" at their disposal? Well, from "me," rather, from the subject who is subjected to them. It is the "I"-less "I" of the narrative voice, the I "stripped" of itself, the one that does not take place, it is he who brings them to light, who engenders these lawmen in giving them insight into what regards them and what should not regard them:

I liked the doctors quite well, and I did not feel belittled by their doubts. The annoying thing was that their authority loomed larger by the hour. One is not aware of it, but these men are kings. Throwing open my rooms, they would say: "Everything here belongs to us." They would fall upon my scraps of thought: "This is ours." They interpellated my story: "Talk," and my story would put itself at their service. In haste, I stripped myself of myself. I distributed my blood, my innermost being among them, lent them the universe, gave them the day, brought them forth to the light of day. Right before their eyes, I became a drop of water, a spot of ink. I reduced myself to them. The whole of me passed in full view before them, and when at last nothing was present but my perfect nothingness and there was nothing more to see, they ceased to see me too. Very irritated, they stood up and cried out, "All right, where are you? Where are you hiding? Hiding is forbidden, it is an offense," etc. [*MD* 14/ *FJ* 28–29]

Law, day. One believes it generally possible to oppose law to affirmation, and particularly to unlimited affirmation, to the immensity of *yes, yes*. Law—we often figure it as an instance of the interdictory limit, of the binding obligation, as the negativity of a boundary not to be crossed. Now the mightiest and most divided trait of *La folie du jour* or of *Un récit?* is the one relating the birth of the law, its genealogy, its engenderment, its generation, or its genre, the very genre of the law, to the process of the double affirmation. The excessiveness [*démesure*] of *yes, yes* is no stranger to the genesis of law (nor to genesis itself, as could be easily shown, for it also concerns a *récit* of Genesis "against the light of seven days" [*MD* 11/ *FJ* 22]). The double affirmation is not foreign to the genre, genius, or spirit of the law. No [*Pas d'*] affirmation, and certainly no *double* affirmation without the law sighting the light of day and the daylight becoming law. Such is the madness of the day, such is a *récit* in its "remarkable" truth [*MD* 5/ *FJ* 9], in its truthless truth.

Now the feminine, the almost generally affirmative gender/genre—"almost always women"—is also the genre of this figure of law, not of its representatives, but of the law herself who, throughout a *récit*, forms a couple with me, with the "I" of the narrative voice.

The law is in the feminine.

She is not a woman (it is only a figure, a "silhouette" [*MD* 14/*FJ* 29], and not a representative of the law) but she, *la loi*, is in the feminine, declined in the feminine; but not only as a grammatical gender/genre in my language (elsewhere Blanchot brought this genre into play for speech ["*la* parole"] and for thought ["*la* pensée"]). No, she is described as a "feminine element" [*MD* 16/*FJ* 34], which does not signify a female person. And the affirmative "I," the narrative voice, who has brought forth the representatives of the law to the light of day, claims to find the law seductive—sexually seductive. The law appeals to him; he likes the law: "The truth was that I liked her. In these surroundings, overpopulated by men, she was the only feminine element. Once she had made me touch her knee—a strange feeling. I had said as much to her: 'I am not the kind of man who is satisfied with a knee.' Her answer: 'That would be disgusting!'" [*MD* 16–17/*FJ* 33–34].

She pleases him and he would not like to be satisfied with the knee that she "had made [him] touch." This contact with the knee (*genou*), as my student and friend Pierre-François Berger brought to my notice, recalls the inflectional contiguity, in the word, of *je/nous*, of the I and the we, the *je* and the *nous*, of an I/we couple of whom we shall speak again in a moment.

The law's feminine element has thus always appealed to: me, I, he, we. The law is appealing, always attracts in its vicinity [*parages*]: "The law appealed to me. . . . To tempt the law, I called softly to her: 'Approach; let me see you face-to-face.' (For a moment I wanted to take her aside.) It was a foolhardy appeal. What would I have done if she had answered?" [*MD* 9/*FJ* 16].

He is perhaps subjected to law, but he neither attempts to escape her, nor does he shrink before her: he wishes to seduce the law to whom he gives birth (there is a hint of incest in this) and especially—this is one of the most striking and singular traits of this scene—he inspires fear in the law. He not only troubles the representatives of the law, the lawmen who are the forensic doctors and the "shrinks" [*les "psy"*]—who demand of him, but are unable to obtain, an organized *récit*, a testimony oriented by a sense of history or his story, ordained and ordered by reason, and by the unity of an *I think*, or of an *originally synthetic apperception accompanying all representations*. That the "I" here was not always accompanying me and does not always accompany itself is by no means borne lightly by the lawmen; in fact, he alarms thus the lawmen, he radically persecutes them, and, in his manner, he conceals from them without altercation the truth they demand and without which they are nothing. But he not only alarms the lawmen, he alarms the law; one would be tempted to say the law herself, if she did not remain here a silhouette and an effect of the *récit*. And what is more, this law whom the "I" frightens is none other than "me," than the "I," effect of his desire, child of his affirmation, of the genre "I" clasped in a specular couple with "me." They are inseparable (*je/nous* and *genou*, *je/toi* and *je/toit*), and so she tells him, once more, as truth: "'The truth is that we can never be separated again. I will follow you everywhere, I will live under your roof (*toit*); we will share the same sleep'" [*MD* 15/*FJ* 31].

We see the law, whose silhouette stands behind her representatives, frightened by "me," by "him"; she is inclined toward and declined by *je/ nous, I/we*, in front of "me," in front of him, her knees marking perhaps the articulation of the (non)pace [*du pas*], the flexion of the couple and sexual difference, but also the contiguity without contact of the hymen and the "mixing of genres."

Behind their backs, I saw the silhouette of the law. Not the law everyone knows, who is severe and hardly very agreeable: this law was different. Far from falling prey to her menace, I was the one who seemed to terrify her. According to her, my glance was a bolt of lightning and my hands were motives for perishing. What's more, the law absurdly credited me with all powers; she declared herself perpetually on her knees before me. But she did not let me ask anything and when she had recognized my right to be in all places, it meant I had no place anywhere. When she set me above the authorities, it meant, You are not authorized to do anything. [*MD* 14–15/ *FJ* 29–30]

"I had no place anywhere," while she had granted me the desire to be in all places. Elsewhere Blanchot designates the non-place and the topical or hypertopical mobility of the narrative voice in this way.

What game is the law, a law of this genre, playing? What is she playing, what is she up to, when she has her knee touched? For if *La folie du jour* plays down the law, plays at law, plays with law, it is also because the law herself plays. The law, in its feminine element, is a silhouette that plays. At what? At being . . . born, at being born *like anybody and no body*.[13] She plays upon her generation and displays her genre, she plays out her nature and her history, and she makes a plaything of a *récit*. In mock-playing herself she recites; and she is born of him, of it, of the *récit* she becomes the law for. She is born of him himself, of it itself, one could even say of her herself, since the gender can be reversed *in the affirmation*: *he* or *she* or *it* is the narrative voice, *him, her, it, I, we*, the neuter genre that subjects and merges itself while giving birth to her, that lets itself be captivated by the law and escapes her, that she escapes and loves, etc.[14] She lets herself be put in motion, she lets herself be *cited* by him/it when, in the midst of her game, she says, pursuing an idiom that her disseminal polysemy conveys to the abyss, "I see the day":

This was one of her games. [He has just recalled that she "once . . . had made [him] touch her knee."] She would show me a part of space, between the top of the window and the ceiling: "You are there," she said. I looked hard at that point.

"Are you there?" I looked at it with all my might. "Well?" I felt the scars fly off my eyes, my sight was a wound, my head a hole, a bull disemboweled. Suddenly she cried out: "Oh! I see the day, oh God," etc. I protested that this game was tiring me out enormously, but she was insatiably intent upon my glory. [*MD* 17/*FJ* 34]

For the law to see the day is her madness, is what she loves madly like the glory, the emblazed illustration, the day of the writer, of the author who says "I," and who brings forth law to the light of day. He says that she is insatiable, insatiable for his glory—he, who is, too, author of the law to which he submits himself, he, who engenders her, he, her mother [*mère*] who no longer knows how to say "I" or to keep memory intact. I am (following) the mother of law, behold my daughter's madness. It is also the madness of the day, *la folie du jour*, for day, the word "day" in its disseminal abyss, is law, the law of the law. My daughter's madness is to want to be born—like anybody and nobody [*comme personne*], whereas she remained a "silhouette," a shadow, a profile, her face never in view. He had said to her, to the law, in order to "tempt" her: "'Approach; let me see you face-to-face.'"

Such would be the "remarkable truth" that clears an opening for the madness of the day—and that appeals, like law, like madness, to the one who says "I" or "I/we." Let us be attentive to this syntax of truth. She, the law, says: "'The truth is that we can never be separated again. I will follow you everywhere, I will live under your roof. . . . '" He: "The truth was that I liked her . . . ," she, law, but also—and this is always the principal theme of these sentences—she, *la vérité*, truth. One cannot conceive truth without the madness of the law.

I have let myself be commanded by the law of our encounter, by the convention of our subject, notably the genre, the law of genre. This law, articulated as an I/we more or less autonomous in its movements, assigned us places and limits. Even though I have launched an appeal against this law, it was she who turned my appeal into a confirmation of her own glory. But she also desires ours insatiably. Submitting myself to the subject of our colloquium, as well as to its law, I sifted "A *récit*," *La folie du jour*. I isolated a type, if not a genre, of reading from an infinite series of trajectories or possible courses. I have pointed out the generative principle of these courses, beginnings, and new beginnings in every sense:

but from a certain point of view. Elsewhere—in accordance with other subjects, other colloquia and lectures, other I/we drawn together in one place—other trajectories could have come to light.

Nonetheless, it would be folly to draw any sort of general conclusion here. I could not say what just exactly has happened in this scene, nor in my discourse or my *récit*. What was perhaps seen, in the blink of time's eye, is a madness of law—and, therefore, of order, reason, sense, and meaning, of day: "But often," said "I," "I lay dying without saying anything. In the end, I grew convinced that I was seeing face-to-face the madness of day. That was the truth: the light was going mad, clarity took leave of her senses; she assailed me irrationally, without control, without a goal. That discovery bit straight through my life" [*MD* 11–12/*FJ* 22].

I am woman, and beautiful; my daughter, the law, is mad about me. I speculate on my daughter. My daughter is mad about me; this is law.

The law is mad, she is mad about "me." And across the madness of this day, I keep this in sight, it—*ça*—keeps me in sight. There, this will have been my self-portrait of the genre.

The law is mad. The law is mad, is madness; but madness is not the predicate of law. There is no madness without the law; madness cannot be conceived before its relation to law. Madness is law, the law is madness.

There is a general trait here: the madness of the law mad for me, the day madly in love with me, the silhouette of my daughter mad about me, her mother, etc. But *La folie du jour*, "A *Récit*?" without *récit*, carrying and miscarrying its titles, is not at all exemplary of this general trait. Not at all, not wholly [*Pas du tout*]. This is not an example of a general or generic whole. Not at all, not wholly. The whole, which begins by finishing and never finishes beginning apart from itself, the whole that remains at the edgeless boundary of itself, the whole greater and less than a whole and nothing, "A *Récit*?" will not have been exemplary. Rather, with regard to the whole, it will have been wholly counter-exemplary.

The genre has always in all genres been able to play the role of order's principle: resemblance, analogy, identity and difference, taxonomic classification, organization and genealogical tree, order of reason, order of reasons, sense of sense, truth of truth, natural light, and sense of history. Now, the test of "A *Récit*?" brought to light the madness of genre. Madness has given birth to and thrown light on the genre in the most dazzling, most blinding sense of the word. And in the writing of *A récit?*, in literature, satirically practicing all genres, imbibing them but never allowing herself to be saturated with a catalog of genres, she, madness, has started spinning Peterson's *genre-disc* like a demented sun.[15] And she does not only do so *in* literature, for in concealing the boundaries that sunder mode and genre, she has also inundated *and* divided the borders between literature and its others.

There, that is the whole of it, it is only what—here, kneeling, I/we, distyle, they say, at the edges of the waters off [*dans les parages de*] literature—"I" can see. In sum, the law. The law summoning: what "I" can sight and what "I" can say that I sight in a *récit* where I/we are, where I summon us [*ou je/nous somme*].

Notes

INTRODUCTION

1. Here I place in italic to remind the reader of words in the keys of *parages* and *eau* that are floating throughout Derrida's text: "*Pay*s*age* sans *pay*s, ouvert sur l'absence de *pa*trie, *pay*s*age* marin, es*pa*ce sans territoire, sans chemin réservé, sans lieu-dit."—*Trans.*

*P*ACE NOT(*S*)

1. The word *pas*, as this text points out, "functions" in French as a noun (with the sense of step, pace, tread, walk, gait, mountain pass, or strait of waters, and so on) and as an adverb of negation, with *ne* present or understood in formal language. In English, the adverbial sense of *pas* can be rendered by a negative prefix such as *non-* or the adjectival *no*, in addition to the adverbial *no* or *not*. Derrida's text explores the various interrelations, intimations, suggestions, allusions, and limits of this French word with itself, its double in its "supposed" two functions, its singular/plural (*le pas, les pas*), and the word *pas* itself (its graphic and sonic forms). The translation can seem to decide which sense and number predominate in a particular passage, particularly those citations taken from Blanchot's *récits*, but it becomes more and more evident that such assurances are precisely what Derrida disrupts in his "proposed" "reading" of "Blanchot's-*récits*." I have tried to signal this "paralysis" (eventually Derrida coins the word *paralyse*, here translated, following Bennington, as "paralys") throughout the translation with reminders in the translation of various French terms, here specifically *pas*.

Pas is rendered by pace/no, no/pace, (non)pace, pace (not), and so forth; by inserting the term within brackets in the text; or by using the term itself "untranslated" in the text. Alternate renderings have been given in the notes in even more "paralytic" passages. The choice of the term "pace" as the first inclination for translating *pas* rather than the more expected "step" (which has been the basis for the published translation of Blanchot texts and for the interrelation with the translation of Heidegger's *Scrhritt*) is to recall Derrida's "*words in*" (understood as *words in the key of*) "*pa, par, para, ra, rage, age.*" I have indicated these

252   *Notes*

"souvenirs" by including at almost random places the French terms in these keys within brackets where the English translation does not provide such reminders.

Pas de . . . (in such phrases as *pas de sens, pas de nom, pas-de-nom, pas de sans*): These phrases head off, for example, in the case of *pas de sens*, in several senses and directions at once. (1) *Sens* refers to sense, senses, meaning, direction. (2) *De* can be understood as a preposition (of a subjective or objective genitive, for example) or as a partitive article. (3) And *pas* falls commonly into the noun "pace(s)," "step(s)," or the adverb of negation. Hence, multiple readings and renderings contaminate one another within the structures of the partitive (*pas de x*, no x) and the prepositional/genitive (*pas de x*, the pace of x, the no of x: the pace that produces/is produced by x, as well as the no that produces/is produced by x). Hence some renderings of the phrase *pas de sens*: no sense, sense's pace(s), sense's "not" (this would not be the same as "no" sense or direction), at times shortened to "no/pace of sense or direction" or as "a pace of/no sense" or finally "(non)pace of (no) sense." Following Barbara Johnson's rendering on *pas de méthode* (see note 23 below), it can be translated as "its paces allow for (no) sense." Somewhat differently and a bit more restricted in reference: no meaning, a pace of meaning, a "not" in meaning (which suggests a knot in meaning) or direction, all of these renderings offered as if it were possible to keep these possibilities partitioned from one another. Therefore, the series can become more and more extensive: no/pace/of/ no/sense/direction, with sense sliding across the slash/virgule and as if marked by an obelus calling into question any stability of sense in this knotted text.

I have silently modified the already published translations of Blanchot's texts to follow the stress of Derrida's readings. And I want to thank Pascale-Anne Brault and Michael Naas for their kind consultation on moments of this text.—*Trans*.

2. The 2003 edition of *Parages* omits "de faire?": "Comment appeler ce que je viens de—de quoi? de dire? de faire?"—*Trans*.

3. "C'est un pas de plus ou de moins sous *venir*." *Sous venir* also suggests "coming back to mind," "memory," "souvenir." It is one *pas* more or less under *venir*, coming back to mind, more or less its souvenir. Farther on, Derrida talks about "the coming-back without memory of a *come*," *le sous-venir sans mémoire d'un* viens (p. 36 of the 1986 edition/p. 33 of 2003 edition; p. 25 of this volume).—*Trans*.

4. For example, *AO* 30, 32, 35, 63/*AtOu* 60, 63, 70, 120.—*Trans*.

5. *Démarche* has the various senses of procedure, walk, step, gait, pace, approach, reasoning in the phrase *la démarche d'un pas*. The *dé-* prefix of *démarche* recalls the arguments regarding negation and dialectics that this piece considers (also see note 1 above). In other words, *la démarche*, like denegation (see Mark C.

Taylor, *nots* [Chicago: University of Chicago Press, 1993], 35–39), could be argued to be a "nonsynonymic" substitute for *pas*. Thus, any rendering of the phrase would be multiply marked by denegation. It could be inadequately rendered by such phrasings as follows: the (dis)procedure of a *pas*, the (non)pace of a no/pace, the (non)reasoning of *pas*, etc.—*Trans.*

6. In his citation of Blanchot, Derrida omits the sentence "Mais ici l'approche était sans approche." I have followed Blanchot's text.—*Trans.*

7. Derrida adds a question mark here, rather than a period, in the 2003 edition of *Parages*.—*Trans.*

8. Derrida adds a question mark here, rather than a period, in the 2003 edition of *Parages*.—*Trans.*

9. In English in the text.—*Trans.*

10. "Et dans son texte si régulièrement, immensément, démesurément. Nous ne cesserons plus de nous y retrouver, de nous y perdre, de nous y noyer."—*Trans.*

11. The 2003 edition of *Parages* mistakenly reads "un magique *intervalle*."—*Trans.*

12. Instead of "the name Thomas [*nom de Thomas*]" Derrida reads "the word Thomas [*mot de Thomas*]." I follow his substitution.—*Trans.*

13. "Le pas, c'est donc le mot pas *et* le pas, *ou* le pas."—*Trans.*

14. In italic in the original.—*Trans.*

15. These passages are taken up with slight changes in *WD* 16–17/*ED* 32–34.—*Trans.*

16. "(que, quoi? qu'est-ce qui va arriver? ou plutôt, car ce n'est pas quelque chose qui va arriver, mais qu'*il* va arriver: que va-t-*il* donc arri-ver?)": In the 2003 edition of *Parages*, a hyphen is introduced in "arri-ver."—*Trans.*

17. *C'était pas . . .* : This phrase can mean "It wasn't . . ." as well as "It was *pas*." The latter part of this sentence makes use of those possibilities: What if it, dialectics, were *pas*? What if it, dialectics, were not?—*Trans.*

18. *A* 329 reads: "*Nous ne devons pas, par des artifices, faire semblant de poursuivre un dialogue.*" *F* 292 translates: "*We should not, by means of artifice, pretend to carry on a dialogue.*" Derrida has substituted the word "sacrifices" for "artifices." I retain his substitution.—*Trans.*

19. *Mot, m'ot*: *mot* = "word," *m'* = first-person singular reflexive pronoun or the first letter of Blanchot's first name (Maurice) + the last letters of the last name of Blanch*ot*.—*Trans.*

20. Five, in the English translation.—*Trans.*

21. Here I place in italic to remind the reader of words in the keys of *parages* and *eau* that are floating throughout Derrida's text: "Vis*age*, riv*age*, nau*frage*, c'est le même *pays*age marin, un *pays*age sans *pays*, sans familiarité, sans ra*cine*."—*Trans.*

22. In English in the text: "l' 'air de famille' (*family resemblance*)."—*Trans.*

23. In partial justification of translating *pas de don* as "gift-knot" in this paragraph here, I refer the reader to Derrida's remarks below (83–84/97 in 1986 edi-

tion/90 in 2003 edition) on *knot* and *not*, as well as to his parenthetical comments in "Border Lines" (123–25/142–44 in 1986 edition/132–34 in 2003 edition) on the untranslatability of *pas*: "*Questions of method* run throughout this book (here, a translators' note: I have published a text that is untranslatable, starting with its title, 'Pas [*Pace Not(s)*],' and in 'The Double Session,' referring to 'dissemination in the folds [*repli*] of the *hymen*': 'Its steps allow for (no) *method* [*pas de* méthode] for it: no path leads around in a circle toward a first pace, nor proceeds from the simple to the complex, nor leads from a beginning to an end ("a book neither begins nor ends: at most it pretends to" . . .). "All method is a fiction." . . . We here note a point/lack of method [*point de méthode*]: this does not rule out a certain marching order [*une certaine marche à suivre*].' The translators will not be able to translate this *pas* and this *point*. Will they have to indicate that this reminder is to be related to what is called the 'unfinished' quality of Shelley's *Triumph* and the impossibility of fixing [*arrêter*] the opening and closing boundaries of *L'arrêt de mort*, all problems treated, in another mode, in the procession above? Will they relate this untranslatable *pas* to the *double knot* [*le double noeud*] of *double invagination*, a central motif of that text, or, along with its entire semantic family, to all the occurrences of 'path,' 'past,' 'pass' in Shelley's *Triumph*?)." See also Derrida's *The Post Card*, trans. Alan Bass (Chicago: University of Chicago Press, 1987), 127.—*Trans.*

24. "Tu n'en as plus le besoin, le désir, le manque 'ne te faut plus'?"—*Trans.*

25. Were the last several words read as "Elle vient de ne pas s'arriver," then the translation would read the "venir de" as the auxiliary of the immediate past: "It has just now itself not come about." The introduction of the break "Elle vient. De ne pas s'arriver" stresses the coming in the not coming about, as well as the sense of "in order not to come about."—*Trans.*

26. Both the 1986 and 2003 editions of *Parages* read: "et donner ce qui viens," but the 1976 original in *Gramma* 3/4 (166) reads: "et donner ce qui vient." I have followed the version in *Gramma*.—*Trans.*

27. *OW* 24: "dreadfully old"/*CQN* 47; *SNB* 15/*PAD* 25.—*Trans.*

28. Cf. *SNB* 28/*PAD* 43: "To play is thus always to play against luck and bad luck—binary logic—for the plurality of the game. But play? yes, play, even if you cannot. To play is to desire, to desire without desire [*désirer sans désir*], and already to desire to play."—*Trans.*

29. *SNB* 81, 133/*PAD* 113, 182.—*Trans.*

30. "Et s'il n'est pas tournant, il éloigne selon des marches immobiles qui ne sont pas, dans leur structure, sous le pas, mais pas elles-mêmes."—*Trans.*

31. "Mais si vous n'arrivez pas à (dire), *viens* . . . "—*Trans.*

32. Cf. *MH* 54/*TH* 58.—*Trans.*

33. "Je n'existe pas avant que s'élève, se hisse, comme le mot ou la mort ('dressée dans la chambre') qui s'appelle, *viens*, surgissant seul, avant toi ou moi,

sans origine et sans fin, sans sujet ni complément. Rappelle-toi: 'Il va vers ce qu'il appelle.' Donc il s'appelle, *viens*, depuis celle à laquelle il dit, l'appelant, *viens*. 'Mais il fait venir? Seulement ce qui demande à venir en l'appel. Il interpelle? Il répond en appelant.' (*L'attente l'oubli*.) Nous avions tout à l'heure reconnu cette équivalence: c'est aussi la mort et le mot 'mort' qui s'appelle dans le *viens: je m'*—appelle mort—je commence ici à parler et à marcher en mon nom. Quand la mort est arrivée, toujours de l'autre, *je m'* n'est plus possible. Mais sans ce qui s'efforce d'un surcroît de force dans *viens*, l'appel de mort *me* précédant, *je m'* (affecte de mon nom) n'est pas encore possible. Je s'appelle toujours *je mort*. Et comme *elle*, il est sans nom avant *viens*, avant de répondre à ce qu'il appelle."—*Trans.*

34. The 2003 edition of *Parages* (p. 83) refers to *SNB*: "c'est pour dire l''admirable progrès' de *Le Pas au-delà*," whereas the 1986 edition (p. 89) refers to what is being laid out regarding the *pace/not beyond*: "c'est pour dire l' 'admirable progrès' du *pas au-delà*." I have followed the 1986 edition.—*Trans.*

35. *Il reste un reste sans reste de ce passage (il y a—pas—rien, un texte, un récit, déjà).*—*Trans.*

36. See Daniel Wilhelm, *Maurice Blanchot: La voix narrative* (Paris: Union Générale d'Éditions, 1974), 270.—*Trans.*

37. I have not been able to locate this citation in Blanchot's texts. Pierre Klossowski, in "Sur Maurice Blanchot," *Les Temps Modernes* 4, No. 40 (February 1949), cites this passage and attributes the citation in footnote 2 (p. 300) to Blanchot's "*La littérature et le droit à la mort*, in *Critique*, XX, janvier 48.*" In *Un si funeste désir* (Paris: Gallimard, 1963), he takes up a selection from this essay and cites this passage on p. 165, n1. After the citation, without any further attribution, he modifies the attribution to the following: "Cf. *La Littérature et le Droit à la mort*, in *Critique*, XX, Janvier 1948." Russell Ford, in his English translation, *Such a Deathly Desire* (Albany, NY: SUNY Press, 2007), 87, n. iii, refers to *WF* 324. In "Literature and the Right to Death," the closest passage changes from third person to first person and reads: "When I speak, I deny the existence of what I am saying, but I also deny the existence of the person who is saying it: if my speech reveals being in its nonexistence, it also affirms that this revelation is made on the basis of the nonexistence of the person making it, out of his power to distance himself from himself, to be other than his being" (*WF* 324). The French in *PF* (313–14) is in italic and reads: "*Quand je parle, je nie l'existence de ce que je dis, mais je nie aussi l'existence de celui qui le dit: ma parole, si elle révèle l'être dans son inexistence, affirme de cette révélation qu'elle se fait à partir de l'inexistence de celui qui la fait, de son pouvoir de s'éloigner de soi, d'être autre que son être.*" The passage by Blanchot in *Critique* 20 (January 1948): 31–32 to which Klossowski appears to be referring is not in italic and is the same as the text in *PF*.—*Trans.*

38. Also: without knowing: *s'avoir* as *savoir*.—*Trans.*

39. "D'un coup. Mais le coup de don, il faut, puisqu'il lui faut l'oubli, qu'il se ré-affirme sans cesse." *Un coup* also has the sense of "a drink" (as in "have a drink") or a "glass" of red wine (*un coup de rouge*), hence the use of "cup" and Derrida's reference to the poison drink in this passage (see note 40 below). In the lines preceding, there are the multiple "translations" of *there is* that connect giving and gift to the givenness of being as forgetting (and of the self-injunction *come*): "there is," "it gives," *il y a, ça donne,* and *es gibt.* —*Trans.*

40. "Donc: pas de don, encore, plus de don. La berge et son bord. Tiens, bois."—*Trans.*

41. English translation reads "although" for "*si*": "I mean I tried to make him understand that, although I was there, still I couldn't go any farther. . . . "—*Trans.*

42. Derrida writes "some twenty pages after," but the French text is only some ten pages after; in the English text, it is some five pages after.—*Trans.*

43. *Sorge* is German for "concern," "care."—*Trans.*

44. Derrida misplaces the "also" in the first phrase in his citation of Blanchot. I have followed Blanchot's text.—*Trans.*

45. "Tu l'entends ici, maintenant, toi-même, au plus près de toi, comme si tu venais de le prononcer mais tu t'en souvenais et t'en souviendras éternellement, dans l'oubli même où il nous aura laissés, quand ce qui enfin à l'autre sera arrivé . . . "—*Trans.*

46. In English in the text.—*Trans.*

47. In the 1986 edition, Derrida indicates a change of speaker twice: "'By his name . . .'" and "'You can't, at this moment . . .'"; in the 2003 edition, he indicates only the second. I have followed Blanchot's text and the English translation, which have neither.—*Trans.*

48. The version of this piece in *Gramma* 3/4 (p. 211) adds in parentheses: "*(pas au-delà)*," which could be rendered as "(pace/not beyond)."—*Trans.*

49. Italic in the French text.—*Trans.*

50. Blanchot's text reads "our name [*notre nom*]." I have followed Derrida's slight change here.—*Trans.*

51. Derrida reads: *à lui-même si bien réapproprié,* and I have added that "re-" to "suit" in the translation.—*Trans.*

LIVING ON

1. In English in the text.—*Ed.*
2. In English in the text.—*Ed.*
3. *Over, above,* and *beyond* were in English in the text.—*Ed.*
4. In English in the text.—*Ed.*
5. As analyzed in "*Pace Not(s).*"—*Trans.*
6. MD 18/FJ 36.—*Ed.*

7. *MD* 17/*FJ* 34.—*Ed.*
8. Taken up in *WD* 72 *"the pane had broken"*/*ED* 117.—*Ed.*
9. *Light* and *life* were in English in the text.—*Ed.*
10. The following parenthetical comment included in the English version translated by Hulbert was omitted in the French version published in *Parages*: "(There are writings entitled, for example, *Entête* [Genesis], the Gospels, Revelation [Apocalypse], and so forth. I would like to speak of them here, to attempt to read them, to move to them from, for example, *The Triumph of Life*, *La folie du jour*, *L'arrêt de mort* . . . and the story, the narrative, of "Living On" as differance, with an *a*, between archeology and eschatology, as differance *in* apocalypse. That will be a while in coming.)"—*Ed.*
11. In English in the text.—*Ed.*
12. In English in the text. All instances of *double bind* are also in English and italic in the French text.—*Ed.*
13. Derrida's addition in brackets.—*Ed.*
14. "The *Sans* of the Pure Cut" is in Derrida, *The Truth in Painting*, trans. Geoff Bennington and Ian McLeod (Chicago: University of Chicago Press, 1987), 83–118 / *La vérité en peinture* (Paris: Flammarion, 1978): 95–135.—*Ed.*
15. Hulbert adds the following explanation: "coined word; cf. *arête*: ridge, cutting edge, backbone, fish bone, arris." In a note to the translation, Lycette Nelson writes about the first occurrence of this term earlier in the text: "What I have translated as 'the edge at which we stop' is Blanchot's word 'l'arrête,' which does not exist as a word, but is a combination of two words. The first of these is 'l'arrêt,' which can mean a place to stop, an arrest in the police sense, or a judicial sentence, as in Blanchot's title *L'Arrêt de mort*. The word 'arête,' on the other hand, indicates a sharp edge (it can also mean a fish bone on which one risks choking). Blanchot takes the same word later in the text, where he qualifies it as 'line of instability'" (*SNB* 139 n10).—*Ed.*
16. Hulbert states that Lydia Davis's translation in *DS* is "quoted throughout, with permission and with occasional modifications for the sake of continuity." I have provided the page references in brackets.—*Ed.*
17. In English in the text.—*Ed.*
18. Smock translates this as Hegel's "early philosophy."—*Ed.*
19. In English in the text.—*Ed.*
20. *Triumph of life, triumph of light, light, night* in English in the text.—*Ed.*
21. In French, all expressible by conjugated forms of the verb *devoir*.—*Trans.*
22. In English in the text.—*Ed.*
23. Derrida uses the singular *parage* here to designate the spacing that he is attempting to describe of/between living, living on (*vivre, survivre*), encapsulated in the spacing of the comma. The word *parage* occurs in English as well, although the senses recognized by the *OED*, from the major derivation of "par-

ity of condition or rank," are lineage, rank, value, equality. Here, *parage* should be understood as the (im)possible state or condition of being beside, alongside, like the unstable line of a coast or a sea, of trying to board or border such a line: para- + age.—*Ed.*

24. The following sentence that began this paragraph in the version Hulbert translated was omitted in the French version published in *Parages*: "Its unfinishedness is structural; it is bound to itself in the shifting binding of the *arrêt*."—*Ed.*

25. The following sentence that ended this paragraph in the version Hulbert translated was omitted from the French version published in *Parages*: "You will find that I have rung some changes on these questions elsewhere."—*Ed.*

26. In English in the text.—*Ed.*

27. In Hulbert's version, not taken up in the version published in *Parages*, there is the following: "here I draw a veil over 'La double séance.'" The reference to Mallarmé is from Derrida's "The Double Session" in *Dissemination*, trans. Barbara Johnson (Chicago: University of Chicago Press, 1981), 175, 214 / *La dissémination* (Paris: Seuil, 1972), 201, 242–43. Johnson translates as follows: "No act, then, is *perpetrated* ('*Hymen* . . . *between perpetration and remembrance*'); no act is committed as a crime."—*Ed.*

28. *AO* 20 "'United: separated,'" 85 "'*reunited: separated*'"/*AtOu* 42, 162].—*Ed.*

29. In English in the text.—*Ed.*

30. The revised and enlarged edition of *Parages* published in 2003 reads: "il ne peut vivre si selon l'unique alliance ni selon la double."—*Ed.*

BORDER LINES

a. *Glas* (Paris: Galilée, 1974), 219b / *Glas*, trans. John Leavey and Richard Rand (Lincoln: University of Nebraska Press, 1986), 195b–96b.—*Ed.*

b. These "Border Lines," in French, are entitled "Journal de bord"—usually translated "shipboard journal," but here also "journal on *bord*."—*Trans.*

c. *Novella* and *short story* in English in the text.—*Ed.*

d. In *Dissemination*, trans. Barbara Johnson (Chicago: University of Chicago Press, 1981), 271 / *La dissémination* (Paris: Seuil), 303.—*Ed.*

e. In English in the text.—*Ed.*

f. Friedrich Nietzsche, "Erste Abtheilung: Vermischte Meinungen und Sprüche," *Menschliches, Allzumenschliches. Ein Buch für freie Geister*, vol. 2, Aphorism 152, in vol. 4:3 of *Werke: Kritische Gesamtausgabe*, ed. Giorgi Colli and Mazzino Montinari (Berlin: Walter de Gruyter, 1967), 77.—*Ed.*

g. Sigmund Freud (1917e), in *Gesammelte Werke* (London: Imago, 1940), 10:428–46; *The Standard Edition of the Complete Psychological Works of Sig-*

mund Freud, ed. and trans. James Strachey (London: Hogarth Press, 1986), 14:243–60.—*Ed.*

h. *Toujours un pas de plus, et pas de thèse*. This "un"translatable "phrase" plays off its telegraphic style, as if each of its "words" was separated by "STOP" to enable and hinder its sense: Always STOP one STOP no/pace STOP (of) STOP more STOP and/is STOP no/pace STOP (of) STOP thesis STOP—*Ed.*

i. In English in the text.—*Ed.*

j. In English in the text.—*Ed.*

k. "Pas plus qu'aucune autre, cette traduction n'est sans reste."—*Ed.*

l. Trans. Bernard Frechtman [(New York: Grove Press, 1969), 27–28].—*Trans.*

m. Mouthful: *bouchée*: John 13:26: "sop," "piece of bread."—*Trans.*

n. In *Writing and Difference*, trans. Alan Bass (Chicago: University of Chicago Press, 1978), 231 / *L'écriture et la différence* (Paris: Seuil, 1967), 340.—*Ed.*

o. Maurice Blanchot, *The Last Man*, trans. Lydia Davis (New York: Columbia University Press, 1987), 9, 12, 2, 3–4, 8, 10–11 / *Le dernier homme*, new edition (Paris: Gallimard, 1957 [1982]), 14–15, 25, 9, 11, 18, 21–23.—*Ed.*

p. In Friedrich Nietzsche, *Unpublished Writings: From the Period of* Unfashionable Observations, trans. Richard T. Gray, vol. 3 of *The Complete Works of Friedrich Nietzsche* (Stanford, CA: Stanford University Press, 1995), 43.—*Ed.*

q. In *Dissemination/La dissémination* 220/249 on syllepsis; 210–11, 233, 281–82/239, 263, 314 on *vitre*.—*Ed.*

r. The following part from Hulbert's text is omitted in the French version published in *Parages*: "to the Mystic Rose in *Miracle de la Rose* and in *Glas*, to the same Mystic Rose in 'The Secret Rose' by Yeats, whose 'Second Coming' should also be cited."—*Ed.*

s. Letter to Regine Olsen, no date (no. 40), in *Letters and Documents*, trans. Henrik Rosenmeier, vol. 25 of *Kierkegaard's Writings* (Princeton, NJ: Princeton University Press, 1979), 85.—*Ed.*

t. In Laure, *Écrits: fragments, lettres*, ed. J. Peignot and le Collectif Change (Paris: Pauvert, 1977, 1979), 296–97.—*Ed.*

u. In English in the text.—*Ed.*

v. Derrida inadvertently states that this article is in *The Space of Literature*, rather than *The Work of Fire*.—*Ed.*

w. In English in the text.—*Ed.*

TITLE TO BE SPECIFIED

1. From the quasi-medieval sense of t-i-t-r-i-e-r liberty is taken in respelling the sixteenth- and seventeenth-century variants of *titler, tytler,* and *titeler* to fashion a homonymy with here and ear. The most obvious ring of "the title (—is—) here" emerges in *le titrier* from *le titre y est*. It remains only the first of the coun-

terfeit sounds we should like to re-assemble in titleer, as the orthography, in remaining faithful to the duplicitous intent (let us say, of a *mauvais titrier*) of "'One who claims or asserts a legal title.' Obs." (*O.E.D.*), has perverse echo in the way an ear would see a sharp point in the history of *title*, equivalence, equivocation, and the variants spinning off it (tickling, titration, etc.). In any case the twice repeated grapheme *tr* of *t i t r i e r* marks another obsessive shape in the French version of the text.

We must recall how "tr" of the essay on Valerio Adami (see Carol James, on page 120 in ["Reading Art through Duchamp's *Glass* and Derrida's *Glas*," *Sub-Stance* 10, No. 2, Issue 31 (1981): 104–28]) generates from the doubly invaginated chaismus of the columns of *Glas*, the *ich* or χ of *Positions*, such that *t* does and does not translate *x*; in any event, too, the tr, τr, χ, etc., traduces the inception of the urgent mark displacing the myth of truth in the title. What had been a deathly inscription is turned into a mobile frame, for the *tr* and χ designate the twists of much of Derrida's writing, whose contour allows us to see in r*écit* a tale or account that will have force in the page to follow, a graphic mannequin of *tr* disengaging a half-trace (*tréci, tré-ci, tri-cé*, etc.) on the grounds of its truth (*vérité*) in American or other translations.—*Trans.*

2. In Conley's translation, Derrida adds the following parenthetical comment regarding his first visit to St. Louis College in Brussels: "(the first time I came here, if I may be allowed to flatter myself with this reminder, was twelve years ago on the occasion to deliver a speech entitled 'La Différance')."—*Ed.*

3. Throughout the French text the law is couched in the feminine gender. Inflections of an allegorical female, a Justicia, pervade so much that it is almost impossible to choose between a *she* and an *it* in the French version. The double bind of the French rendering therefore could have a cacophonous ring in the English if we rightfully put forward *she* in *its* place.—*Trans.*

4. In English in the text.—*Ed.*

5. This title can be translated in at least two ways: "Of/On the Right to Literature" and "From Right to Literature."—*Ed.*

6. "Pas de sens et pas de lieu, donc."—*Ed.*

7. His "I" is *son* "*Je*": as elsewhere, the text echoes an impossible pairing of identities, and all the more when different personal pronouns shift over each others' surfaces. Here "his 'I'" avers to be the space of a dream, a *son-je*; later, the knee of Justice will thrust through Blanchot and Derrida in the shape of a *je-nous*, a catastrophic violation of the law of the shifter.—*Trans.*

8. *MD* 10–11: "Outdoors, I had a brief vision:" to "All that was real: take note."—*Ed.*

9. In English in the text.—*Ed.*

10. In English in the text.—*Ed.*

11. In English in the text.—*Ed.*

12. Here *à préciser*, which we render as we do above, invaginates the field of *pré, près, prêt, présence*, etc., specified in allusion to *La Fabrique du pré.*—*Trans.*

LAW OF GENRE

1. In English in the text.—*Ed.*
2. "Genres, 'Types,' Modes," *Poétique* 32 (November 1977), 408; in Gérard Genette, *The Architext: An Introduction*, trans. Jane E. Lewin (Berkeley: University of California Press, 1992), 45 / *Introduction à l'architexte* (Paris: Seuil, 1979), 49.
3. The 2003 edition of *Parages* drops the letter *a* and reads "*physis* précisément—que commerce" rather than as the 1986 edition: "*physis* précisément—que comme race."—*Ed.*
4. The 2003 edition of *Parages* reads "le principe ou l'instruction classificatoire" rather than as the 1986 edition: "le principe ou l'instrument classificatoire."—*Ed.*
5. In this respect, the second footnote on p. 271 in Philippe Lacoue-Labarthe and Jean-Luc Nancy, *L'absolu littéraire* (Paris: Seuil, 1978) [*The Literary Absolute*, trans. Philip Barnard and Cheryl Lester (Albany: State University of New York Press, 1988), 142 n15] seems to me, let us say, a bit too equitable in its rigorous and honest prudence.
6. This value of *inclusion*, simple or double, will lead to some nuances or complications in the work that takes up this article of 1977. Cf. G. Genette, *The Architext: An Introduction* 72ff. / *Introduction à l'architexte* 76ff.
7. In *The Architext* and *Introduction à l'architexte*, this passage reads: " . . . belong to . . . what we now call *pragmatics*."—*Ed.*
8. The word *récit* occurs five times, although Derrida indicates four times in the French text. Derek Attridge made the change in *Acts of Literature.*—*Ed.*
9. In English in the text.—*Ed.*
10. The previous two paragraphs were added in the 1986 and 2003 editions of *Parages.*—*Ed.*
11. See especially 91 and 144 n26 / *L'absolu littéraire* 276.
12. First published on its own, separately (in *Première Livraison*, 1976), the text so titled was reinscribed in *The Writing of the Disaster* 72, also cf. 114–16, 125–28/*ED* 117, 176–79, 191–96.
13. *À naître, à naître* comme personne: *naître*: to be born, also homophonically *n'être*: (not) to be; *personne* has the senses of "person," "anyone" or "no one." In her translation, Ronell uses the ellipsis to draw the reader's attention to the "being" in "being born."—*Ed.*
14. "En se jouant elle récite; et elle naît de celui pour lequel elle devient la loi. Elle naît de celui-là même, on peut dire de celle-là même puisque son genre peut s'inverser *dans l'affirmation*, *il* ou *elle* est la voix narrative, *lui, elle, je, nous,*

le genre neutre qui se laisse attirer par la loi, s'y assujettit et la fuit, qu'elle fuit et qu'elle aime, etc." The references within these two sentences are complicated by the translation from the two genders of French to the three of English. Blanchot, for example, writes about the "intrusion of the other—understood as neutral—" marked in the "narrative *il*," which is masculine (or impersonal) in grammatical gender and translated by *he* or *it*. The narrative voice (*la voix narrative*), whose pronouns and modifiers are feminine in French, is Blanchot's designation for this intrusion (*IC* 385/*EI* 564–65) and could be translated by *she* or *it* in English (and in a sense in French too). (The same translation possibility that gathers together all the problematics of personification and prosopopeia, of anthropomorphism and human exceptionalism recurs here in the choice of pronoun for *la loi*, law, and of course for *le récit*; elsewhere for *la pensée*, thought, and *la vérité*, truth.) Hence, the at-least-dual grammatical gender in the "narrative voice" is being re-marked by Derrida, as well as the at-least-double reference of the masculine pronouns and modifiers of *il* to the "narrative voice" of the *récit* and to the *récit* itself, *le récit*.

Two paragraphs later, *la mère*, the mother whom he is (following), returns us to the sea, *la mer*.—*Ed.*

15. On "Petersen's rose window of genres," see Genette, *The Architext* 51–56/ *Introduction à l'architexte* 56–60. Citation here from 55/60. Disc/rose window is 54/58.—*Ed.*

Cultural Memory in the Present

Henri Atlan, *Sparks of Randomness, Volume 1: Spermatic Knowledge*
Rebecca Comay, *Mourning Sickness: Hegel and the French Revolution*
Djelal Kadir, *Memos from the Besieged City: Lifelines for Cultural Sustainability*
Stanley Cavell, *Little Did I Know: Excerpts from Memory*
Jeffrey Mehlman, *Adventures in the French Trade: Fragments Toward a Life*
Jacob Rogozinski, *The Ego and the Flesh: An Introduction to Egoanalysis*
Marcel Hénaff, *The Price of Truth: Gift, Money, and Philosophy*
Paul Patton, *Deleuzian Concepts: Philosophy, Colonialization, Politics*
Michael Fagenblat, *A Covenant of Creatures: Levinas's Philosophy of Judaism*
Stefanos Geroulanos, *An Atheism that Is Not Humanist Emerges in French Thought*
Andrew Herscher, *Violence Taking Place: The Architecture of the Kosovo Conflict*
Hans-Jörg Rheinberger, *On Historicizing Epistemology: An Essay*
Jacob Taubes, *From Cult to Culture*, edited by Charlotte Fonrobert and Amir Engel
Peter Hitchcock, *The Long Space: Transnationalism and Postcolonial Form*
Lambert Wiesing, *Artificial Presence: Philosophical Studies in Image Theory*
Jacob Taubes, *Occidental Eschatology*
Freddie Rokem, *Philosophers and Thespians: Thinking Performance*
Roberto Esposito, *Communitas: The Origin and Destiny of Community*
Vilashini Cooppan, *Worlds Within: National Narratives and Global Connections in Postcolonial Writing*
Josef Früchtl, *The Impertinent Self: A Heroic History of Modernity*
Frank Ankersmit, Ewa Domanska, and Hans Kellner, eds., *Re-Figuring Hayden White*
Michael Rothberg, *Multidirectional Memory: Remembering the Holocaust in the Age of Decolonization*
Jean-François Lyotard, *Enthusiasm: The Kantian Critique of History*
Ernst van Alphen, Mieke Bal, and Carel Smith, eds., *The Rhetoric of Sincerity*

Stéphane Mosès, *The Angel of History: Rosenzweig, Benjamin, Scholem*

Alexandre Lefebvre, *The Image of the Law: Deleuze, Bergson, Spinoza*

Samira Haj, *Reconfiguring Islamic Tradition: Reform, Rationality, and Modernity*

Diane Perpich, *The Ethics of Emmanuel Levinas*

Marcel Detienne, *Comparing the Incomparable*

François Delaporte, *Anatomy of the Passions*

René Girard, *Mimesis and Theory: Essays on Literature and Criticism, 1959–2005*

Richard Baxstrom, *Houses in Motion: The Experience of Place and the Problem of Belief in Urban Malaysia*

Jennifer L. Culbert, *Dead Certainty: The Death Penalty and the Problem of Judgment*

Samantha Frost, *Lessons from a Materialist Thinker: Hobbesian Reflections on Ethics and Politics*

Regina Mara Schwartz, *Sacramental Poetics at the Dawn of Secularism: When God Left the World*

Gil Anidjar, *Semites: Race, Religion, Literature*

Ranjana Khanna, *Algeria Cuts: Women and Representation, 1830 to the Present*

Esther Peeren, *Intersubjectivities and Popular Culture: Bakhtin and Beyond*

Eyal Peretz, *Becoming Visionary: Brian De Palma's Cinematic Education of the Senses*

Diana Sorensen, *A Turbulent Decade Remembered: Scenes from the Latin American Sixties*

Hubert Damisch, *A Childhood Memory by Piero della Francesca*

Dana Hollander, *Exemplarity and Chosenness: Rosenzweig and Derrida on the Nation of Philosophy*

Asja Szafraniec, *Beckett, Derrida, and the Event of Literature*

Sara Guyer, *Romanticism after Auschwitz*

Alison Ross, *The Aesthetic Paths of Philosophy: Presentation in Kant, Heidegger, Lacoue-Labarthe, and Nancy*

Gerhard Richter, *Thought-Images: Frankfurt School Writers' Reflections from Damaged Life*

Bella Brodzki, *Can These Bones Live? Translation, Survival, and Cultural Memory*

Rodolphe Gasché, *The Honor of Thinking: Critique, Theory, Philosophy*

Brigitte Peucker, *The Material Image: Art and the Real in Film*

Natalie Melas, *All the Difference in the World: Postcoloniality and the Ends of Comparison*

Jonathan Culler, *The Literary in Theory*

Michael G. Levine, *The Belated Witness: Literature, Testimony, and the Question of Holocaust Survival*

Jennifer A. Jordan, *Structures of Memory: Understanding German Change in Berlin and Beyond*

Christoph Menke, *Reflections of Equality*

Marlène Zarader, *The Unthought Debt: Heidegger and the Hebraic Heritage*

Jan Assmann, *Religion and Cultural Memory: Ten Studies*

David Scott and Charles Hirschkind, *Powers of the Secular Modern: Talal Asad and His Interlocutors*

Gyanendra Pandey, *Routine Violence: Nations, Fragments, Histories*

James Siegel, *Naming the Witch*

J. M. Bernstein, *Against Voluptuous Bodies: Late Modernism and the Meaning of Painting*

Theodore W. Jennings, Jr., *Reading Derrida / Thinking Paul: On Justice*

Richard Rorty and Eduardo Mendieta, *Take Care of Freedom and Truth Will Take Care of Itself: Interviews with Richard Rorty*

Jacques Derrida, *Paper Machine*

Renaud Barbaras, *Desire and Distance: Introduction to a Phenomenology of Perception*

Jill Bennett, *Empathic Vision: Affect, Trauma, and Contemporary Art*

Ban Wang, *Illuminations from the Past: Trauma, Memory, and History in Modern China*

James Phillips, *Heidegger's Volk: Between National Socialism and Poetry*

Frank Ankersmit, *Sublime Historical Experience*

István Rév, *Retroactive Justice: Prehistory of Post-Communism*

Paola Marrati, *Genesis and Trace: Derrida Reading Husserl and Heidegger*

Krzysztof Ziarek, *The Force of Art*

Marie-José Mondzain, *Image, Icon, Economy: The Byzantine Origins of the Contemporary Imaginary*

Cecilia Sjöholm, *The Antigone Complex: Ethics and the Invention of Feminine Desire*

Jacques Derrida and Elisabeth Roudinesco, *For What Tomorrow . . . : A Dialogue*

Elisabeth Weber, *Questioning Judaism: Interviews by Elisabeth Weber*

Jacques Derrida and Catherine Malabou, *Counterpath: Traveling with Jacques Derrida*

Martin Seel, *Aesthetics of Appearing*

Nanette Salomon, *Shifting Priorities: Gender and Genre in Seventeenth-Century Dutch Painting*

Jacob Taubes, *The Political Theology of Paul*

Jean-Luc Marion, *The Crossing of the Visible*

Eric Michaud, *An Art for Eternity: The Cult of Art in Nazi Germany*

Anne Freadman, *The Machinery of Talk: Charles Peirce and the Sign Hypothesis*

Stanley Cavell, *Emerson's Transcendental Etudes*

Stuart McLean, *The Event and Its Terrors: Ireland, Famine, Modernity*

Beate Rössler, ed., *Privacies: Philosophical Evaluations*

Bernard Faure, *Double Exposure: Cutting Across Buddhist and Western Discourses*

Alessia Ricciardi, *The Ends of Mourning: Psychoanalysis, Literature, Film*

Alain Badiou, *Saint Paul: The Foundation of Universalism*

Gil Anidjar, *The Jew, The Arab: A History of the Enemy*

Jonathan Culler and Kevin Lamb, eds., *Just Being Difficult? Academic Writing in the Public Arena*

Jean-Luc Nancy, *A Finite Thinking*, edited by Simon Sparks

Theodor W. Adorno, *Can One Live after Auschwitz? A Philosophical Reader*, edited by Rolf Tiedemann

Patricia Pisters, *The Matrix of Visual Culture: Working with Deleuze in Film Theory*

Talal Asad, *Formations of the Secular: Christianity, Islam, Modernity*

Dorothea von Mücke, *The Rise of the Fantastic Tale*

Marc Redfield, *The Politics of Aesthetics: Nationalism, Gender, Romanticism*

Emmanuel Levinas, *On Escape*

Dan Zahavi, *Husserl's Phenomenology*

Rodolphe Gasché, *The Idea of Form: Rethinking Kant's Aesthetics*

Michael Naas, *Taking on the Tradition: Jacques Derrida and the Legacies of Deconstruction*

Herlinde Pauer-Studer, ed., *Constructions of Practical Reason: Interviews on Moral and Political Philosophy*

Jean-Luc Marion, *Being Given: Toward a Phenomenology of Givenness*

Theodor W. Adorno and Max Horkheimer, *Dialectic of Enlightenment*

Ian Balfour, *The Rhetoric of Romantic Prophecy*

Martin Stokhof, *World and Life as One: Ethics and Ontology in Wittgenstein's Early Thought*

Gianni Vattimo, *Nietzsche: An Introduction*

Jacques Derrida, *Negotiations: Interventions and Interviews, 1971–1998*, ed. Elizabeth Rottenberg

Brett Levinson, *The Ends of Literature: Post-transition and Neoliberalism in the Wake of the "Boom"*

Timothy J. Reiss, *Against Autonomy: Global Dialectics of Cultural Exchange*

Hent de Vries and Samuel Weber, eds., *Religion and Media*

Niklas Luhmann, *Theories of Distinction: Redescribing the Descriptions of Modernity*, ed. and introd. William Rasch

Johannes Fabian, *Anthropology with an Attitude: Critical Essays*

Michel Henry, *I Am the Truth: Toward a Philosophy of Christianity*

Gil Anidjar, *"Our Place in Al-Andalus": Kabbalah, Philosophy, Literature in Arab-Jewish Letters*

Hélène Cixous and Jacques Derrida, *Veils*

F. R. Ankersmit, *Historical Representation*

F. R. Ankersmit, *Political Representation*

Elissa Marder, *Dead Time: Temporal Disorders in the Wake of Modernity (Baudelaire and Flaubert)*

Reinhart Koselleck, *The Practice of Conceptual History: Timing History, Spacing Concepts*

Niklas Luhmann, *The Reality of the Mass Media*

Hubert Damisch, *A Childhood Memory by Piero della Francesca*

Hubert Damisch, *A Theory of /Cloud/: Toward a History of Painting*

Jean-Luc Nancy, *The Speculative Remark (One of Hegel's Bons Mots)*

Jean-François Lyotard, *Soundproof Room: Malraux's Anti-Aesthetics*

Jan Patočka, *Plato and Europe*

Hubert Damisch, *Skyline: The Narcissistic City*

Isabel Hoving, *In Praise of New Travelers: Reading Caribbean Migrant Women Writers*

Richard Rand, ed., *Futures: Of Derrida*

William Rasch, *Niklas Luhmann's Modernity: The Paradox of System Differentiation*

Jacques Derrida and Anne Dufourmantelle, *Of Hospitality*

Jean-François Lyotard, *The Confession of Augustine*

Kaja Silverman, *World Spectators*

Samuel Weber, *Institution and Interpretation: Expanded Edition*

Jeffrey S. Librett, *The Rhetoric of Cultural Dialogue: Jews and Germans in the Epoch of Emancipation*

Ulrich Baer, *Remnants of Song: Trauma and the Experience of Modernity in Charles Baudelaire and Paul Celan*

Samuel C. Wheeler III, *Deconstruction as Analytic Philosophy*

David S. Ferris, *Silent Urns: Romanticism, Hellenism, Modernity*

Rodolphe Gasché, *Of Minimal Things: Studies on the Notion of Relation*

Sarah Winter, *Freud and the Institution of Psychoanalytic Knowledge*

Samuel Weber, *The Legend of Freud: Expanded Edition*

Aris Fioretos, ed., *The Solid Letter: Readings of Friedrich Hölderlin*

J. Hillis Miller / Manuel Asensi, *Black Holes / J. Hillis Miller; or, Boustrophedonic Reading*

Miryam Sas, *Fault Lines: Cultural Memory and Japanese Surrealism*

Peter Schwenger, *Fantasm and Fiction: On Textual Envisioning*

Didier Maleuvre, *Museum Memories: History, Technology, Art*

Jacques Derrida, *Monolingualism of the Other; or, The Prosthesis of Origin*

Andrew Baruch Wachtel, *Making a Nation, Breaking a Nation: Literature and Cultural Politics in Yugoslavia*

Niklas Luhmann, *Love as Passion: The Codification of Intimacy*

Mieke Bal, ed., *The Practice of Cultural Analysis: Exposing Interdisciplinary Interpretation*

Jacques Derrida and Gianni Vattimo, eds., *Religion*

The authorized representative in the EU for product safety and compliance is:
Mare Nostrum Group
B.V Doelen 72
4831 GR Breda
The Netherlands